WATERS
CLOSE
OVER US

WATERS CLOSE OVER US

A journey along the Narmada

HARTOSH SINGH BAL

FOURTH ESTATE • *New Delhi*

First published in India in 2013 by Fourth Estate
An imprint of HarperCollins *Publishers*
A-75, Sector 57, Noida, Uttar Pradesh 201301, India
www.harpercollins.co.in

2 4 6 8 10 9 7 5 3

P-ISBN: 978-93-5029-705-6
E-ISBN: 978-93-5029-706-3

Hartosh Singh Bal asserts the moral right
to be identified as the author of this work.

The maps in the book are not to scale and are for
representational purposes only.

Typeset in 10.5/14 Calibri
by Jojy Philip, New Delhi 110 015

Printed and bound at
Saurabh Printers Pvt. Ltd.

For my sons Nihal and Nirvaan and my nephew Samrath
so that they may carry some sense of the land
my father and his father before him made home

Waters close over us, a name lasts but an instant.
Not important whether the generations hold us in memory.
Great was that chase with the hounds for the unattainable
meaning of the world.

'Winter', Czeslaw Milosz

I

Almost two decades ago, as I waited for the tea to come to a boil at one of the dhabas that line the single street that winds its way through Amarkantak, a young Bengali turned to me with a question. I had sensed his curiosity the moment I entered.

'I nearly became a mathematician,' I told him.

He looked up, his face suddenly very animated. 'No, no, that is not the path for you.'

He offered to read my hand. I just nodded, pretending not to understand; any answer would only have prolonged the conversation.

A vague sense of indecision and a desire to be on my own had brought me to Amarkantak. The town itself was no more than a collection of a few shops along the path leading to the source of the Narmada in the highlands of central India. A trickle of pilgrims from the fertile Narmada Valley that lay below provided enough business to sustain its residents.

Like so many of the pilgrims, I had grown up along the Narmada, and journeys through the forests that still exist on its banks are among my earliest memories – the soft sheen of rain on the trees, the sunlight playing on sal leaves, a green different from any other in the forest. I felt at home by this river, among these hills, surrounded by this vegetation. I would spend my days walking without end along the river, or to one of the many ashrams that dot the town and the surrounding forest. The source lay barely a few kilometres from where I was staying.

A few days after the encounter at the dhaba, I was woken up at five in the morning. I thought the chowkidar at the guest house was drunk. I had been up very late at night only because he had insisted on taking me along to the local church.

He had ushered me to the front and seated me on one of the foldable metal chairs that made up the first few rows of the open-air congregation in the church compound. The guest house was run by a state-owned aluminium company that had taken a lease on the bauxite mines in the nearby forests. Some of the employees took up the remaining chairs. Behind them, seated on durries spread on the ground, replicating the hierarchy of the company, were the workers on daily wages, in the main Gond tribals from nearby villages.

After a few introductory remarks, the main speaker of the evening was introduced. He stood on a podium, a tall striking figure, clad in a spotless white kurta-pyjama, with a shawl draped across his right shoulder. He didn't need a mike, his voice carried easily.

He was, he said, the only son of the Pushkar head priest. From the banks of the holy lake in the desert of Rajasthan to this hill tract was a long journey, but he seemed at ease. He was among the highest of Brahmins, descended from a line that went back generations to the time of the great sages. He wanted for nothing, he said. His parents doted on him. In college he excelled in everything, he was what everyone aspired to be. He was even offered a role in a Bollywood film. While in college, he became attracted to a young woman. She was not of the same caste, and to make matters worse, she was Christian, so by implication, in this part of India, a low-caste convert. She was devoted to him, but she was equally devoted to her faith. She was even willing to provoke his temper by asking him to follow the one true path. As he spoke, he sought to indicate the anger with which he, born to the family of the Pushkar high priests, would have greeted such a suggestion.

His parents opposed the marriage, but once he had set his mind on something, he was not to be deterred. At their home, she was treated worse than chattel, he said, but she had given up everything but her faith to be with him. She was convinced that she would bring him around to Essu. When he said the word, his voice dropped in pitch and his angry countenance gave way to an expression of great calm.

He would slap her. At times she would fall at his feet, begging him to accompany her to church, and he would kick her face. Again his expression changed, conveying grief and horror at the man he had once been. Even now, so many years later, this is how I remember his story. I took no notes and I cannot recall the event that triggered a change of heart. But I remember the tears streaming down his face, the tears that welled up in every eye in the congregation as he spoke of his wife's faith, a faith that was now his, a faith that he had come to preach in Amarkantak. By the time he finished, darkness had long descended. He must have spoken for several hours, but no one had stirred.

It took me a long while to go to sleep. So when I was woken up at five in the morning, after what seemed like a few minutes of sleep, I thought the chowkidar must have been drinking through the night.

'*Nahin baba, kuch log aain hain darshan ke liye* (Some people have come to see you, baba).'

For him I was a bureaucrat's son, and so baba I would be. It perhaps said something for the aims of a civilization that the same word should apply to a venerable elder and the children of the powerful, but the confusion was more than semantic. My visits to the ashrams in the vicinity of this small town had given rise to a perception that I had decided to renounce the world. A young man from a relatively privileged background, preoccupied with holy men, no other explanation made sense here.

Now there were two men at the door, seeking darshan. Groggy-eyed, I walked to the door, unprepared for what awaited me. Before I could say anything, they bowed to touch my feet. I squatted on the ground to forestall them. They reached for my feet, I tried to shuffle back, stumbled and fell. Sprawled on my arse, a lame man and a blind man clinging to my feet, I had no choice but to bless them.

Ridiculous though it may have been, even then I was struck by the power of faith and where it took men. It seemed, whether we liked it or not, we were constantly being shaped by the narrative of others. A woman could make a preacher of a high-born Brahmin, the faith of two men could invent a faithless guru.

After that first journey, I came back several times to the banks of the Narmada as a journalist. The largest network of dams in the country was slowly coming up along its course. In the ensuing debate, almost every aspect of the notion of progress had been thrown open to question, but as I talked to people and read about the Narmada, it became clear that this was not the first time that opposing ideas had clashed on these banks. And I felt there was a narrative unique to the Narmada that naturally wove together these conflicts into a story, the parikrama.

~

Pilgrimage is an ancient practice, common to almost every religion. But within the Indian tradition, its appeal is easy to see. It recognizes no barriers of wealth or caste. At one point in the wandering narrative that makes up the immense length of the Mahabharata, one of the seven great sages of legend, Pulastya, educates the celibate warrior Bhishma, 'O lord of men, that rite, however, which men without wealth, without allies, singly, without wife and children, and destitute of means, are capable of accomplishing and the merit of which is equal unto the sacred fruits of sacrifices, I will now declare unto thee, thou best of warriors! O thou best of the Bharata race, sojourns in tirthas (holy places, but literally places where one can cross over, from one bank to another or from this world to the next) which are meritorious and which constitute one of the high mysteries of the rishis, are even superior to sacrifices.'

A parikrama – literally a going around – whether it is of a temple shrine, a mountain or a lake, is the culmination of almost every Indian pilgrimage, and the most sacred part of the journey. The Narmada is the only river in India to merit a parikrama.

In the course of my travels along the river, and in the writing of this book, I did my share of reading about rivers; books on the Mekong, the Nile, the Thames, the Meander, the beautifully named Magdalena in Colombia, Marquez's river. And it seems to me that even though the relationship between civilizations and rivers has been intimate everywhere, the sense of the sacred that we have inherited down the centuries is unique to us.

The Nadistuti or the river hymn in the Rig Veda sings of ten rivers as they flow westwards from the Ganga. It lists the Yamuna and Saraswati, as well as the Beas, Ravi, Chenab, Jhelum, and the Indus. Thousands of years later, in our times, the list has changed. The seven sacred rivers are the Ganga, Yamuna, Saraswati, Narmada, Godavri, Kaveri and since 1947, the Krishna instead of the Indus. In this change lies the history of a civilization, the slow abandonment of its northern moorings, the long intellectual journey southwards in the subcontinent. In this journey, the Narmada would have been the first non-Vedic river to enter the Indo-Aryan awareness of the subcontinent. But its sanctity seems to predate this awareness.

For people who live along these banks, the Narmada is the other magnet of Hinduism, a counterpoint to the Ganga. It cuts through the heart of peninsular India, in a landscape already in place aeons before the Himalayas began their upsurge, long before the Ganga could even be conceived. Fed entirely by rain, it flows through terrain intensely familiar to Kalidasa – *Rewa's streams spread dishevelled at Vindhya's rocky foothills, like ashen streaks on an elephant's flank.* Of its other fourteen names, Rewa, the leaping one, is the best known, but for most of its course the river is just Narmada, the giver of delight.

The parikrama can commence anywhere along its banks. The pilgrim must keep the sacred shrine, here the river, to the right while walking. A pilgrim on the Narmada parikrama never breaks the journey, stopping only for the four months of the monsoon when flooding makes travel impossible. Barefoot, depending for food and shelter on the hospitality of those who dwell by the river, the pilgrim will go over to the other bank only at the source at Amarkantak or where the river meets the Arabian Sea at Bharuch. By the time the journey ends, at the same place where it began, a pilgrim would have walked 2,700 km.

Today the vast majority of pilgrims cut short the time for the journey, taking buses where possible, but a few persist. Less than a kilometre from the source of the Narmada at Amarkantak, where the river is but a trickle, I met Chhote Lal Thakur.

He and his companions had been on the Narmada parikrama for ten months. Still in his twenties, he had been shaped by the journey – a long flowing beard untouched since the day he set out, a slender frame stripped of spare flesh. His son should now be two, he said, but he had not spoken to his family since he began the parikrama.

He was surprised by the question I put to him.

'No, no one stopped me. When Narmada Mai calls, who would do so? If you want to write,' he tells me abruptly, 'you should write about the Shulpan jhadi.'

This is Bhil territory on the border of Madhya Pradesh and Gujarat, the most feared stretch of the entire parikrama. The Bhils are a tribal people who occupy the lower reaches of the river and are closely related to the Gonds of the upper Narmada. The Gond territory is still heavily forested, and has remained peripheral to what is seen as the mainstream of Indian history. The Bhils have been less lucky. Their territory has served as the crossing point across the Narmada for armies from the north of India headed to the south. It has left them with a long history of brigandage and some part of the tale Chhote Lal related could be the tale of any medieval pilgrim.

'On the very first day that we entered the Shulpan jhadi,' he said, 'the Bhils took away everything we had. We had already donned the sadhu's garb, knowing what awaited us. We told them, whatever we had, they were free to take. They took away our clothes, shawls, the vessel of holy water, they only left behind the image of the Mai.

However, once we crossed Shulpan jhadi, more was given to us than they took away.

'For eleven nights we walked naked through the wilderness, fire our only solace in the cold. It may have been a brush forest once, now it is desiccated, nothing grows there; the poverty of the people is there for us to see. Yet, each day the Bhils would give us one roti among the six of us. *Mai ki kripa thi* (It was the Narmada's blessing), we did not feel hungry.

'Walking in this fashion, we reached the edge of the sagar (literally sea, the term that every pilgrim now uses for the immense reservoir created by the Sardar Sarovar Dam on the river). It is not possible to walk along the banks. It took us four hours in a motorboat to cross the sagar.'

In a few moments he had spanned several centuries. Time after time, pilgrims spoke to me of the canals that have sprung up as a result of the dam. A pilgrim is not supposed to ford the waters of the Narmada, but the argument goes that in the same way that the waters of a tributary are not the waters of the Narmada, the water in the canal is not the water of the Narmada. Tradition may have settled the argument, but the builders of these canals have not seen fit to plan for the pilgrims. Thousands have to walk tens of kilometres to cross the canals at the nearest bridge.

The dam is only one of many being constructed along the river, and has resulted in a new set of displaced people, not willing ones such as the pilgrims but those known simply as PAPs (Project Affected Persons). Over the years, I had reported my fair share of such stories; the exodus from Harsud – a town sentenced to drown; the mock city of vast tin sheds near Barwani – constructed by farmers who believed compensation would be awarded in proportion to the size of their dwellings; the sixty-two pilgrims washed away on a full moon night because auspicious occasions are not the concern of the engineers who monitor the discharge from the dams.

These thoughts floated through my mind as Thakur spoke, while his companions proceeded to bathe in a small tank by the stream. My thoughts and his words were rudely interrupted by an inmate from a nearby ashram. 'Everyone bathes in the stream, *tum saale gandu especial ho* (are you fuckers special), stop dirtying the tank.'

A day later I went to meet the mahant who ran the ashram. He sat cross-legged on a sofa, his arms folded over an enormous pot belly, watching the day's cricket being summed up on the private news channel Aaj Tak which had just started beaming to a large part of the country till then only used to Doordarshan. At the end of the programme, after chiding his disciples for their overenthusiastic support for the Indian team, he turned to me.

He had come here, he told me, a pilgrim on the parikrama. He had taken up residence at this place. By her grace, he said, as he meditated in the shade of a tree that still stands in the ashram compound, disciples sought him out, contributing their land and wealth to the service of the Mai. First he set up this ashram for pilgrims to the town, then came the school and hostel for tribal children, followed by the hospital that stands at the edge of the town.

The man who had taken me to meet the mahant worked with the local municipality. He had sat silently through the audience and as we emerged outside the ashram, he asked me to follow him. At the edge of the ashram, he turned along an open sewer that flowed past the hostel. We followed it to the banks of the river where, separated by a thin mud embankment from the flowing water, the effluvia of the sadhus bubbled in a cesspool, ready to overflow into the river. Unknown to the pilgrims, barely a few hundred metres from the source, the river was as much shit as it was sacred.

I didn't have to ask the question. As we walked away, my companion offered an explanation of his own.

A sadhu, he began, accompanied by two disciples reached a town late at night. The townspeople greeted him and his disciples in the prescribed manner, providing them with the best they could offer. As he left the town in the morning, he blessed them, *'Ujjodo'* (be uprooted) much to the shock and surprise of his disciples.

The next night they reached another town where they were

greeted by taunts. Children hurled stones at them, they slept in the open and went hungry. Leaving town in the morning, he turned and blessed the denizens, *'Baso'* (settle and prosper). The astonished disciples could no longer keep silent and asked him why?

The sadhu smiled and said, 'If those who know right conduct are uprooted, they will travel the world, taking along with them the manners we so require. The others, who do not know how to behave, let them stay in one place and suffer each other.'

It was a story that also applied to the pilgrims and those displaced by the dam, but the conclusion it suggested was not something I had any faith in.

~

It was the parikrama that brought Marietta to these banks. 'I was living in Himachal Pradesh when I read Gita Mehta's book *River Sutra*. It immediately clicked in my mind that if the Narmada actually exists, if there is a parikrama, then I will do it. At that time I was staying in a small hut in a remote village. When the lease ran out in late 1998, I came down for the parikrama. Later I wrote to Gita Mehta that her book had changed my life. She wrote back to say that I was not the only one inspired by her book. She had written the book without going to the Narmada, without seeing the river, but Narmada calls through the book.

'From the time I was very young, seventeen or so, I read the Gita and the Dhammapada. I grew up in the south of England just outside London. No one around me was interested in Indian culture. I first came here in 1982; in twenty-three years I have been back to London just once, to extend my visa.

'I stayed on at this Amarkantak ashram after finishing the parikrama. I am doing service at an Adivasi school 20 km from here, providing care to the little children. For me, this is home. I love this ashram. It is peaceful here, by the Narmada.'

When I first went looking for her at a local ashram, I was told she was away teaching at the school. I returned a few days later and the sadhus at the ashram pointed to a tiny hut at one end of the ashram compound. Dressed in a white sari, she did not seem taken aback in the least to find a stranger seeking to talk to her about the parikrama.

'It took me over three years to complete the entire parikrama. I walked the entire length barefoot. I still don't know whether it is more painful to stub my foot on a stone or have a thorn drive into my heel. I had malaria four times; once it was very serious. I suffered from typhoid and malnutrition as the food did not suit me.'

I figured her to be about sixty when she began the parikrama. It would have been no easy journey for someone that age, walking through the hilly and forested terrain.

'I would walk no more than six to seven hours daily. If I found a wonderful place, I would stop. Once I stopped at 6.30 a.m. I would sometimes arrive weeping at a village, a physiological reaction to hunger. A sweet cup of tea would take care of it, but it would alarm the villagers no end. Whenever I stopped, flies would surround me and people would cluster around asking me the same questions I answered every day. It was one experience the Indian parikramawasis did not suffer.'

As she paused, she must have noted the question on my face. The actual experience of the parikrama seemed to have been very different from the romantic impulse that set her off when she read Gita Mehta's book. She answered with a digression of her own.

'A Gond accompanied me for much of the way. He did so on his own. His grandson was crippled, he could only shuffle around on his bottom. I got him treatment, he was fitted with calipers and can now walk. He is doing much better. What his grandfather did was pure seva. This then is the real miracle of the Narmada, not the apparition of some old woman who points the way on the parikrama.'

It was Marietta, or Mira as she is now called, who told me about Kosi. I had asked her if she had heard of Verrier Elwin. It was a natural question to ask of an Englishwoman.

An English priest influenced by Gandhi, Elwin and his friend Shamrao had come to the Mandla district in the 1930s to work among the tribals of central India. They had set up base less than 15 km from Amarkantak. Elwin went on to become the foremost documenter of tribal life in central India and then in the north-east. After Independence, his association with Jawaharlal Nehru ensured that he played a key role in shaping this nation's tribal policy.

Not only had Mira read Elwin, she told me that another inmate at the ashram was related to Elwin's first wife. 'Kosi's son Vijay died last year, and I was asked to accompany her to the ceremony because I was from the same community, but having read Ramachandra Guha's biography of Elwin, I am not so sure about that. I am told she is very unwell, a visit might be just what she needs. You know my grandfather-in-law was the last native speaker of Manx and linguists from all over the world would come to see him. He lived to ninety-four only because of that.'

She told me of a local tailor who may have once stitched clothes for Elwin. I went along the Amarkantak main street asking after a tailor who may have once worked at the ashram where Mira was staying. It did not take very long to locate him. A portly man who immediately offered me tea, he seemed much too young to have stitched for Elwin.

He had never met Elwin, but he knew of him. 'Everyone knew of *bade bhaiyya* (elder brother). I was a young boy when he used to work here,' he said, searching his memory for details. '*Buzurg kehte the ke pakkad ke chai pila dete the* (the elders say he used to force people to sit down and drink tea). No one ever drank tea in this region before his arrival.'

It seems there is little we can do to shape the way the world remembers us. Influenced by Gandhi, Elwin had already renounced his Christian past when he started his work among the Gonds. But by the time he met Kosi, he had come to believe that the Gandhian prescription of abstinence made little sense in the world he now inhabited. He had entered the world of the Gonds, and he fell in love with Kosi. As for the wisdom of the move, it was his choice; he was thirty-seven, she was barely out of her teens.

Writing about his marriage in his later avtar as an anthropologist, Elwin recounts the vows read out by the Gond head priest.

He is English. He has come from another land to love us. From how great a distance have you and he come together, over land and sea, over mountain and forest, drawn together by fate. To you he is Raja; to him you are Rani, and because of you two we are all of royal blood. And listen again, brother! Today you eat her tender flesh; tomorrow do not despise her bones. Never leave this girl, nor leave this country, for she is yours and this land is yours.

But as his knowledge of tribal India deepened, his marriage with Kosi began to come apart. He would eventually be able to live out only part of the marriage vows. He never did leave this country, but he did leave this girl. Guha in his biography writes: 'Kosi Elwin was very much her own woman; independent, intelligent and self-willed, and in some matters vastly more experienced than her husband. Her view was that sex was her right; she'd "shout and rage, get tight, brag of her lovers, scorn V's skill and then expect a night of passionate love".'

Their first son was named Jawahar after Nehru, a friend of Elwin's; the second son Vijay was conceived in 1945, while Elwin was away studying the tribes of Orissa. In all likelihood, as Mira had noted, he was not Elwin's son though he bore his name. By 1948, the marriage was clearly coming apart.

~

I set out to see her the morning after my conversation with the tailor. The roads in MP then ranked among the worst in the country, for a good reason. This stretch of barely 15 km to Raitwar took over an hour. But once there, it was easy to locate the hut where Kosi stayed.

The girl who opened the door looked surprised to find a stranger at the door. The last time someone in search of a narrative came to this village hut in Raitwar, she was not even ten; now she was seventeen. Her name, she said, was Akrita Elwin. She was Vijay's daughter. She invited us in. The hut was bare but clean. The lack of possessions should have prepared me but when Akrita disappeared inside to summon her grandmother, there was nothing to foreshadow the shock of Kosi's appearance. Unable to stand, she shuffled in, dragging herself along the ground on her arms, her feet trailing below. She hauled herself over the step that led into the room and dragged herself to a corner, seating herself on the floor, leaning against the wall.

She said she felt over a hundred years old. It was an exaggeration but it rang true. Akrita's father Vijay, she told me, had died a year earlier of a burst ulcer. His elder brother Jawahar had died in the same fashion several years earlier. 'We had named him after the prime minister. Nehru met me in Delhi while I was pregnant and said that if it was a boy we must name the child after him.'

A few years ago, she had hurt her back in a fall. She managed to start walking after treatment but fell down and hurt herself again. There was no money to resume the treatment. Since then the family – Kosi, her daughter-in-law Santi Bai and her three children Akrita, Pramod and Arun – had lived on the money Santi earned by working on daily wages at nearby farms.

Even the pension, started in 1981 when the poet Dom Moraes had visited Raitwar, had been stopped for nearly a year. Shocked by the state of a family he had once known in Bombay where Jawahar had been his schoolmate, Dom Moraes got the MP government to sanction a pension from the department of culture for the family of a 'writer and artist'. The sum of Rs 600 a month stopped arriving in March 2005, shortly before the death of Vijay. With the family struggling to make ends meet, the MP government finally agreed to release the Rs 6,000 due to Kosi after I wrote about her.

As Santi related these facts, Akrita returned to the room with a glass of black tea, sweetened with gur. She apologized for the lack of milk and sugar in the house; she needn't have, I knew the Gonds had no fondness for milk in their tea. She said she knew nothing about the man whose name she bore. All she knew, she said, was that 'he wrote books in English.' And, she added, no one in the family now read the language.

In such surroundings, even though Kosi was more than willing to speak about the past, it was impossible to discuss evenings spent in the company of Jawaharlal Nehru or late-night revelries at the Taj Palace in Bombay.

From the perspective of that hut, Elwin's immersion in Gond culture remains a troublesome fact. In *Story of the Warrior and the Captive*, Borges writes of Droctulft, a barbarian who abandons his colleagues and dies defending the city they had besieged – Rome. Borges asks us to imagine not the individual Droctulft but the generic type formed from him. And in that measured flight of the intellect which has already given the language an adjective, he writes, 'Suddenly he is blinded and renewed by this revelation, the City. He knows that in it he will be a dog, or a child, and that he will not even begin to understand it, but he also knows that it is worth more than his gods and his sworn faith and all the marshes of Germany.'

Elwin too gave up his gods, his sworn faith, and he never returned to England. He never aimed to impose the civilization he brought with him, never did he seek to belittle a culture that in the context of this story Borges would have termed savage. Yet, in the space that he created for himself, he changed some lives irrevocably, and by no means for the better.

Droctulft was a man and a barbarian, Elwin a civilized man. He carried within him far less violence, far less intent to destroy, yet like the cup of tea that bears his memory, it is difficult to say what a man leaves behind.

No wonder Guha cautions that 'in the prevailing political climate, it is all too easy to represent the Elwin-Kosi encounter as one of the anthropologist exploiting his subject, the Oxford scholar dominating his tribal wife, and the Englishman being arrogant towards the Indian. These are all gross simplifications of a complex story.' Perhaps.

It was to the banks of the Narmada that India's foremost visionary Sankara journeyed to attain the realization of Advaita – non-duality. But such reconciliation is not always available in a valley where the agriculturist first encountered the forest dweller, the Indo-European north faced the Dravidian south and the Afghan battled the Gond. Circumstances differ but if each encounter was a love story, it was also a tragedy where the burden of loss weighed far more on one side. In each case, was a script such as Kosi's already written out at the start? It is a question that a traveller with a notebook, looking outwards rather than inwards, could at least hope to ask.

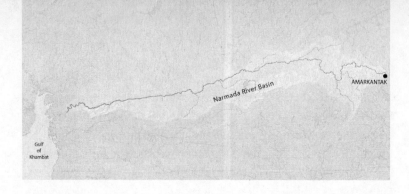

Narmada River Basin

AMARKANTAK

Gulf
of
Khambat

II

Whitewashed temples surround the sacred pool at the source of the river. Stone steps lead to the edge of the pool where a shrine stands half-submerged. Near the main temple, pilgrims have lined up beside a small stone statue of Nandi, waiting to crawl under its belly; success indicates divine favour. To my eyes, the Lord here seems to believe that the slight shall inherit the earth. As I stand and watch, I don't even think of giving it a try.

No one crowds the complex. Not the faithful who would once have thronged the pool but now inhabit the bathing ghats that have been constructed further along the stream. Not the importuning Brahmins common at many of the most important shrines of Hinduism. The British administrator W.H. Sleeman, better known for his encounter with the thugs, had noted over 150 years ago that bathers emerging from the 'Nerbudda', the name that the river actually goes by among a large number of those living along its banks, 'gave a trifle to these men ... but in no case was it demanded, or even solicited with any appearance of importunity, as it commonly is at fairs and holy places on the Ganges'.

This has much to do with the nature of faith in this region. Central India lacks the multitudes that define the Indo-Gangetic plain. Figures convey some sense of the difference. Over 700 persons inhabit every square kilometre along the Ganga, while the number is less than

200 in this region. In the tribal areas that lie along the banks of the upper Narmada, the population is even sparser. Faith here is far more personal, far less demonstrative. The temples themselves reflect this, they are unassuming conical structures gleaming white in the sun. From their pinnacles colourful pennants flutter in the breeze. These are not shrines built to awe; rather, in their whitewashed exterior and their diminutive size, they speak of a faith that comes from the heart.

An older temple complex looms just a few hundred yards to the south. It rises from the edge of another pool, certainly once sacred, that has been fenced off by the Archaeological Survey of India after a curious pilgrim drowned in the dirty, still water. These temples are clearly born of a classical heritage. The Kalachuri kings, contemporaries of the Chandelas who built Khajuraho, constructed them around the twelfth century AD. Almost five centuries later, the Rewa dynasty, their very name derived from the river, built the temples that now stand at the source.

It is difficult to say how the old temples would have once looked; their worn stone façade no longer boasts of the ambitions of kings, while time has made them part of the landscape. On my first visit here, when this book was not even an idea, I would often sit by the plinth of the Karnamath temple at the summit of the complex. It dominated the Amarkantak horizon and as langurs clambered around and a gentle breeze blew in from the sal forest, it was difficult not to be swayed by the impulse that draws men to religion.

A decade later, Rakesh Sahu was the ASI man on duty at the complex. In his mid-thirties, with features that did not mark him out from many of the Gond pilgrims, he was glad to have someone to talk to. When I asked him about the conflicting claims to the source of the river, he did not question the faith that took the pilgrims to the new source; all he said was that he was present when the old kund was drained and cleaned in 2005. 'It is around 35 feet deep. When the water was pumped out, it began to fill back at the rate of about 1.5 feet a day. This kund seems to be connected to the pool that devotees now believe is the source; whenever that pool is emptied for cleaning, the level in this kund falls.'

It was the rise and fall of water that still brought a few of the faithful to the old complex. Sahu pointed to one of the smaller temples still standing within. 'Sahib, on any one Monday in the month of Sawan (July–August), this shivling is immersed in water that rises up by itself from the earth. This is what people mean when they say Shiva bathes in the Narmada once a year.'

In the face of my scepticism, he said, 'I have seen it with my own eyes.'

Stories of miracles were abundant in this landscape, only a few stood up to scrutiny. But, for the pilgrims, the world of miracles was as real as the world I shared with them. This view of the world magnified the powers of those who claimed to work such miracles.

At the heart of this complex lay an ashram built by the Juna Akhada, the fraternity of naked Naga sadhus who lead the march of the sadhus at every Kumbh. The ASI was involved in a complex court battle to throw them out. 'I keep out of their path, they are unpredictable,' says Sahu. 'Our job is always at risk, how can one man look after the security of such a complex?'

He pointed to a new temple that towered over the old complex. An ugly edifice, garish and multicoloured, it marred the Amarkantak horizon. It was built, illegally, by the Kanchi Sankaracharya. The aesthetic that shaped the classical temples, whether of the north or the south of India, was born over several generations in the interplay of trained hereditary craftsmen and a lettered elite. Somewhere in the last five hundred years, the elite that nurtured this heritage vanished in north India. The new temple was an attempt by the Sankaracharya to imitate a model he did not understand with materials he did not comprehend. Even done well, the great classical temples of the south would be incongruous here, but this was a bad imitation adorned with bathroom tiles.

Sahu's disdain had little to do with aesthetics. 'One of our officers lost five salary increments for allowing this construction. What was he to do? Whenever he would come here to demolish the complex, the police would refuse to help him. Can one man bring down a temple with his bare hands in defiance of the wishes of a government?

'But even so, I am glad to be here. This is my hometown and in my job the problems can be worse. I was earlier posted at a shrine deep in the jungle, hundreds of kilometres from here. You must go see the temple, it houses an 8-foot shivling with Shiva's face carved on it. It is a seventh-century shrine surrounded by thick jungle. There is no habitation around for miles. My nights were spent in a hut built and maintained by the ASI guards who had been posted there over the years. Each day was like the passing of a year.'

He had come back to find that the contempt the Sankaracharya had displayed for the architecture of Amarkantak had been played out across the landscape in different ways. 'Things have changed, there are too many vehicles, and the forest is retreating. A few years ago, the sal borer attacked the trees. They had to be cut down, but for each tree that was affected, the contractors cut down ten that were not. The jungles have been thinned out. I am thirty-four years old, sahib, and I remember the times during the rains when we would not see the sun for months. Water would suddenly start bubbling from the earth and each new spring would continue to gush forth for months.'

Uphill from the source, the soil is boggy, water seems to seep out everywhere. It is possible to locate the beginnings of the river anywhere on this hillside. The Kalachuri temples mark one choice for the origin of the river. A new dynasty, seeking to impose its own order on the river, built another set of shrines close by. As far as the pilgrims are concerned, this is now the source of the river. Except for that one day in Sawan, they prefer to walk past the older complex. Even the few that wander in do so with a tourist's eye. It would not always have been so, but today the older complex is dead simply because there is no one alive to tell its tale.

~

Accompanied by an entourage of 360 mules and a host of Gond attendants, Rewa Nayak and Nayakin had wandered through the jungle for an entire day before they came to rest by the spring. It was exactly as Rewa Nayak had seen it in his dreams, and the bath in its waters miraculously cured the itching that had long plagued his body. That night, as he slept restfully for the first time in years, a young girl appeared in his dreams – I have granted you solace, build me a temple.

In the morning, rested, he forgot his dream. He tried to stir his men to load the mules but they slept into the afternoon. There would not be time enough to leave the jungle by nightfall. As Rewa Nayak slept by the spring for another night, the young girl again appeared in his dreams – You have forgotten my temple. In the morning Rewa Nayak asked his men to begin work. These were the temples that gleamed white at the source.

I heard the story recited by Ram Prasad Dhruve, a Pardhan Gond in the village of Sonpuri. For the Pardhans, the story of the Narmada temples begins with the Rewa kings. Nayak is the word they use for a king and the little girl is the river deity.

It was easy to see why the older temples did not draw the Gonds: the classical aesthetics they were born of came from another world. But the lack of any mention of the older temple complex raises interesting questions about their presence in this region. They are a people of Dravidian origin who once spoke a language akin to Tamil and Telugu. By the fifteenth century, Gond dynasties were certainly ruling in the town of Mandla, a hundred kilometres further along the river's course. If oral tradition is reliable, and it often is, the Gonds may well have come to the region around Amarkantak only after the twelfth century.

They are usually referred to as a tribal people but, for those who associate the word tribe with the inhabitants of a forest, this is misleading. The Gonds number over ten million and some are indeed forest dwellers but many made the move to agriculture centuries earlier. From them have come people who have founded dynasties, ruled kingdoms and today are beginning to find space in the regional and national legislatures. If they are a tribe, they are a tribe much in the way that the Mayans or the Aztecs were a tribe.

The Pardhans who told the tale of the temple are both priests and genealogists to the Gonds. Ram Prasad Dhruve's village of Sonpuri lies barely thirty kilometres from the source of the river. When I first met him in the village, there was little to mark him out. Like so many others, he tended his fields for much of the year, and his concerns were the concerns of farmers everywhere: would the rains be on time, would the harvest be bountiful? It was only when he set out every other year on a long journey to visit his patrons that he came alive to his calling.

As he told me, the journey could take him several months because these patrons, the jajmans, are scattered over a vast territory and some live several hundred kilometres from his village. They await his arrival and if by the third year they do not see him, they send for him. Calamities, they believe, befall households where the ruling deity of the Gonds, Bada Deo, has not been invoked. But it is only their Pardhan who can make the music that summons Bada Deo.

In a world spun out of stories, the Pardhans relate several tales of why this should be so. In the version Ram Prasad recites, seven Gond brothers working on their father's fields see a handsome young man ride through the fields mounted on a white steed. Fearing for their crops, they give chase. Only the youngest, fearful and hesitant, stays back. At the edge of the fields, the horse and rider vanish. It is then they realize they have seen Bada Deo incarnate. Angered, he has taken refuge in the saja tree.

The brothers pray and plead, they offer sacrifices. It does not work. Eventually the youngest gathers enough courage to find out what has happened. He goes into the jungle and fashions a string instrument out of a branch of the khirsari tree. In his hands it soars, producing a music none of them has heard before. Pleased, Bada Deo appears before them. 'This instrument will be called the bana, and whenever you play it, I will become manifest.'

From that day on, the brothers tell the youngest, he would not have to work on the fields. 'You will get your share of our produce for playing the bana. Even when we die, you will share our property. Our children will follow the same rules with your children.' The Pardhans are the descendants of the youngest son.

The genealogies of his Dhruve jajmans and the art of playing the bana are the patrimony of Ram Prasad Dhruve, as they are any Pardhan's. A father's jajmans are partitioned equally between his sons.

When Ram Prasad does arrive at the home of any one of his jajmans, he is welcomed with due ceremony. An offering of grain awaits him, new clothes and, if a rare jajman has the means, even silver, gold, cattle and the gift of land. But most importantly, ample amounts of mahua, Bada Deo's gift to mankind, await him.

The story goes that Bada Deo happened to venture out in the world on a day the king had chosen to feed his entire populace. He found men lying somnolent by the roadside, sapped of energy. To ensure they would never again feel so, he gifted them the art of distilling mahua from the flowers of the mahua tree. From that day on, joy, laughter and dance found a home in the world. No religious ceremony of the Gonds has taken place without mahua ever since.

Seated at the centre of the courtyard in his jajman's home, Ram Prasad unveils the bana and awaits the offering of mahua. The reverence is appropriate: no other instrument is Bada Deo incarnate, no other liquor is his spirit. After a sip of mahua from a cupped sal leaf, Ram Prasad begins to tune the plaintive cry of the bana, played much like a fiddle. Then, with a stroke of his bow, he begins the invocation of Bada Deo.

He sings the genealogy of his patrons. Their origins are his origins. He sings of the valour of the dead, of battles fought, of kingdoms founded and forts built, a recitation of deeds that have come down the generations to the men sitting before him. In the day or two he spends there, he adds to his knowledge of the clan the names of the newborn and the newly dead.

Once every three to five years, he will gather together all his patrons in an open clearing at a designated spot. The spirits of those who have died since the last such gathering have yet to find release. The memory of each death is enshrined in a particular object called a kunta. The jajmans arrive bearing the kuntas, which are then hidden in and around the clearing. Dressed in new clothes, reclining against a set of new bolsters, Ram Prasad begins the invocation of Bada Deo. To the sound of his playing, the spirit of Bada Deo finds a host among the gathering.

The spirit seeks water. Charged by its presence, the host runs towards the nearest source of water, a well, pond or river, and plunges in. Such is the power of the spirit, Ram Prasad relates, that the host has the strength to leap back out of the water, even from a well.

Then, trident in hand, the spirit seeks the memory of the dead. Each kunta, wherever it is hidden, is prised out and brought to the centre of the gathering and placed in a basket slung from a pole. Three days later, the kuntas are immersed in water and the spirits of the dead finally find release.

So Ram Prasad Dhruve told me, and I believed him. The art of storytelling exists to suspend disbelief. He was inheritor to this art in a way that is almost lost to us. Every pause, every gesture, every exclamation is inextricably bound to a narrative that is recreated at each telling. Not every Pardhan can play the bana and not every Pardhan is a master storyteller, but the few who combine the two skills are well known among the Gonds.

One night, as I watched, a Pardhan from the distant village of Garkamatha threw the assembled Pardhans of Sonpuri a challenge. 'You are wise and learned, you are the repositories of stories. I ask you a few simple questions: where is there water without mud, where is the fire that doesn't singe?'

The questions were taken seriously, the answers debated, but it was only a ritual leading up to the stories. In an open courtyard under the clear night sky, just a kilometre from the shores of the Narmada, a Pardhan Gond answered these questions by relating the story of Ganga's descent from the heavens. It was in Shiva's matted locks that there was water without mud, and the fire that did not singe resided in the story of Prahlad, the devotee of Vishnu who did not forsake his devotion in the face of torture by his father Hiranyakashipu.

As he narrated the tale of Ganga's descent, he asked another question, 'Why is the water of the Ganga so pure?' and proceeded to relate the story of Vishnu's Vamana avatar. Vishnu in the form of a dwarf asked for a mere three strides of land to vanquish the pride of the ruler of the earth. Granted the boon, Vishnu became manifest and having spanned the earth, his foot penetrated the heavens. Brahma, aware of Vishnu's presence, washed his foot and collected the water. This became the sacred water of the Ganga.

The Pardhan was not done. Once again he turned to the assembled audience and asked if they knew why Vishnu had to assume the form of a dwarf. He then began another story, part of a stream without beginning, without end.

For the Sonpuri Pardhans some of these stories were new, but by the end of the evening they had made them their own. The Pardhans are storytellers and a memory honed on genealogies accommodates everything in its own fashion. Among such people, it is difficult to talk of borrowings and influences. Many of the stories they tell are told in one form or the other in different parts of India. It is often claimed that these stories have filtered through to the Gonds from the people they lived in close contact with over the centuries, much as I witnessed the absorption of new stories in the course of that night, but the truth may well be otherwise.

It makes sense to come to this truth from across the globe, for the stories have spread far. Between June and August 1977, another storyteller, blind in a way that belongs to the epics, spun his own set of tales. In those two months Borges delivered seven lectures at the Teatro Coliseo in Buenos Aires. He began his third lecture by speaking of the discovery of the East by the West and concluded by saying, 'It is a book so vast that it is not necessary to have read it, for it is a part of our memory ....' He was talking of The Thousand and One Nights.

In the course of this lecture Borges noted, 'It is the work of thousands of authors, and none of them knew that he was helping to construct this illustrious book ....' and then summoned a fact from his infinite library. It is a note transcribed by Baron von Hammer-Purgstall. 'He speaks of certain men he calls *confabulators nocturni,* men of the night who tell stories, men whose profession it is to tell stories during the night. He cites an ancient Persian text which states that the first person to hear such stories told, who gathered the men of the night to tell stories in order to ease his insomnia, was Alexander of Macedon.'

The tales that form the core of *The Thousand and One Nights* go back to the twelfth-century Kashmiri text *Kathasaritasagara*, The Ocean of Stories. The author of the *Kathasaritasagara*, Somadeva, relates that his book is based on a much older source, the *Brihat Katha* by Gunadhya, which dates back to the first century BC.

The story of stories goes that Gunadhya was a sage residing in the forest who composed seven volumes of tales told over 700,000 verses. He chose to relate his tales in the Paisachi language. This language, probably of Dravidian origin, did not find favour with the king who was a scholar of Sanskrit. So the sage retired to the jungle and started relating his tales to the animals gathered there. As soon as he finished reciting one volume, he would consign it to the flames. Six volumes were so consigned when an ailing king was forced to send for him.

Immersed in the tales, the animals had forgotten to feed themselves. Deprived of game meat, the king had fallen ill. His courtiers reached just in time to save the last volume that engendered the *Kathasaritasagara*, which in turn gave rise to *A Thousand and One Nights*.

There is reason to suppose Paisachi was a Dravidian language spoken between the Narmada and the Godavari, and Gunadhya would certainly have found himself at home among the Gonds, who in many of the regions they inhabit remain forest dwellers. But even if such speculations remain open to debate, sitting among the Pardhans in the heart of Gondwana is as close as any of us can ever get to the storytellers of the nights.

~

The title of Salman Rushdie's *Haroun and the Sea of Stories* (the sea of stories is nothing but the *Kathasaritasagara*) is a homage to the ancient art of storytelling. When Haroun finally reached the source of all stories, Rushdie writes, he 'looked into the water and saw that it was made up of a thousand thousand thousand and one different currents, each one a different colour, weaving in and out of one another like a liquid tapestry of breathtaking complexity ....'

In so linking words to colours, Rushdie had unknowingly intuited the fate that has now embraced the ancient tradition of storytelling among the Pardhans, the possible forebears of Rushdie's forebears.

~

In 1979, J. Swaminathan, poet and painter, had just taken charge of Bharat Bhawan, a new cultural centre set up in Bhopal, the capital of the central Indian state of Madhya Pradesh which encompasses the greater part of the Narmada's course. He sent out a team of young artists to travel through the tribal areas of the state, in the belief that traditional crafts of the tribals could be looked at purely in terms of their artistic merit.

While in Patangarh, a village that lies less than a kilometre from Ram Prasad Dhruve's home in Sonpuri, their eyes fell on a painting of Hanuman on the walls of a hut. It was an innovation they were not prepared for; geometric designs on the floors, clay reliefs on the walls, all these were expected, but representational painting, they believed, was unknown. They found out that the painting was the work of a young Pardhan Gond named Jangarh Singh Syam.

A few months later Jangarh was headed to Bhopal. Accompanying him was his wife Nankusia, who was from Sonpuri. They had been married a few years earlier after a long courtship. Today Nankusia lives and paints in the same few rooms that they were first allotted, adjacent to one of the government bungalows in Bhopal's Professor Colony.

The room where I met her was bare, lit only by the pale-blue glow of a flickering tubelight. She sat on a rug on the floor facing us, while her children, Japani and Mayank, sat to one side listening to their mother talk of their father.

'We were from neighbouring villages. My sister had been married to his brother but it did not work out. He first saw me at a family wedding in Patangarh and then started visiting our house regularly. My parents thought he was there to meet my brother but even then he would joke that he would marry me.

'I would laugh at him. I was young, barely fourteen or fifteen, but I was on the taller side and he was short. Yet I could not help but notice him. He could play the flute so well, the tabla, the dholak. Even today I have his instruments lying with me.'

As memory transported her far from Bhopal to her village, the children hung on to every word. They must have heard the story several times but these words, and these memories were their only link to a father they barely got to know.

'One day when a group of us had gone to see the Dussehra at a nearby village, the two of us fell behind the rest while returning late at night. He promised to drop me home saying that he just had a bit of work to take care of in his village. We went to his aunt's house. On some pretext or the other, he kept me there till morning. In Sonpuri, word spread that I had run away with him.

'A week later, when I was working in the fields, my mother took me away. I was sent to stay with relatives in the village of Garkamatha where I had already been betrothed. A few months later, I met Jangarh again at a village fair. He asked after me and I told him I could not imagine being married to anyone else. He took me to his village, but I could not stay at his house. His father was opposed to the marriage but came around after consulting a local healer. Before anything could be done, he fell ill and died. We got married shortly after.

'We were badly off at the time. His sister and her two children had been abandoned by her husband. We were supporting the entire family, and the only work we could do was labour on other people's fields. Jangarh would even go out to help with the earthwork for erecting electric poles. He would spend the day digging and ferrying earth.

'Things began to change when we moved to Bhopal. At first we lived in a slum before Swaminathan found us this place. He made sure he was in regular touch with Jangarh. He would ask Jangarh to think of deities in the village such as Durga and paint them. He would give him paper and paint; all of Jangarh's earliest paintings are on paper.'

Mayank leaned forward, listening even more intently. He had inherited his father's talent.

'Whenever Jangarh painted, he was totally obsessed. He would work all day long at Bharat Bhawan and start his own work in the evening. He would often use material from the stories he had heard or he would ask elders to relate such stories.'

The evolution in Jangarh's art from these early paintings on paper is a vindication of Swaminathan's judgement. For a Pardhan to go from relating stories to illustrating them was an understandable step. For him to be shaped by Swaminathan's vision is to be expected under the circumstances, but Jangarh's talent was his own. Till Swaminathan's intervention, tribal art had been studied in India mainly for its insight into a 'tribal world' but no one had ever become the individual presence that Jangarh carved out for himself. Within a decade his murals adorned the dome of Bharat Bhawan and the open halls of the Madhya Pradesh Legislative Assembly. In 1989, he was the Indian representative at the 'Hundred Magicians of the Earth' exhibit at the Pompidou Art Centre in Paris.

A Japanese institution that had taken up the study of another traditional painting form that had travelled from village walls to canvas, the Mithila art of Bihar, extended Jangarh an invitation.

'He first travelled to Japan for about ten days. He really liked it, so much so that we named our daughter Japani. He then went back to Japan for three months. On his return I went to receive him at

Calcutta. He did not say much but he told me he had felt very lonely because everyone spoke angrezi [she uses the term to refer to a foreign language].

'For some reason the woman from Calcutta who had organized his trip kept his passport with her. She kept asking him to make another trip to Japan. He gave one excuse after another. He finally agreed to go. He told me that this would be the last time and on his return he could think about leaving his job and devoting himself fully to being a painter. He also kept saying he needed to get his passport back.

'From Japan he would write to me but we rarely spoke on the phone. He was not happy there. He wrote that he wanted to come back but that the people there wanted him to extend his visa by another six months. He felt things had changed since his last visit. People related to him differently. He asked me to write to him in our language because he felt his letters were being read. Then he wrote saying that his departure had been finalized and he would be arriving shortly.'

Her face had tightened.

'I still remember the date, it was 1 July 2001 when I got a call from him. He didn't say a word on hearing my voice, he just started crying. When I asked him what was wrong, all he said was that he was missing the children.

'The next day I got a call from the passport office. They asked if there was anyone else at home, so I gave the phone to his nephew. I thought they were calling about extending his visa. I had no idea how these things worked. I told his nephew not to let them extend the visa. It was then we learnt that Jangarh was dead.'

There are those who claim he was murdered. Nothing was ever clearly heard from Japan. Even the money to fly the body back had to be sent by the MP state government. The post-mortem conducted in Bhopal was never made public, though relatives claim it ruled out hanging as a cause of death.

It is difficult to sort out the truth from invention in the mystery that surrounds his death. I checked with the doctor who conducted the post-mortem; he confirmed that the death was due to hanging. He also clarified that the death had taken place on 3 July, two days after Nankusia recalls receiving the call. He was very sure of the dates, and I believed him because of a single telling detail. He could still remember the coffin which was used to ship Jangarh's body home from Japan. 'I have never seen anything so exquisite.'

Several years have passed, the story has been retold often and, in the minds of the grieving relatives, conjectures have become certainties. With neither the Japanese nor the Indian government interested in an enquiry, the mystery surrounding Jangarh's death may never be cleared.

Certainly, he seemed depressed in Japan and was under medication. A degree of paranoia was inevitable in surroundings where he understood no one. He was initially staying with some painters from Bihar but later he was on his own. For a man rooted in community, used to the ease of social interaction in India, there could have been few places more alien than Japan. That first journey from his village to Bhopal should have been far more difficult than the voyage to Japan, but it wasn't so. Even more than village and tribe, it is the language that we speak and the people who surround us that allow us to feel at home.

'I don't know what they did to him. No one ever called me from Japan, no one ever wrote to me. The woman from Calcutta did not even take my calls to her mobile. My husband had faced and dealt with extreme poverty in Patangarh. He had dug and carried earth to pull himself out. Such a man would not go to Japan and die. If he had to die, he would die in Patangarh or in Bhopal. He had three children, a good job, his paintings were selling and he commanded respect. Would he commit suicide in Japan? No, I don't think so – I don't believe it.'

In that room, in her presence, with her children looking on, I found it difficult to believe it as well. A man who showed the world how 'each coloured strand represented and contained a single tale' seemed to have been defeated by a silence he could not understand, a silence that still surrounds his death.

III

Jangarh's story does not end quite so simply; no story does. His life continues to echo beyond his death, setting in motion events that are changing a few villages and several lives, while manufacturing an idea of being Gond for the outside world.

It was in pursuit of this story that I had driven my three companions 400 kilometres from Bhopal in an old beat-up Maruti 800. Seated beside me was John Bowles, a collector of Gond art, but driven by motives well removed from those that bring wealth to Christie's. In the rear were our hosts, Nankusia's brother Subhash Vyam and his wife Durga, both painters whose work hangs on the walls of John's California home, part of perhaps the largest such private collection in the world.

Spun out of myth, these paintings need interpretation for the untrained eye, work John had undertaken for more than a decade. He had only been hampered by his Hindi, which while passable could do with some additional help. My journey from the source of the Narmada seemed to intersect perfectly with his journey to the source of Gond art.

At Patangarh, a dirt track branched off the main road and headed towards Sonpuri. It was already dusk and deep ruts carved out by tractors and jeeps threatened to sink the car up to its axle. Boulders that would not trouble off-road vehicles obstructed its path. It took half an hour of anxious driving before the road flattened out at the summit.

The path ran straight through fields dotted with yellow, and we found ourselves atop a low plateau, driving through villages quite unlike the habitations of non-tribal India. Each hut stood in isolation from the rest, surrounded by a field or two, hedged off by lantana. The main landholdings of the village seemed to lie below on the plains. A chequerboard valley of fields, mustard and green, gently sloped down to a tributary of the Narmada, and then rose again towards the blue hills where the fields met the forest. As we neared Sonpuri, the last light of dusk still glowed in the sky, tints of red and orange played on the cirrus clouds at the edge of the horizon. Subhash told us the Narmada lay barely a kilometre or two away.

Shovels and pickaxes were brought out to open up a path for the car from the road to Subhash's house. It was dark by the time we were parked and safely inside. It was only by the morning light that we realized that the mud hut where we were to stay over the next ten days deserved a place of its own in the history of this art.

The hut was constructed much like any other in the village – built up on all four sides with the rooms opening out onto a central courtyard. But its exteriors and interiors were adorned by murals that far exceeded the expectations the team from Bharat Bhawan would have brought with them to Patangarh. At the entrance stood Dehri Devi, goddess of the threshold, in the kitchen Chulha Deo, god of the hearth. Gond painters in Bhopal had given faces to the gods (only Bada Deo is never so represented; when the Pardhans depict him, it is always in the form of the baha). Now vivid and multicoloured, they had returned home.

We shared a room in one wing with Subhash's elder brother Pyare Lal and his family. Durga, Subhash and his aged parents occupied a room adjacent to the kitchen in another wing. Domesticated jungle fowl and cattle were almost on par with the humans in residence, with one wing to themselves. We found soon enough that here the days had an unhurried rhythm. We would eat two meals, both in the kitchen, seated on the floor. Durga Bai cooked, and while gender differences were lax in the village, many of the attitudes of the outside world had crept in. There was only room for three people at a time and Subhash, John and I always took precedence. The food was basic: bajra roti, ample amounts of rice, spicy curried vegetables and occasionally fish from nearby streams, less than an inch long, cooked and eaten whole in a curry.

The evenings would unfold in the courtyard at the centre of the hut. A single bare bulb lit in our honour would easily dispel the vivid night sky; the nearest large town was a hundred kilometres away. As the mahua began to flow, more and more people from the village would join us. Distilled from the flowers of the mahua tree, it is a clear liquid, like gin, with a heady aroma. It can be brewed to differing strengths, but in Sonpuri it needed no dilution with water. During our stay in the village, we grew used to imbibing mahua at any time of the day – after a long walk, during a session of storytelling or just at our ease. Not once were we afflicted by a hangover.

At some point in the evening, the gathering would move into the room we shared with Pyare Lal's family. Ram Prasad Dhruve would unveil the bana and the mahua would begin flowing. Women and men from the village would continue trooping in late into the night, some to listen to the stories, others because they were fascinated by our presence. The bana seemed to catch fire as the mahua seeped in. The Gond women were unafraid to look us in the eye, and there was a charge to their glances. It was easy to see why Elwin stayed on.

John was the first white man to have stayed in these villages for any length of time since Elwin had set up an ashram in Patangarh in the 1940s. Even in less remote parts of India, John's greying blond hair and his piercing blue eyes would have attracted attention. If this were not enough, he was equipped with a laptop, an oversize camera that I was later glad he had carried and a water-purifying pump that offered the entire village entertainment each evening.

His worry about the water only added to our hosts' belief in the frailty of all city dwellers. They would insist on using their precious supply of firewood to warm up water for our baths out in the open. John, out of sheer laziness or perhaps thanks to his being young in the sixties, did not believe in bathing in the morning. He bathed at the end of the day, a practice that made no sense to our hosts.

A day after receiving a late-night call from California on his cellphone (mobile telephony having outstripped electricity in its coverage of this region), he tried telling them a tale of his own. Explaining that the earth is like a very large ball, he said, 'If we start drilling a hole from this hut right through, we will probably end up close to my house in America on the other side. Things are upside down there, if it is evening here, it is morning there.' An enormous burden seemed to lift off their shoulders; this, they exclaimed, explains why he bathes in the evening!

It was a reminder, in a place where no such reminder was needed, that the world here was made whole only through stories. In our room Pyare Lal had begun illustrating the creation myth of the Gonds. The figures he painted were cramped and intense, a complete contrast to the far more expansive work of his son Gangaram which adorned the outside walls. Both Gangaram and Pyare Lal could trace their craft back to the extended school of art fostered by Jangarh in the very rooms where I had sat and heard Nankusia speak in Bhopal.

While Jangarh worked at Bharat Bhawan, one by one his relatives came to live with him in Bhopal. It was often difficult for them to find work when they arrived from the village, so he set them to work on his paintings. He would begin by asking them to fill in a prescribed colour after he had sketched the design. In time he would step back to allow them to sketch parts of the painting or pick the colours of their choice. It was much like the atelier of a master artist in the medieval era.

It was only later that I came to realize how closely, if unknowingly, Jangarh had recreated the medieval model. In the courts of Rajasthan and Himachal, away from the Mughal court, writes the art historian B.N. Goswamy, '... nearly everything there appears to have been made within families of painters: "family workshops", so to speak, not necessarily located in the state capital or nearby, and not made up of artists of different extractions or backgrounds. Artists could be working in their family homes: a small town or a village, perhaps ....'

As the demand for their work grew, more and more painters emerged from his village of Patangarh. Many of them were fleeing the poverty that had driven Jangarh to manual labour. Subhash recalls his childhood; 'I barely studied till the fifth standard. Pyare Lal and my father were both doing work on barkhi for other households. That meant that for a sum of about Rs 1,000 a year, they would live in that household and do all that was asked of them in the fields. As you can imagine, it was not an easy life: the demands could be extreme and there was no dignity to it. But we had no choice. Our fields had been mortgaged and even brass vessels had been pawned. I took up a number of odd jobs to sustain the family.'

It was during this time that Jangarh saw some of the clay figurines Subhash had made and managed to find a place for him in Bhopal. Durga Bai was also encouraged by Jangarh to paint. Now, shortly before our trip, Durga Bai had been to Frankfurt, Pyare Lal to Calcutta.

Jangarh's own village of Patangarh lay barely a ten-minute walk away. What happened in this one home in Sonpuri was repeated on a much larger scale in Patangarh. As the Pardhans in the village saw the success and wealth that came the way of Jangarh, a painter sprung up in almost every Pardhan household in the village.

In Patangarh, we visited the parents of Bajju Syam, probably the best-known of the Gond painters after Jangarh. John told me of Bajju's recent visit to London; it had resulted in a book – *The London Jungle Book* – in which he had painted and written about the city with much bemusement and some sympathy, but in a way that was his own, and owed something to this setting. 'Times have changed, I live in a city now, and I have been on a plane to London. That's not to say I'll throw my tradition away. I can't – it's in me. The new is done with the old in the blood. So even the pictures I draw of London – they will have a Gond twist, be a Gond view of London.'

～

Even before we started off on the drive from Bhopal, John and I had figured we needed to make sure we gave no cause for offence out of ignorance. Subhash suggested we could begin by hosting an evening for the village elders where the mahua would flow freely. It was a suggestion that went down well with John, who had been worried ever since reading an account of BBC journalist Mark Tully's visit to Patangarh in the company of Jangarh.

Almost a decade and a half earlier, Tully and Jangarh had travelled the same route that we had taken from Bhopal to reach Patangarh. Tully describes an evening of drinking and dancing that had seemed to flow smoothly till the village headman Sahiba Singh Tikam intervened. Cornering Tully for failing to foot the bill, he accused him of being kanjoos, stingy.

On reaching the village, we consulted the young headman of Sonpuri. He suggested we host an evening of traditional dances though he could not openly allow the distribution of mahua. A couple of years ago, he told us shamefacedly, Sonpuri was declared a model village during a visit by the chief minister of the state. Four handpumps were to be constructed in time for her visit. She arrived two days early, much to the surprise of the officials. Only one of the pumps was functional by then, the other three were never installed. In return for a pledge to forego mahua, the villages were given indoor toilets and biogas plants to fuel their homes. Eleven such plants were installed. During our stay, we found not one worked, no one used the indoor toilets and their decision to forego mahua had made them the butt of jokes in the surrounding villages.

The next day, after nightfall, we walked to the village school. We found a few young men making desultory attempts to install lighting and a sound system on a small stage. Bollywood music was blaring in the background as they worked. It didn't seem an auspicious start to an evening of traditional dance and music.

As the night wore on with little or no sign of progress on stage, Subhash appeared no less bewildered. John and I cracked nervous jokes about our search for authenticity. Just when we had given up hope, the distant roll of a drum and the sound of a flute heralded the dancers as they stepped out of the shadows along a village path. The Bollywood music faded away.

The dancers were attired in cream kurtas and dhotis, their headwraps a sparkling yellow or a deep red. A few were barefoot, others were in sneakers. As the drum began its beat, they hitched arms and began swaying to its sound, slowly picking up the rhythm as they circled the men playing the instruments at the centre of the stage. Their movements grew more vigorous, there was an abandon to their dancing.

When the men were done, the women began. They moved to a different rhythm, slow and haunting. Their singing took precedence over the dance. They sang of the beloved invited to partake of the mahua, of the aborted marriage of the Narmada. By now almost the entire village had gathered around the stage.

A few days later, when we walked to Patangarh, news of the evening had already preceded us, but it did not seem to have had the intended effect on all the residents. We stopped at the shrine to the village deity situated under a banyan tree at the entrance to the village. Remains of an old temple lay scattered around us, a few of the idols that had once been part of the temple made up the open-air shrine. As I walked up to speak to some men from the village, John stayed back to take a closer look at the idols.

Suddenly one of them turned to him and launched forth in English, 'You white man, too big to say "Ram, Ram" to a native.' We were all taken aback as he continued to harangue John over the next few minutes. Then as suddenly as he had flared up, he calmed down, and walked over to embrace John. 'I am just joking. We are like brothers.'

When the introductions were done, we found out this was the same Sahiba Singh Tikam. The years had made him no less formidable and the mahua he had been drinking from early in the morning did not help. Now that he had our attention, he told us his sister Leela was Elwin's second wife, the woman Elwin married after divorcing Kosi. He was also first cousin to Jangarh.

Seated by the banyan tree, he pointed to a spot a few hundred metres away. This was where Elwin had once lived and worked but the school he had started no longer existed, and the ashram had returned to the soil. Here, as we soon found out, a stray act of patronage by Elwin may have had a far more lasting impact than the two decades of work carried out in these buildings.

It was Sahiba Singh who set us off on the trail. Overriding the mumbled complaints of his companions, he told them to keep quiet while he spoke. 'You have no idea what these people are looking for.' He again pointed in the direction where the ashram once stood, 'The walls of the ashram had work in clay that was extraordinary. No one had seen anything like it in this village. Figurines of clay, reliefs on the wall, work on the doors, windows, it was all done by a woman that Elwin had especially brought here from Sadvachappar. Her name was Dasahi. The women in this village would all visit the ashram and slowly they picked up many of the designs and techniques that Dasahi had used. Jangarh's mother was one of them. Jangarh's father was my mother's brother, I know what I am telling you.'

Seeing that we were listening keenly, he paused long enough for us to send for more mahua, and then resumed, 'My sister may not be in touch with me but I have to say Elwin was a great man. It is only because of him that people like you come to this village. These people could never figure him out, they never knew where his money came from. He would lie in his bath and write up his notes on a typewriter and they thought he was printing currency.'

The old man we first met at Sadvachappar certainly thought so. 'He would lie naked in warm water and print notes.' Dasahi, he asked, yes of course, and pointed to another hamlet that we had left behind on the main road. As we turned to leave, he told us that he deserved some mahua for the information he had imparted.

Elwin had lived in Sadvachappar before he moved to Patangarh. He had left, Guha notes in his biography, after 'local reformers wanted the Gond to wear the sacred thread, abstain from liquor, give up music and dance ... coming to Patangrah from Sarwachappar was like abandoning a conventicle of the Plymouth Brethren for a cocktail party.' On the evidence of our visit, the local reformers had lost the battle.

As we walked back to the main street, we attracted a throng of villagers interested in our piquant quest. Someone said we should speak to a man sitting by the roadside, his crutches lying next to him. He was, we were told, the oldest man in the village.

'Dasahi, yes, her name was Dukhala Bai Markam, she was my aunt. If you follow me, I can show you her work. Some of it still survives on the walls.' We walked with him to a hut just a short distance from the main road. Another relative of Dukhala's, Aghanya Bai, joined him.

She started weeping as she began chanting the names of her relatives and her aunt. 'Gone, they are all gone, those times will never come back, this is all that survives.' Behind her on the wall, dabs of colour still peeping through several coats of whitewash, was a clay relief of a six-armed Shiva, trident and drum in hand, magnificent even in what remained.

Dukhala Bai never married. She probably had no conception of artistic immortality. She, in turn, must have learnt the rudiments of her art from someone in her family, but like Jangarh, her genius was her own. In some way then, it was true, as John noted, that an act of patronage by an Englishman connected Dukhala Bai to Jangarh and the paintings that hang in his California home.

~

One morning, accompanied by Subhash and Rajendra Kushram, a boy from Patangarh who had been extremely curious about the purpose of our stay, we set off for the Narmada. As we walked along a path that sloped gently towards the river, Subhash spoke of the land that had been cleared just a few generations ago. His grandfather, he said, had cleared their fields that lay below the village. Tall grass once grew till the very edge of the jungle, which had now receded. They still fetched firewood from the forest, setting out early in the morning. It took them the entire day to reach the jungle, chop wood and travel back. But the nostalgia for the jungle lived on. It was evident in the scenes Pyare Lal had painted on the walls of the hut. He was a man of few words, a farmer and a peasant before he was an artist. He was up early to let the cattle out to graze, supervise the ploughing of the field, sacrifice a chicken if the crop so required, and it was when he was done with these duties that he painted.

Amidst the panels that detailed the creation myth of the Gonds, there was one that did not fit in. When we asked him about it, he talked of a time when he was very young. 'It was almost forty years ago that I went to the jungle for the first time. We spent the night there by a stream. In the morning, when I went to fetch water, I saw this bird holding an antelope at bay as they circled each other. I have never again seen anything like it. I just wanted to convey a sense of what it was like then.'

For them, unlike the agriculturists of non-tribal India, the jungle had never been a menacing place. Yet, on this walk, they told me the riverbank had once held certain taboos. The terrain we were walking through was mostly jungle then, Subhash related. 'Even ten or fifteen years back our elders would caution us against wandering along the banks of the river early in the morning or close to sunset.' This was tiger territory in living memory and the precautions made sense.

We had heard exactly the same words a few days earlier when we had gone to Garkamatha, ten kilometres upriver. 'A few decades earlier we would go to the river only at midday. This was where the spirits dwelt. Now there are too many men and the spirits have left the world.'

When we finally reached the riverbank, we found the Narmada no more than a large stream, the water barely up to our waist. Even in November the afternoon sun was warm enough for us to laze in the water, stepping out only to talk to two passing parikramawasis. Nirmalananda Puri and his companion had been on the parikrama for six months. They were observing the traditional norms, walking barefoot and staying close to the bank.

Nirmalananda was the younger of the two, but also the more articulate. He was twenty-nine years old, from Ferozepur in Punjab. He left his home to join the Dasnami sect when he was seventeen. He said all this in English. 'I then studied for my MA in philosophy at the Benares Hindu University. I have been to Holland, Germany, Spain and Switzerland with my guru. I have decided to settle down in Mandla at the end of the parikrama, I have already bought land for my ashram.' I asked what had brought him from the banks of the Ganga to this parikrama. He quoted from the Upanishads and then translated for me, 'The *Chhandogya Upanishad* says that one must renounce the world on the banks of the Jahnavi, and meditate by the Rewa.' Subhash and Rajendra touched his feet.

My mind went back to the evening at Garkamatha where to our surprise one of the Pardhans broke away from his recital of traditional myths to sing Sankara's invocation to the Narmada. We were suddenly transported to another world – to the strains of the bana, a Gond was reciting a Sanskrit composition. At some point of time in the eighth century, the story went, Sankara had attained enlightenment on the banks of this very river. The Pardhan told us he had learnt the invocation from the parikramawasis who passed by, often staying the night in the village.

Their numbers had increased as the forests withered away and the dangers of the parikrama lessened. Not only had more of the outside world filtered in with them, the Gonds themselves were venturing forth. In Garkamatha no one had ever been on a parikrama till a decade back, now more than fifteen men from the village had completed the journey.

As we walked back in silence, it seemed to me that many different worlds were encroaching upon Sonpuri. The fields that we had been walking through were jungle once, now their very fertility would soon aggravate the problems of surplus and hierarchy. Men like Subhash had brought in money from the outside, whether as painters or men employed by the government, and the idea of a surplus was being created.

Subhash had managed to free his fields from mortgage but this was only a step away from buying new fields. A lack of hierarchy and an equitable distribution of meagre resources had long marked the village we had been staying in. Now for the first time, a few brick-and-mortar houses were coming up. Some men were doing better than the rest.

In such a world, it made little sense to worry about the impact of the market on the art of the Pardhans. Patronage, whether by their jajmans or by the market, had always shaped their attitudes. On our first evening in Sonpuri we were repeatedly told, 'You are like gods, we have been blessed by your presence.' It was a statement that left us wondering about our presence in their midst.

Over the next few days we realized there was a formulaic aspect to this utterance. The realization that should have been obvious at the very beginning came to us with time. For them we were much like their jajmans, and in the case of John this was really true. A language honed under other circumstances was now directed our way. As patrons, the same munificence that the jajmans displayed was expected of us. The Pardhans, Subhash's maternal uncle Ajju Ram told us 'are here to relate stories. The eyes see, the ears hear, the nose smells and we tell stories.' In much the same manner as their patrons, it was implicitly assumed that at the very least we would keep the mahua flowing. It was a year during which, they told us, the price of mahua had touched a new high. In some small measure, we may have contributed.

In this context, the demon of authenticity always raises its head. Is such an art truly 'primitive', is it tailored to a certain demand? I could only think of what the team from Bharat Bhawan had first found when they came here. Jangarh had painted an iconic representation of Hanuman carrying a mountain. To those familiar with the Ramayana, the context is immediate. Laxman lies dying in the battlefield, only the Sanjivani herb can bring him back to life. Even two decades ago, a Pardhan in Patangarh did not need to be told that Hanuman had neither the time nor the patience to search out a particular herb in the densely forested hillside, so he uprooted the mountain. Jangarh was born to this context, and it is in this context that this school of painting survives. Without the outside world looking in, men such as Jangarh may have been consigned to a life of hard physical labour and much that is valued today may well have been permanently lost.

On our way back, Rajendra stopped at Patangarh, saying he wanted to show us something. He reached Sonpuri later in the evening and took out a notebook. It resembled the register that schoolteachers use to keep attendance. Page after page had been filled with neat, tightly spaced handwritten sentences in Hindi. There were twenty stories in the notebook, tales he had heard his grandmother narrate. It had taken him six to seven days of uninterrupted work to write down each story. Now he wanted to know if his work had any worth.

I didn't really have to give him an answer. He began the work because he had seen the artists who returned from Bhopal ask their elders to repeat stories they had once heard when they were children. The stories today had a new value. A Pardhan artist may well paint a Hanuman, but he will do so rarely. The buyers of their art can buy a Hanuman painted by an artist anywhere in India, but only a Pardhan can depict a Sanphadki – a snake that takes flight for the first and last time on reaching the age of one hundred, its mere shadow enough to cause paralysis.

~

In Delhi, a year after our visit to Sonpuri, I hesitantly accompanied John to an exhibition of Gond painting by Dawat, Jangarh's son-in-law, whom we had met at Nankusia's home in Bhopal. I knew these exhibitions ensured the painters made a living, but there was something disconcerting about seeing the art discussed in such settings. Perhaps my mind was made up by the mention of a bana player on the invite.

The paintings had been put up on display on a well-lit proscenium. There were people milling around, I could hear snatches of conversation. It took a while before my eye fell on a figure sitting in an ill-lit corner of the stage. I could make out the bana and the white turban, and then suddenly I recognized Ram Prasad Dhruve.

He looked shrunken and withdrawn in these surroundings. None of those wandering amid the exhibits were paying him any attention. John and I sat down to listen. He couldn't make out faces in the dark but the presence of a few figures listening gave him some heart, his voice picked up. But it couldn't last. What was a bana player without mahua or an audience that added its voice to his own?

His face lit up when he finally saw us. Dawat came over, and told us he had travelled all the way from Bhopal to Sonpuri to bring Ram Prasad to Delhi.

At the end of the evening, they accompanied me home. For Ram Prasad everything around him was new, the cars, the headlights, the stream of traffic, the roundabouts of New Delhi. I did wonder what this world looked like through his eyes but we did not share a vocabulary that would allow for such a discussion. At home, after I settled them in, he emerged from his room to find out where he could go to piss. I showed him how the flush worked.

We finally sat down to a bottle of Russian vodka, which was more familiar territory for Ram Prasad. He wanted to know how this mahua had been made. He seemed sceptical when I said it was distilled from potatoes. Anyone who has known the heady smell of the mahua flower would find it difficult to imagine potatoes could yield a comparable liquor.

After the ritual offering to the bana, we drank the vodka. A few glasses of one part vodka to one part water cleared his doubts, and he began to play. The haunting, plaintive sound transported me back to Sonpuri. Some of the stories were ones we had heard before, others were new. The story of the friendship between a dung beetle and a bumblebee, of the dung beetle's shame when he sees the beautiful home his friend lives in, a reminder through song and story of our duty as jajmans.

John and Dawat were soon ready to sleep, but Ram Prasad seemed to derive strength from the vodka. The more he drank, the more awake he was, the more lively his playing, the more animated his stories. After the bottle was over, we pulled out another half bottle of cheap Indian vodka, and we no longer bothered with the water. When I couldn't keep awake any longer, Ram Prasad Dhruve looked at me, a little disappointed, and then reluctantly disappeared into a room to try and sleep.

In the morning, as they prepared to leave for the train station, we sat over a morning cup of tea. As always, I found it difficult to discern what Ram Prasad was thinking. Whenever he was not playing the bana, he preferred silence. I asked him the question that had been playing in my mind ever since my conversation with Dawat the night before.

I had told Dawat he should have brought someone younger with him, someone who would be more familiar with this world. He had shrugged his shoulders and said there was no one among his compatriots who played the bana. The young Pardhans found it demeaning to depend on their jajmans for a living. Ram Prasad Dhruve was the last of the bana players in Sonpuri.

There was a note of regret in Ram Prasad's voice. 'No one wants to learn the bana. Some are happy farming, the others want to paint. I worry for my jajmans. Without my bana, how will they worship Bada Deo? The gods will trouble them.'

What the new patrons of the Pardhans did not seem to realize was that the thousand thousand thousand and one different currents, each one a different colour, would no longer cohere without the bana.

IV

Past Sonpuri, fed by the rivulets that race through the forests and fields on its banks, the Narmada swells from a waist-deep stream into a mighty river. Headed westwards to the sea, only once does it change course, suddenly lurching south to meet its tributary, the Banjar. The two large rivers collide almost head on. The impact is enough to knock the Narmada back on its westward course. Along this arc described by the Narmada, on the far bank from the Banjar, surrounded by water on three sides, lies Mandla.

When the Pardhans sing the history of the Gond clans, they begin with the history of the 'king of the fifty-two forts' who ruled from the city of Mandla. Today this is almost the edge of Gond territory. Further west, the Gonds begin to give way to a non-tribal peasantry who farm some of the most fertile land in the country. But five centuries ago, Mandla lay at the heart of a vast Gond kingdom that today survives only in the songs of the Pardhans.

At the Jabalpur museum, an old map of undivided Madhya Pradesh, from a time when political correctness was not in fashion, displays the distribution of the tribal population in the state. The south-eastern quarter is shown as inhabited by the Gonds. This includes the long southward projection, now Chhattisgarh, which the map claims is home to the 'most primitive Gonds'.

The area around Amarkantak along the upper course of the

Narmada has among the highest density of Gond population in the state. This density starts decreasing as the river proceeds westwards, shrinking to a tiny southern corridor along the river encroached by the 'less tribal' portion of the state. The corridor, though, doesn't entirely disappear, rather it melds into the Bhil region of the state, linking up to the other large tribal group in the state.

Like the painting of the Pardhans, the map tells a story.

Through the early history of the Indian subcontinent, the Narmada Valley was home to a number of classical cities that lay along the trade routes that connected the two great cities of the Mauryan Empire, Pataliputra in the Indo-Gangetic plain and Ujjayini that lay on the edge of the Narmada Valley. After the breakdown of the empire, a number of these cities flourished as city states, before declining in the face of new kingdoms that lasted till the early medieval period. For much of this period, the bulk of the population of the valley remained tribal.

Through constant interaction with these cities and civilizations, the Gonds eventually founded a kingdom of their own. Fifteen kilometres upstream of Mandla, at the Ramnagar fort, where every room and terrace seems to have been designed with a view of the Narmada in mind, stands a stone tablet listing the history of the dynasty. The first name on the tablet is Yadav Rao.

According to a legend documented by Sleeman, Yadav Rao, a young Gond from the lands south of the Narmada, had once gone on a pilgrimage to Amarkantak. Walking through the forest, he saw three Gonds, two men and a woman, walking ahead trailed by a gigantic monkey. The monkey dropped a few peacock feathers at his feet. Yadav Rao picked them up. At night, Narmada in the guise of a goddess appeared in his dreams. She told him that he had actually seen Ram, Laxman, Sita and Hanuman. The peacock feathers he had picked up, she said, prophesied that he would be king.

Yadav Rao followed the advice of the river goddess and took up a job with the local ruler of Garha, a few kilometres from Jabalpur. The king had only one offspring, his daughter Ratnavali. He called a gathering of eligible men where the kingfisher, an auspicious bird, would select the groom. Let loose in the assembly of men, the bird alighted on Yadav Rao's head.

The legend seems to point to the same northward movement of the Gonds that their Dravidian language attests to, but the Rampur stone tablet imposes a chronology of kings that extends back to the third or fourth century AD. The names that follow Yadav Rao on the list seem apocryphal, matching the penchant of all Indian dynasties to seek sanctity in a distant past. It is only the figures of the medieval period that seem to reflect historical personages.

A historian of the Gonds, Suresh Mishra, places the beginnings of this dynasty in the fifteenth century. He argues that the presence of the Gonds as rulers in this region seems to coincide with the disappearance of the powerful Kalachuri dynasty, the very same dynasty that had built the older, now abandoned, temples at the source of the Narmada at Amarkantak. While the Kalachuris reigned from Jabalpur, he argues, they would hardly have let an independent principality exist barely a few kilometres away at Garha. Mishra's argument only reconfirms what the legend of the Rewa temples related by the Pardhans suggests, that they arrived in this region after the twelfth century.

Certainly, by the mid-sixteenth century, the Gond kingdom was larger than Ireland and Wales put together. Further to the west was the kingdom of the Malwa sultans who figure far more in canonical renditions of Indian history because they guarded the main route across the Narmada to the Deccan. Somewhere between 1556 and 1560, the last of the independent Malwa sultans, Baaz Bahadur, attacked the Gond kingdom, then ruled by the legendary queen Durgawati. He was beaten back, his army put to the sword, but the battle fatally weakened both the Afghans and the Gonds. Within a few years the Malwa principality fell to Akbar and in 1564 Durgawati died fighting Akbar's general Asaf Khan.

After the defeat of Durgawati, Asaf Khan stormed Chauragarh, the seemingly impregnable fort of the Gonds. Akbar's chronicler Abul

Fazl provides a contemporary account. 'When the brilliancy of the Rānī's rule was extinguished, and when in the very height of her rule the hand of destruction flung the dust of annihilation on the head of that noble lady, Ā(s)af Khān after two months, and when his mind was at rest about the Miyāna country proceeded to the conquest of Caurāgarh fort. This fortress was replete with buried treasures, and rare jewels, for the collection of which former rajahs had exerted themselves for many ages. They thought these would be a means of safety but in the end they were a cause of destruction. The soldiers girded up the loins of courage to capture this golden fort, and from the love of these treasures they washed their hands of life and eagerly followed Ā(s)af Khān. The Rānī's son who had left the battle-field and was shut up in the fort, came out to fight on the approach of the army of fortune; but the fort was taken after a short contest' (Abul Fazl, *Akbarnama*).

While Mandla and Rampur are easy to visit, Chauragarh is even more inaccessible today than it was five hundred years ago. No buses ply the route, few outsiders know of the existence of the fort that local villagers call Chaugan. On my first visit I was, after much questioning, directed to a dirt track through a dense forest. It was not terrain that my Maruti was designed to handle. With every passing kilometre the road seemed to fall further into disrepair, melding into the surrounding forest. Crossing a river bed, the car sank into the wet sand. I waited for an hour before a passing tractor hauled me out.

I returned a year later with John, and made sure we hired an SUV. A long detour on a narrow dirt track winding around fields, miles further along from where I had abandoned the track, finally got us to the base of a hill. The climb to the fort took an hour, the path briefly levelling out at the summit of a hillock before it climbed up to the fort. From the top, with the Narmada Valley spread out below, it would have been easy to spot any approaching army miles away. Within the walls, remains of large perennial baolis were still visible.

The royal palace in one corner of the fort complex was in ruins. From the glimpses of paint on the façade and the work on the stone pillars collapsed amidst the encroaching jungle, it was easy to tell that the Gond had borrowed from the older dynasties in this region. They seemed to have done what every new set of rulers did in this land – use existing material for their construction. Amidst the ruins of the royal palace lay carved pillars that seemed to date back to the Kalachuri period.

From an independent kingdom to a feudatory of the Mughals, this was the beginning of a slow decline. Fort by fort, the kingdom fell away. Looking for a more secure capital, the subsequent rulers first shifted to Ramnagar on the banks of the Narmada where the palace housing the stone tablet still stands, and then back to Mandla in 1699. It was the takeover of Mandla by the Marathas in 1781 that brought an end to the dynasty. By 1820 the Marathas had given way to the British.

In an account of his travels in 1835, W.H. Sleeman writes of an encounter with the last queen of this dynasty, Laxmi Kumari, 'Her husband, Narhari Shah ... died a prisoner in the fortress of Kurai, in the Sagar district, in 1789 AD, leaving two widows. One burnt herself upon the funeral pyre and the other was prevented from doing so, merely because she was thought too young, as she was not then fifteen years of age ... She is now about sixty years of age, and still a very good looking woman. In her youth she must have been beautiful. She does not object to appear unveiled before gentlemen on any particular occasion; and, when Lord W. Bentinck was at Jubbulpore in 1833, I introduced the old queen to him. He seemed very much interested, and ordered the old lady a pair of shawls. None but the very coarse ones were found in the store-rooms of the Governor General's representative, and his Lordship said these were not such as a Governor-General could present, or a *queen*, however poor, receive; and as his own "toshakhana" had gone on, he desired that a pair of the finest kind should be purchased and presented to her in his name ... when I returned in 1835, I found that the *rejected* shawls had been presented to her, and were such coarse things that she was ashamed to wear them, as much, I really believe, on account of the exalted person who had given them, as her own.'

Bentinck was the man credited with the end of sati, but Sleeman does not seem to record what this survivor of the practice may have had to say to Bentinck.

Despite their knowledge of this kingdom, the British seemed to view the tribals much as the rest of India continues to do today. In an excellent paper titled, 'Race, Caste and Tribe in Central India: the Early Origins of Indian Anthropometry', the scholar Crispin Bates describes an exhibition held in Jabalpur in 1866-67, thirty-eight years after Bentick banned sati, modelled on the Great Exhibition at the Crystal Palace in London in 1851. Bates's tone, with the restraint proper to a historian, says more than any analysis of British attitudes would. 'Samples of produce, archaeological finds and handicrafts were brought to Jubbulpore from all over the Central Provinces, together with live examples of the various "aboriginal tribes" that were judged to be characteristic of the different parts of the territory.'

Perhaps Narhari Shah knew what the future held. Heirless, in 1779 he found an infant abandoned by the banks of the Narmada. He adopted the boy and named him Narmada Baksh (the gift of the Narmada). Narmada Baksh never sat on the Mandla throne but he was declared heir to the property of Laxmi Kumari. When the Bundela Rajputs fought the British in 1842, the records speak of a rebel named Narmada Baksh.

~

The ruler of the Gond dynasty best known to the outside world, Durgawati, was the daughter of a Chandela Rajput king. The willingness of a status-conscious Rajput king to give his daughter in marriage to a Gond ruler reflected the power of the dynasty. The marriage set a pattern which was replicated among the Mandla feudatories, creating a ruling community – the Raj Gonds.

On the road from Narsinghpur to Hoshangabad, a right turn led us to the village of Kareli, located a few kilometres from the Narmada. Here it was easy to find the house we had gone looking for; everyone knew where the Raja sahib lived.

It was constructed on much the same pattern as the hut we had stayed in at Sonpuri, but magnified manifold, it was more an earthen palace than a hut. The large entrance led to an open courtyard, cut in half by a large wall beyond which lay the private quarters of the family. A tractor was parked to the left, and cows were tethered along the wall. We were ushered into the wing on the right, where the Raja sahib seemed to spend much of his time and received visitors. The entire wing was one vast room, with its dark expanse barely visible from where we were seated near the doorway. An old ceiling fan slowly spun from the rafters, a huge bed was placed on a raised earthen platform. The furniture was old and finely worked.

The raja emerged from the dark of the room. His swarthy complexion belonged to the Gonds, but his features carried the impress of his Rajput forebears. His name, he told us, was Raja Lal Devi Singh Judeo, and his family once ruled from a palace in Fatehpur, an hour-long journey along the road we had just left.

According to Roper Lethbridge's *The Golden Book of India*, a compilation of the genealogies of the ruling families of India, 'The Fatehpur Jagir is said to have been conferred on an ancestor by Raja Kamal Nain, Gond Raja of Mandla in 930 AD. A sanad from the Raja of Mandla dated 1500 AD is still in the possession of the family.'

However efficiently historians may muster up their facts, they can claim little control over memory, which constructs a narrative of its own. This terse entry subscribed both to the mythological origins of the dynasty, hence the date of 930 AD, and the demands of the historians, who would rather place reliance on an actual document that dates to 1500 AD.

Judeo told me that sixty-six generations of his family had ruled over Junagadh in Gujarat before they migrated to Rajasthan in 805 AD, on their way to Mandla. 'At Fatehpur we ruled over a jagir of 750 villages. After Independence our privy purse amounted to Rs 2 lakh a year.'

In 1969 Indira Gandhi abolished the purse, something that still rankled with Judeo. 'I am in correspondence with the home ministry. The decision was illegal, I want the privy purse restored.'

He sent someone to look for copies of the letter, and then turned to me. As if admitting that he was fighting a world he didn't understand, he asked me, 'You live in Delhi, do you think you can find out why they have not been replying to my letters?'

He didn't wait for my answer; another member of his bedraggled retinue had returned with the memorabilia of the estate the family once ruled.

Surrounded by cows, flea-ridden pi-dogs, a rooster and several hens, we gazed at the court insignia, the royal seal, the royal ring and the gold zari work on the sherwani his grandfather had worn to attend the durbar of King George V in 1911 in Delhi.

As he posed for a few pictures, royal sword in hand, he spoke of memories triggered by the artifacts. 'I was born in Fatehpur. My eldest brother was married while we were still living there. But we could no longer go on living there. In 1960 we paid Rs 75,000 just for the whitewash. We needed to employ twenty-five people.'

A couple of days later I remembered his words as we assembled again to travel to Fatehpur. The raja was accompanied by the local police inspector and a private guard armed with a 12-bore gun slung over his shoulders, a belt of cartridges strapped diagonally across his chest.

The journey took much longer than it should have. The raja stopped to pray at every temple along the way. This Raj Gond devotion to Hinduism was something the BJP had put to good use. The raja told me Dilip Singh Judeo in Chhattisgarh was a cousin, as were all the Gond ministers in the BJP government in MP. The raja himself was an office-bearer in the Narsinghpur district unit of the BJP.

At one of the halts, I asked a man accompanying us whether the raja was married. He told me the raja had been married for forty years, and his wife lived in a hut behind the whitewashed wall that ran the length of the the courtyard. She had an attendant to see to her needs, but in the forty years she had lived there, no one other than the raja and the attendant had ever seen her.

The road eventually left the habitations and temples behind and headed into a sal forest. We parked near an abandoned baoli, close to a large stone building that had once housed a garrison. In 1842, Fatehpur had fallen to the British after a cannonade destroyed the garrison's resistance. The raja, who had heard the story passed down the generations, showed us where the British had positioned their powerful cannons and shelled the palace.

We walked towards the palace. In the forty years of its abandonment it had already turned to ruin. The jungle was encroaching, the walls and roofs had caved in. In the Indian climate, none of this had taken very long.

One of the men who accompanied us from Kareli had been a retainer when the raja's father still held court in Fatehpur. He showed me the kacheri, the courthouse, where the raja would dispense justice, the quarters where food was once cooked, the stables and the storehouse for the weapons. Here, history was decaying faster than memory.

~

For the forty years between the Maratha conquest of Mandla and their defeat by the British, the Narmada Valley was thrown into turmoil. The series of Maratha losses culminating in their final defeat led to the decommissioning of irregular troops. These troops had never been paid a regular salary; instead, they were given a share of the plunder during the campaigns. This decommissioned cavalry became the core around which thousands of brigands and freebooters gathered, and the poorly documented but vivid legend of the Pindari was born.

Contemporary Indian accounts are scarce, and British accounts are riddled with the need to justify colonial occupation, especially after the event. Accounts, written at a time when the possibility of war was open, seem a more realistic appraisal of the foe the British were to soon meet in battle. Just such an account of the Pindaris – The Pindaris, with the author identified only as an officer in the service of the honourable East India Company – was published in 1818 and written in the years immediately preceding the British campaign against the Pindaris:

> It is only of late, that these bandits have become really formidable, and they may now be looked upon as an independent power, which if properly united, under an able commander, would prove the most dangerous enemy that could arise to disturb the peace and prosperity of India.

> The climate and the hardy habits of these plunderers render tents or baggage unnecessary encumbrance, each person carries a few days possession for himself and for his horse, and they march for weeks together, at the rate of thirty and forty miles a day, over roads and countries impassable for a regular army. They exhibit a striking resemblance to the Cossacks, as well in their customs as in the activity of their movements. Their arms are the same, being a lance and a sword, which they use with considerable dexterity; their horses, like that of the Cossacks, are small, but extremely active; and they pillage, without distinction, friends as well as foes. They move in bodies seldom exceeding two or three thousand men, and hold a direct undeviating course until they reach their destination, when they at once divide into small parties, that they may with more facility plunder the country, and carry off a large quantity of booty; destroying, at the same time, what they cannot remove. They are frequently guilty of the most inhuman barbarities, and their progress is generally marked by the smoking ruin of villages, the shrieks of women, and the groans of their mutilated husbands. At times they wallow in abundance, while at others they cannot procure the necessaries of life; and their horses, which are trained to undergo the same privation as their master, often receive a stimulus of opium when impelled to uncommon exertion. Night and the middle of the day are dedicated to repose; and recent experience has shown us that they may be surprised with effect at such hours. Fighting is not their object, they have seldom been known to resist the attack even of an inferior enemy; pursued they make marches of extraordinary lengths, and should they happen to be overtaken, they disperse and reassemble at an

appointed rendezvous; or if followed into their country, they immediately retire to their respective homes. Their wealth and families are scattered over that mountainous tract of country which borders the Nerbudda to the north. They find protection either in the castles belonging to themselves, or from the powers with whom they are either openly or secretly connected. They can scarcely be said to present any point of attack, and the defeat or destruction of any particular class would only effect the ruin of an individual, without removing the evil of a system equally inveterate in its nature, and extensive in its influence.

The Pindaris seem to have dispersed into the general population after their defeat. But in Narsinghpur, local talk connects them to the Jat family that founded the town. When we told Judeo that we were going to meet the Jat sardars of Narsinghpur, he scoffed at the claim. '*Woh to looteray the* (They were looters).'

We went to meet Rao Raj Kishore at his large haveli in Narsinghpur. His old world manners had no touch of the buccaneer. Family tradition suggests his ancestor arrived here in the eighteenth century. 'He built the temple to Narsingh, our family deity, hence the name of the town.'

The date made sense. Under the Gonds, all the chieftains were Raj Gonds. Only under the Marathas, in the confusion of the Pindari years, could a Jat chieftain have staked a claim to territory in this region. While many of the Pindaris seemed to have been of Afghan origin, they had Jats in their ranks – the most prominent of the Pindari bands was the one led by a Jat named Chitu. We hesitantly asked the Rao about the possibility of a Pindari connection. He said he had no idea what brought his ancestors to Narsinghpur, but he could not rule out the possibility.

Amar Farooqui, in his study *Sindias and the Raj: Princely Gwalior c. 1800-1850* writes, 'The two most important Pindari chiefs, Chitu and Karim Khan ... had accepted grants from Sindia in the rather remote and inhospitable Narsimhapur area ... Until about the last quarter of the eighteenth century it was unsettled and sparsely populated. Narsimhapur town, originally known as village Gadariya Kheda ("settlement of shepherds") began to develop only during the 1780s.'

The Rao, accompanied by his son, generously showed us around the haveli. Unlike the abandoned ruins of Fatehpur, this double-storeyed haveli was in good condition. As he lit a wick that set a kerosene-powered fan going, the son told us that all the old artifacts were kept in working condition. Pointing to the old guns that had been pulled out of the shelves for us to inspect, he said they were cleaned regularly and fired once a year.

There was an easy lack of formality about the family, very distinct from the Rajput ways. The Rao's wife asked me about my journey along the Narmada. The idea of the kind of permanent purdah which we had just left behind a few kilometres away in Kareli seemed far removed from the setting. She spoke to us of the difficulty of adjusting to this life when she first moved here from Delhi. Her son added that all their relatives lived in and around Delhi and all their marriages still took place with the Jats of the region.

This only seemed to add to the evidence connecting the family to Chitu. In his Master's thesis, 'Pindari Society and the Establishment of British Paramountcy in India', Philip F. McEldowney had put together a brief biography of the Pindari leader:

> Chitu, the other outstanding Pindari leader of the Independent Period, was born a Jat near Delhi. Dobble Khan, whose sons led Barun' B durrah, bought Chitu as a slave and then adopted him as his son. Eventually Chitu acquired the leadership of Barun's group ....
>
> In February (1817) most of the Pindari leaders surrendered to the British authorities. Only Chitu escaped ... Near the end of February 1819 his body was brought to Malcolm. He had been attacked and killed by a tiger.

Past the lamps and the guns, the Rao stopped in front of a sword that occupied a shelf of its own. The Arabic calligraphy was very intricate. The local Shia community, he told us, had a name for it – Tega, and held it in very high esteem. Each year the Muharram procession began from this house, in the presence of this sword.

The explanation for the custom, it seemed to me, lay in the camaraderie that appeared to have existed in the Pindari bands between the Hindus and Muslims, and the devotion of each band to its sardar. I was, I now believed, talking to Chitu's descendants. Their wariness in acknowledging their Pindari connections seemed misplaced to me. Less than fifty years after his death, Chitu had already become a figure of legend.

In a poem written 'on the Nerbada 1866,' the British ICS officer Alfred Lyall has his 'Old Pindaree' lament:

> And if I were forty years younger, with my life before me
>   to choose
> I would'nt be lectured by Kafirs, or bullied by fat
>   Hindoos;
> But I'd go to some far-off country where Musalmans still
>   are men
> Or take to the jungle, like Cheettoo, and die in the tiger's
>   den.

~

The Rao even in his hospitality embodied the process that has transformed the plains of the Narmada over the past 300 years. The loss of the Mandla kingdom and the subsequent turmoil meant that the Gonds had largely ceded this territory to outsiders.

Over much of the fertile plains of the Narmada Valley, a set of rulers ranging from Jat sardars of Narsinghpur to the British and the Marathas invited agriculturists from other parts of the country to come, clear the forests and farm the land. This was how the 'less tribal' region had grown to encompass the Narmada.

It is only where the fertile plains recede into the hills of Jhabua that another tribal community, the Bhils, dominates the landscape along the river. While the Dravidian language of the Gonds, Gondi, now spoken mainly by the 'most primitive' branch of the community, is still part of the living memory of the entire tribe, the Bhils speak an Indo-European language. It is not clear if their original language belonged to a different language group, but the tribe retains no memory of any other language.

Unlike the Gonds, who interacted with the Rajputs through a few families who came to the Mandla court as powerful feudatories, the zone of interaction among the Bhils and the Rajputs is immense, ranging from Rajasthan to Madhya Pradesh. The interaction has produced the Bhilalas. Much like the Raj Gonds among the Gonds, the Bhilalas are a privileged community among the Bhils. Given their geography, they are far more numerous and form a much larger percentage of the Bhil tribe. This has only furthered their familiarity with Hinduism, already fostered by geography. It has also resulted in a gradation even within the Bhilalas, with those at the very top claiming an exclusively Rajput status, largely cut off from any contact with the Bhils.

At the very end of my journey along the Narmada, I met the Bhilala ruler of Mandhata, the ancient city that once occupied the summit of the island of Omkareshwar, the island where this book, like all parikramas of the Narmada, will end.

I travelled twice to Omkareshwar in the course of writing this book. Somewhat astounded by the rapid changes that had come to the island with the construction of a dam at its very tip, on my second visit I travelled with NDTV journalist Radhika Bordia and her crew, who documented these changes in a half-hour episode.

At the end of the filming, Radhika and I were invited to dinner by the king of the island. He lived in a house on the south bank of the Narmada, on a cliff that projected out over the river. What was once the kacheri had become the Maharajah Guest House run by Shivcharan Singh Chauhan, the raja of Mandhata. According to the mythological history of Mandhata, Chauhan's ancestor had established the dynasty in the eleventh century after he married the daughter of the local Bhil chieftain, Nathu Bhil.

When we reached at the appointed time, there seemed to be no one around. The area around the entrance was strewn with garbage, the path to the guest house led through the semblance of a garden. The rooms were lined up along a long corridor. As we walked its length, the raja's daughter stepped out from the shadows. She was dressed in a sari, her hair pulled back and tied, the roots betraying a touch of grey.

She said she had been living here for the past year. She had grown up in her maternal uncle's house in Gujarat, and as the change in diet and atmosphere had not suited her, she tired easily, she said. As if on cue, her father, the king stepped into the room. He held a cane in hand, he seemed almost a dwarf, well under five feet, shrunken in proportion to his domain. He made up for his height by the expansiveness of his moustache. Its magnificent handlebars would have shamed even the Raj Gond raja of Fatehpur. He must have been past sixty, but it did not show in his demeanour. He was a man permanently living out the part of a Rajput with his overdone gallantry aimed at Radhika while his daughter and I served the part of a privileged audience. In a younger man it would have grated, but under the circumstances, it was almost endearing.

'I have killed sixteen tigers,' he began. 'Among Rajputs, this matters a lot. Actually, one I never found, so make it fifteen. My younger brother Shailendra, the one in the palace, he could never fire a gun.'

We had already learnt that the current generation of the Chauhans had fallen out, and the property dispute had gone to court. Shivcharan's younger brother Shailendra had possession of the royal palace on the island. As the raja spoke, there was a childlike glee on his face. He was looking to settle scores with his brother, not through the deviousness of the courts, but through the barrel of a gun. After all, among Rajputs, he had made it clear, killing tigers counts for a lot.

'I was allowed to hunt only after my father tested me on a fish. There is a particular fish that can move backwards. The shot has to go clean through the head. So I set out on a boat and when I got the fish, my father asked to see it. The bullet had gone clear through, right where it is meant to. He looked at me and said, "Now you can go hunt a tiger."

'My brother told my uncle, "Look, my elder brother hunts so well, help me out." So he was taken to a nearby jungle. He was on the slope of a hill on a bullock cart, a gully lay at the bottom of the slope, and on the far bank, level with him, was a herd of spotted deer, one of them standing in isolation. He opened fire, puffs of sand rose in the air several feet from the target. My uncle told the bullock cart driver, "Take us back quickly. If this man faces a tiger, the tiger will have us for a meal."

'All I ever wanted to do was hunt, and the palace constricted me. My father would allow me a gun only one day a week and only ten cartridges. My mother interceded and said to him, "But you loved to hunt." And he said, "Yes, and I would go away for ten days at a time. I don't want him to do that, the gaddi would be neglected." So I thought over this and told my mother, "Our farm (which is the land we owned away from the island) is going waste, someone needs to look after it." My mother spoke to him, and he said, "Yes, go and do it." Then my mother added, "There are leopards all over the place, give him a weapon." He thought and thought and said, "Okay". Ever since, I have moved between the farm and this old courthouse and prison that is my home.'

Dinner had been served in the adjacent room. Old photographs of the hunt hung on the wall. All of us, except his daughter, were sipping beer, and he was telling us stories of the foreigners who would come and stay with him. His daughter added he was obsessed with foreigners, and indeed he was, much as he was with the hunt. He ran through the varying temperaments of different nationalities, describing them as he would describe various animals on a hunt. He spoke of the boat rides he had arranged for them up the river; of midnight swims amidst crocodiles, leopards playing in the torchlight by the riverbank, camping out, wild nights of alcohol and dancing.

The dinner over, the attendants cleared the table and left for the night. Finally, with complete calm, when we were by ourselves, the Rajput daughter, free of the prying eyes of her courtiers, poured herself some beer, and urged Radhika to have some more. 'It is only light beer.'

The raja opened the door from the room to the cliff that projected over the river. We stepped out. It was beautiful. The moon was out, the river was flowing below us and the island was barely visible to our right.

The raja stepped back into the room, and emerged holding a gun. He sat down and pointed to the river. 'On such nights, when I am by myself, I like to sit here with my gun at hand. Sometimes I fire into the river. There is nothing quite like it.'

He urged the gun on us, asking us to give it a try; we gently declined. I was left with the image of a tiny raja, gun in hand, firing into the river on a moonlit night, a look of quiet joy on his face. A few months later, Radhika called me from Bombay. He had landed in the city, and was seeking her help to buy cartridges of a prohibited bore.

V

If the history of kingship along the river had now been reduced to
its last remnants, piquant and tragic at the same time, I expected
something else entirely from the ascetic quest along the Narmada.
On an earlier trip to Amarkantak, I had visited several of the sadhus
who lived there. It had left me with the impression that the quest may
still have something genuine at its core along the Narmada, where
there was little money to be made in the trade.

Carried along by the memory of an ashram in the wilderness, built
out of wood and thatch, surrounded by a garden of herbs and coffee
shrubs, I followed the pilgrim path past Amarkantak. Just outside the
town, a turn into the sal forest took me away from the river. The path
levelled off here after a slight climb.

It was early in the morning and I had only the sound of the wind
through the sal for company. At the end of a brisk twenty-minute
walk, the path descended slightly. A clearing opened up before me,
a stream flowed through it, and at the far edge stood the ashram.
The coffee shrubs at the entrance seemed strangely at home in the
herbarium surrounding the hut. The herbs jostled with papaya trees
for space and as I stood there, I could recall the earlier visit.

It had been the baba's day of silence. It was just past dawn when
he had welcomed me into the hut, the biting cold even sharper in
the clearing surrounded by sal trees. The dhuni, more smoke than

fire, burnt at the centre of the hut. A trident stood beside it, planted in the soil. Attired in loincloth and ashes, Phakkad baba sat by the dhuni, the smoke lit up by a ray of the rising sun slanting through the roof. I sat there in silence while the baba warmed up some water, tossing in some tea leaves and herbs from the garden as it came to a boil. The brew had a refreshing warmth. When I was done, he raised his hand in blessing.

The silence had left enough of an impression to bring me back a decade later. The baba was away, only a disciple was around. He welcomed me to the hut, the brew he offered me instantly invoking the memory of my past visit. Phakkad baba, he told me, had been away for a long time and he had no idea when he would return.

His name was Shiv Patel. He was glad to have someone to talk to, he said, sometimes days would pass without a visitor. Bare-chested, his hair tied in a topknot, a single fold of white cotton cloth wrapped around his waist, he had the appearance of an ascetic but not the bearing. With time, he would lose the deferential manner he now adopted with visitors such as me.

He had come here from Rattanpur in Chhattisgarh, which lay less than a hundred kilometres away. He was worried about the baba. 'It's been six months since he left,' he told me, 'it is the longest he has been away since I came here.' There was nothing he could do but wait. If anything had happened to the baba, he would not be able to go on. He was not yet ready to take over the ashram.

He said he was a brahmachari being initiated in the ways of a sadhu. The term implied an abstinence from all forms of sexual release. It was the first and most basic requirement of a sadhu's life, but often it was observed in the breach, the lustful sadhu a common figure in Indian popular culture. He seemed uncomfortable with the topic.

He was more at ease talking about what he had left behind. 'I come from a family of six brothers and one sister; they did try and stop me, but from my childhood I had been attracted to the company of sadhus. I studied till standard X and I had been working since. For eight years I peddled copper utensils, sandalwood and stone idols to people. Tired of the lure of the world, I felt the urge to renounce it. When I started attending camps organized by a sadhu from Gujarat, my family got worried. They tried to get me married off.'

This was a common enough story, marriage was always the Indian solution for reining in a young man who refused to settle down. Again, it was difficult to ask him about his aversion to marriage. 'I realized they might force me to do so and then I would be tied down with no possibility of breaking free. What is the point of renouncing the world after marriage?'

His was a story I was to hear again and again: *Duniya ke moh se ub gya tha* (I had grown tired of the lure of the world). He couldn't elaborate on it, it was not a sentiment he seemed to have examined. It was something that had sprung fully formed into his consciousness.

'I left home, came to Amarkantak and became a disciple of the baba. I have been living here since. With his permission I have gone back home once but I have not told them where I live. I spend the day in the baba's seva. He barely sleeps, so whenever he wants me to do something, even if it is just a cup of tea, I do it. This could be at three in the morning or at noon.'

Along with his initiation as a sadhu, he was picking up the knowledge of herbs which had given Phakkad baba a reputation as a healer in Amarkantak. 'He is well versed in the healing power of shrubs, roots and herbs. He grows some of them in the garden, some he gathers from the forest. I learn by watching what he does.'

The knowledge of herbs and the knowledge of texts melded into one in his account. The baba in turn seemed to have acquired a knowledge of both in a similar fashion. 'He is illiterate but he can expound at length on any religious text. He was associated with an *akhada* (religious order) based in Amarkantak but he broke away and came to this spot thirty-five years ago; he never went back. He is the one who has insisted that no permanent structure made of concrete, not even a temple, should come up here. Now he does not keep good health. Unlike him, I want to get ordained in a religious order if babaji is willing. Of course, I will return here. I do not intend to wander from place to place.'

The various sects of sadhus have been divided into these akhadas since the time of Sankara in the eighth century AD. Shiv Patel did not want to be bereft of such an association, neither did he want to give up the rewards of his long apprenticeship. When Phakkad baba died, this ashram would be his, and he would inherit the work of a healer that brought the faithful here.

I did not think I could learn much more from Shiv Patel. I could understand the attractions of the life he had chosen. In many ways, he would enjoy far greater power and prestige than he ever would have as a peddler. But it also seemed that the religious quest had here been reduced to a mundane apprenticeship with little or no sense of the larger questions that may have once motivated it.

~

The ascetic goes back to the earliest surviving memories of Indic culture. A Rig Vedic hymn (10.136) sings of the kesin – a long-haired ascetic:

> Kesin holds fire, holds the drug, holds sky and earth.
> Kesin reveals everything, so that everyone can see the
>   sun.
> Kesin declares the light.
>
> These ascetics, swathed in wind, put dirty red rags on.
> When gods enter them, they ride with the rush of the
>   wind.
>
> Crazy with asceticism, we have mounted the wind.
> Our bodies are all you mere mortals can see.

But in the vast corpus of the Rig Veda, this hymn is an exception. Many of the Vedic hymns are concerned with the proper performance of sacrifice, which is what truly brings merit to men. This requires an elaborate array of priests, each invoking one of the four Vedas: the Hotra, who invokes the gods through Rig Vedic hymns; the Udgatra, who sings the hymns from the Sama Veda; the Adhvaryu, who stakes out the sacrificial space in accordance with the formulas of the Yajur Veda; and the Brahmin, who must make sure no mistakes are made and the sacrifice indeed follows the directions given in the Atharva Veda. Eventually, the entire priestly class was subsumed under the term Brahmin.

The kesins invoked in the hymn, crazed with asceticism, swathed in wind, stood in contrast to the Brahmins. These were probably the men who gave rise to the Upanishads, the Buddha and Mahavira. It was they who put the entire Vedic order into question.

We have contemporary testimony not just from India but from Roman sources that bears this out. Thanks to Wikipedia, it is easy to track down the original texts in translation. The story is related by Nicolas of Damascus and has been noted down by Strabo in Book XV of his *Geography*:

73. He says that at Antioch, near Daphne, he chanced to meet the Indian ambassadors who had been despatched to Caesar Augustus ... that the gifts carried to Caesar were presented by eight naked servants, who were clad only in loin-cloths besprinkled with sweet-smelling odours; and that the gifts consisted of the Hermes, a man who was born without arms, whom I myself have seen, and large vipers, and a serpent ten cubits in length, and a river tortoise three cubits in length, and a partridge larger than a vulture; and they were accompanied also, according to him, by the man who burned himself up at Athens; and that whereas some commit suicide when they suffer adversity, seeking release from the ills at hand, others do so when their lot is happy, as was the case with that man; for, he adds, although that man had fared as he wished up to that time, he thought it necessary then to depart this life, lest something untoward might happen to him if he tarried here; and that therefore he leaped upon the pyre with a laugh, his naked body anointed, wearing only a loin-cloth; and that the following

words were inscribed on his tomb: 'Here lies Zarmanochegas, an Indian from Bargosa, who immortalised himself in accordance with the ancestral customs of the Indians.'

Plutarch notes the inscription on the tomb to this Indian, leaving us in no doubt about his origins:

'ΖΑΡΜΑΝΟΧΗΓΑΣ ΙΝΔΟΣ ΑΠΟ ΒΑΡΓΟΣΗΣ'

(Zarmanochēgas indos apo Bargosēs – The Sramana master from Barygaza in India)

Sramana was the name the ancient Indian texts used for those who were the likely intellectual descendants of the kesins. Later Roman sources corroborate and build on the story of the Sramanas. Porphyry, writing two centuries later, relates in Book IV of *On Abstinence from Animal Food*:

> For the polity of the Indians being distributed into many parts, there is one tribe among them of men divinely wise, whom the Greeks are accustomed to call Gymnosophists. But of these there are two sects, over one of which the Bramins preside, but over the other the Samanaeans. The race of the Bramins, however, receive divine wisdom of this kind by succession, in the same manner as the priesthood. But the Samanaeans are elected, and consist of those who wish to possess divine knowledge ... All the Bramins originate from one stock; for all of them are derived from one father and one mother. But the Samanaeans are not the offspring of one family, being, as we have said, collected from every nation of Indians ....

He goes on to relate the customs of the Sramanas:

> The Samanaeans are, as we have said, elected. When, however, any one is desirous of being enrolled in their order, he proceeds to the rulers of the city; but abandons the city or village that he inhabited, and the wealth and all the other property that he possessed. Having likewise the superfluities of his body cut off, he receives a garment, and departs to the Samanaeans, but does

not return either to his wife or children, if he happens to have any, nor does he pay any attention to them, or think that they at all pertain to him. And, with respect to his children indeed, the king provides what is necessary for them, and the relatives provide for the wife. And such is the life of the Samanaeans. But they live out of the city, and spend the whole day in conversation pertaining to divinity. They have also houses and temples, built by the king ....

Porphyry was a Syrian mathematician of the third century AD who advocated a neoplatonism that spoke of an ultimate reality beyond thought or language, the shades of Indic thought in this belief too obvious to be easily dismissed. Certainly there seems to be some evidence that the Christian mystic traditions owe something to a Sramana from Barygaza.

Barygaza, the city of his origins, was but the Roman name for the port city of Bharuch, or Bhrigukach, at the mouth of the Narmada.

~

In form, if not spirit, Shiv Patel embodied the Sramanic life. He was not a Brahmin but that made no difference to his being accepted as an apprentice. He had also left his village and family behind but I could not see him spending the whole day debating the true nature of divinity; it seemed to be a question that lay outside his ken.

In the face of my scepticism, I was asked to go see one of the solitary sadhus of Amarkantak, an aged man known for his unpredictable temper and his solitary nature. He lived in a small cottage on the banks of the river, well outside town. I borrowed a bicycle to get to his hut.

Perhaps, I was hoping, somewhere in the transition from apprentice to sage came the knowledge and the equanimity in the face of death that the Romans saw in the Sramana. He lived by a loop in the river where the Narmada, still a thin trickle, had nearly doubled back on itself. A miniature oxbow lake was in the making, and the small hut stood nearly enclosed by the river on all sides.

He was called Sitaram. He was not given to speaking about his past, the townspeople said. His constant refrain – Sita-Ram-Sita-Ram – had become his name. I waited for him to emerge from the hut. He was old and emaciated, his white beard scraggy and undone, a towel draped perfunctorily over his shoulder to conceal his nudity. Hearing I was a journalist, he started off, 'Yes, some local journalists had come here once; I hurled stones and chased them away, the matherchods (motherfuckers).'

Feeling he had suitably chastened me, his conversation wandered off elsewhere before coming back to the same incident. Apparently a local newspaper had published a report saying he was spreading the use of ganja among the youth, and it had led to the collector of the district landing up at his hut. Sitaram had, I was told later, hurled the same abuse at the head of the district administration.

'I then told the journalist that my curse would last generations. Beware, set right what you have started. He apologized. As for ganja, what ganja, I use the chillum and I take bhang and datura. It is the food of the sadhus as it is Shiva's food. I told the journalist that I don't take away your food, why are you depriving me of what I live on. It is our food to resist the temptation of kamdeo (the god of love and lust).'

Even as he spoke, he seemed to be acting out the role of Shiva's ascetic, the unprovoked rage being part of what was expected of him. But all it had taken for him to talk had been my silence. It seemed to me that of all the temptations in the world, the desire to speak of oneself to a ready audience may be among the most difficult to resist.

He told me of his days in Bombay. 'Now that I think, as I wait to die by the Narmada, a madman who lives beside the Mai, how life is and how easily it could be otherwise. But we find our own fate. I remember travelling by the local train in Bombay, hanging out of the door. The train passed perilously close to an electric pole, the man hanging out of the compartment ahead was struck on the head. I remember the moment vividly, his head split open, parts of his brain splattering my face, my clothes. I thought of Ram, the pole brushed my hair, I was safe.

'One day in the city, on a double-decker, I raised the cry of thief when someone attempted to steal the little I had. The crowd brushed me aside and nearly beat him to death. Now I keep silent. After all, even the thief is looking for a way to live. And then, after all this, I came to an ashram in Amarkantak, fell from the roof and nearly lost my eye. To have gone through all that and nearly have my eye taken off at this sacred spot ... we meet our own fate.

'I live by myself. I ask for nothing, yet the other sadhus resent this,' he says, turning to me at the end of his monologue. He has one final word of advice. 'Write as you would about your mother. People do not write ill of their mother even if she is a whore; this mother is sacred, a gift of the gods.'

~

After meeting Sitaram, I cycled to the adjacent ashram on a whim. The sant in charge welcomed me in, offered me some water and showed me his leg. It was in a cast and he seemed rather morose. I commiserated with him. The world was in decay, he told me, and the time for the great ascetics was in the past. His guru, he said, had lived for more than a hundred and fifty years, a man all Amarkantak held sacred. 'While in dhyan, he would slowly levitate till his head touched the roof. Each day, he would bring out his entrails and wash them. Who among the sadhus and mahatmas of Amarkantak can do this today?'

It was not a question I could answer. It seemed more and more to me that to be a sadhu was in most cases the last refuge of a layabout, the prestige of a tradition ensuring both respect and free food. Certainly I met none who had studied the texts with a questioning rigour, and I met no one who could hold his own in philosophical debate. Some were like Shiv Patel, picking up a ragtag bunch of knowledge about herbs and healing, while acquiring the ability to quote from various texts of Hinduism. Much of what they had to say was the trite nonsense any Indian can recite in the name of Hinduism. Men like Sitaram could at times offer a native wisdom, but really it was nothing beyond the experience of a life lived under difficult circumstances.

On the other hand, the Sramana who made the journey to Antioch was heir to a tradition of intellectual ferment that extended back at least five hundred years, if not longer. The subcontinent of the fifth century BC is almost impossible to summon up today but enough evidence exists to glimpse the times. The writing of the earlier portions of the Vedas was already in the distant past. Thousands of young men had left their families behind to seek new answers to the mystery of existence. It is these men that Porphyry is describing when he speaks of the Samanæans. Their ensuing quest resulted in an array of dizzying speculation that covered a vast range of human thought, so much so that the subsequent development of philosophy in the subcontinent has only taken up a few of the streams to emerge, the others now seem lost to us.

There were the Charvakas, unfairly consigned to ignominy because they survive only through the criticisms of their opponents. They were materialists and were unyielding even in their premises. They refused to entertain the plausibility of explanations that could not be fully justified. The suggestion that A causes B only because repeated observations have shown A is followed by B did not seem tenable to them. A million or even a billion such observations, as far as they were concerned, still did not suggest that A implied B.

At this time, the Upanishads were still being composed. Their dizzy intellectual flight was to embrace pantheism as well as monism, hinting at worlds and possibilities that lay beyond the power of thought. In between these extremes stretched a whole array of systems in dispute, their differences settled by the power of the intellect. Disagreements were debated in public, with the loser embracing the school of thought of the winner. No dispute ever was settled by force, even if a particular scholar enjoyed the patronage of the local ruler.

While these different schools of Sramanic thought were often at odds with each other, the one thing they did have in common was their opposition to the Vedas as revealed texts and their dismissal of the efficacy of sacrifice. The only sacrifice they believed could lead to knowledge was a sacrifice of desires. It was only through restraint of the body and the mind that true knowledge could be glimpsed.

What I had noted with Shiv Patel seemed to be true in general. The form of Sramanic practice seemed to survive in the sadhus, but it was bereft of the spirit and intellect that animated the Sramanic view of life. Some of the differences between the Sramanas of the text and the sadhus I had met were simply a question of class and education. Very few of the men who become sadhus today can boast of an education that prepares them to deal with the learning of our times. Often they are from families that see a monastic order as one way to feed an extra mouth.

The monastic orders themselves have lost their tradition of learning, far more concerned as they are with the order of precedence at the Kumbh mela. Members of each akhada are caught up with their rise within the bureaucracy, aspiring to designations such as mandaleshwar and mahamandaleshwar, hoping for salvation through clerkdom, or even better, the patronage of a politician. It is difficult today to imagine someone from a well-off background abandoning the world in the manner of the Buddha or Mahavira.

Perhaps out of sympathy for my quest, even the waiters and the manager at the MP Tourism hotel I was staying at came up with recommendations of their own. One day the manager at the hotel told me that I must go and see Mohanji Maharaj – he was Uma Bharti's guru and she often came to seek his advice. I knew enough about Uma Bharti to be interested. Her own rise to power as the chief minister of MP had come about through a combination of religious demagoguery and personal charisma; it was another matter that her fall was as quick and spectacular as her rise. I made the trip to Mohanji Maharaj.

He lived in a small hut on the ridge above the source of the Narmada. On the other side of the ridge lay the origins of the river Son, which heads eastwards to meet the Ganga. This ridge literally parts the country in two: water falling on its western slope eventually makes it to the Arabian Sea, and rain falling a few feet to the other side heads to the Bay of Bengal.

I walked along a freshly laid road, courtesy Uma Bharti's visits to Mohanji's cottage. He was the first sadhu in Amarkantak I met who did not sport a beard. He had been part of the Ramakrishna Mission. Work for the institution left him, he said, with no time for spiritual practice. He was a Brahmin and 'it was my parents who infected me with faith'. He insisted on inserting a few words of English in his conversation.

'I was a postgraduate student in Indian philosophy before I joined the Ramakrishna Mission. I was in Haridwar for ten years and I realized that sadhus, sants had taken up the dharma out of a desire for selfish gain. I finally came here because my body belongs to the banks of the Narmada. Sadhus never disclose their beginnings but my attachment to this river dates back to a very early age.

'I tell people to worship nature, a living god. There is nothing indirect about what we get from the sun; there is a direct benefit from wind, the earth, rivers; these are living gods and the body is made of the same essence. The Puranas say that just the darshan of the Narmada gives you the same benefits that you obtain from bathing in the Ganga. In this era of decay, in this kaliyug, the Narmada grows in strength; that is why, of the seven sacred rivers, it is the only one to merit a parikrama. There is no pollution in the Narmada, the Ganga is filthy after Haridwar, the Yamuna is a sewer after Delhi. Let the scientists research this subject.'

Seeking to lend strength to his arguments, he searched for an intellectual parallel. 'No one believed in Darwin's theory till he asked why the apple fell downwards. It used to fall downwards earlier as well, but the answer arose only in Darwin's mind.'

Newton and Darwin were the new gods, and in this world he was unsure of himself. Hoping to impress me with his learning, he wanted to summon these names to his aid. After all, the gods of Hinduism were interchangeable. I was left almost certain that the tradition had long run its course.

VI

A red-haired mannequin in a black sari was guarding the entrance to the shop. The sari, carefully draped to reveal an ample cleavage, only served to highlight the attempted allure of white plastic. The signboard above proclaimed: Timarniwala & Sons, Clothes Shop. I was seated on a mattress on the floor, leaning my back against shelves lined with bales of cloth, listening to the shop owner in Gadarwara talk about his first cousin, Rajneesh Chandra Mohan.

The origins of the self-styled Bhagwan had been far from my mind when I set out from Bhopal a few days earlier, months after my stay in Sonpuri. The route I had chosen led to Jabalpur, with the river to my right. As always, at the beginning of the trip I was haunted by the fear of finding nothing of worth in a town where I knew no one. But the state of the road left little room for my anxiety to play itself out, enforcing a pace of progress that prevented me from overlooking the small nondescript sign at the edge of the road. Osho Tirth, it said, pointing to the village of Kuchwada.

For a moment, I hesitated. The ardous drive had tired me out and I was unsure of the village road that lay ahead. Osho had never interested me, and his exploits seemed to belong to another world. I had a vague recollection that he had taught at the university in Jabalpur, but I had never been curious enough to find out more. It was the serendipidity of this signboard where I least expected it that led me to reconsider.

It took me less than half an hour to reach Kuchwada. Some five hundred yards short of the village was the gate to Osho Tirth, the 'pilgrimage' at Osho's birthplace. Visitors, a signboard announced, were allowed ten minutes to stroll around the site after paying Rs 5 for entry. The boy at the gate pointed me to the library across the road.

It was a white-domed structure, odd in these rural surroundings. The sun poured in through the skylights and wasps buzzed in and out as I looked through the enormous volume of words that Rajneesh had regurgitated in the course of his life. Vedanta, Buddhism, the Gita, Kabir, the Sufis, the Bible, Mahavira, the writings of Nanak – nothing had been spared his attention.

I soon struck up a conversation with the only other person in the hall – Swami Prem Ashish from Kathmandu. We talked as he took me into the main compound, past the first gate. Rajneesh's acolytes from Japan had built the complex and their influence was visible in the architecture. But even so, as we passed a second gate, the huge, pale-blue, pyramid-shaped mediation hall caught me unawares.

I was not allowed entry into the hall, Ashish told me apologetically, but he said I should meet Swami Satyatirth Bharti who ran this tirth. He was an old associate of Rajneesh, which for Ashish seemed to be a matter of some importance. I wrote out a note about my travels, which was dispatched to the swami. As we awaited his reply in the canteen, Ashish talked about his own initiation into the cult of Osho.

It was in Kathmandu, six years after he had finished high school, that he first heard of Osho. Someone he knew had taken 'sanyas' at a camp run by Osho's followers. It seemed a strange thing for a young man to do, he said, most of his friends worked odd jobs and, like the young anywhere in the world, were interested only in sex and alcohol. His curiosity aroused, he started reading the literature handed out by the commune. Something in what he read appealed to him, so he went to attend a meditation camp.

For the first two months, he said, it was just an hour of meditation in the morning and an hour in the evening. Within the first week he gave up meat. No one forced him, he said. In fact, friends at the camp told him not to; they said nothing should be given up so quickly or so easily. But, he added, he could not help doing so and soon enough, gave up alcohol. Now even the taste of eggs made him vomit. 'I am being purified internally.'

He spoke with ease, nothing in what he said seemed designed to convince me. He suggested I should try a meditation camp. Sanyas, he told me, does not require giving up anything. It was a strange definition of a word that means renunciation, but then, he was a sanyasi only in the sense that he had gone through Rajneesh's version of sanyas.

Sanyas, he quoted Rajneesh, does not require change. Osho's meditation is not worth a penny if it does not affect a person despite meat or alcohol. All it requires is sincerity, and he didn't seem to be joking as he said this. Yet, he did seem to believe that in the end, giving up meat and alcohol was the result of his sanyas.

I was a bit taken aback by my first encounter with a follower of Osho. True, there was an earnestness about him that I found appealing but the whole experience that Prem Ashish described, starting with his new name, left me uneasy. It seemed designed to take away the hardships from a quest that through the centuries had required much effort and had asked much of the self.

Within the commune there were no saffron-clad hippies, and sex seemed far from the mind of my companion and the men running the tidy dining hall. If there was anything that did startle, it was the architecture – the Japanese gates, the white-domed library, the blue pyramid hall in a dusty village, among red-tiled mud huts, lacked any feel for the surroundings, much like the temple the modern-day Sankaracharya had built in Amarkantak.

Taken together, the simplification of a rigorous quest and the architectural toys that went with it reminded me of the fad of new maths that had swept through academia: the claim that maths, in fact all learning, should be fun. This, as became obvious soon enough, was a deception. However much you may disguise the fact, learning the alphabet or the multiplication tables could never be other than a certain amount of work. I am not sure whether the same held true for the quest that went by the name of enlightenment. I am not even sure if the quest has any meaning, but certainly the struggle to achieve it had produced some of the most enduring thoughts of a civilization.

As I waited, word arrived that the swami could not see me. Ashish was crestfallen. The swami, he told me, received several injections for the illnesses plaguing his body, and this made it difficult for him to meet outsiders. As I got up to leave, he apologized for any hurt that might have wittingly or unwittingly come my way in the time I spent at the Osho tirth.

~

Rajneesh spoke, and spoke without end. Many of his books had been dictated to his followers. His autobiography, compiled from his own outpourings on his life, is extensive. It starts with a conceit that can only come to the truly enlightened, the memory of his past lives. Past lives existed, he said, because he could remember them.

When he began to speak of this life, he did so in the same way. A great man's birth in the Indian way must be heralded by portents and omens, yet how was this to be reconciled with rationality? In our times, the pretence to rationality was impossible to give up if a man was to be taken seriously.

Two important events presaged Rajneesh's birth. His mother, five months pregnant, accompanied by her brother, was headed to Kuchwada, to her parents' home, where she was to stay till the birth. They had to cross the Narmada in spate.

The boatman refused to ferry the family across. The myth of Kansa attempting to kill his newborn nephew Krishna had ensured an Indian superstition against travelling on water with a sister's son. They waited by the river for a few days till a holy man intervened.

He touched Rajneesh's mother's feet, recognizing the greatness of the child she was carrying. Rajeneesh added that as far as he was concerned, the holy man befooled the boatman. In his telling, even as a portent of his future greatness was being revealed by a holy man, he sought to distance himself from it.

A month later, the Narmada in spate flooded the village. The flood exceeded anything in living memory. 'The rains were so heavy that the ocean was not able to take the water as quickly as it was coming, so the water at the ocean front was stuck; it started flowing backwards. Where small rivers fell into big rivers, the big rivers refused to take the water, because they were not able even to contain their own water. The small rivers started moving backwards.'

The floodwaters of the Narmada entered his grandparents' house, reaching up to the second floor where his pregnant mother lay on a bed. The waters reached up to his mother's stomach and then receded. He was born 'almost a sant' in the village, and even the elderly lined up to touch his feet.

His grandparents asked his parents that he be allowed to stay with them, a solace in their old age. He was indulged, nothing was required of him, nothing was forced upon him. He lived in this house, with his grandparents and an elderly manservant for company. The family was by far the richest in the village, and there was no question of playing with the other children.

Rajneesh wrote of being a lonely child, 'I was absolutely alone. It was not company, it could not be company ... I was left to myself ... my grandparents would not allow me to mix with the village children. They were dirty, and of course they were almost beggars. So there was no way to have friends. That caused a great impact. In my whole life I have never been a friend, I have never known anybody to be a friend. Yes, acquaintances I had.'

After his childhood in Kuchwada, he went to school at Gadarwara where his parents lived. The family had continued with the business that had been started by Rajneesh's grandfather. Everyone in town seemed to know where his cousins lived. Two clothes shops, identical to each other, stood side by side in the crowded bazaar of Gadarwara. I picked one at random. It was late in the evening and there were no customers around. The shop attendant seated me on the floor, as he would any customer. The cousin was having his dinner upstairs.

My eyes kept wandering around the shop, from the olive-green tiles back to the fair-skinned mannequin. I imagined a factory somewhere, churning out an unending stream of such mannequins. Aware that in this country, even the children, rejecting the faces around them, reached for the blonde visage of a Barbie, sari shop owners across the country had settled on this buxom redhead.

The man who descended the stairs leading down from the first-floor house to the shop floor was one among them. He apologized for keeping me waiting. He sat down beside me. Nothing in him hinted at any relationship with a god-man; he was any shopkeeper anywhere in India.

He seemed to have repeated the story several times earlier; I sat through a sketchy hagiography. Not once did he call his cousin by his name as he talked to me. 'Osho was brilliant. He studied from primary school to his matriculation here in Gadarwara. He had a great memory, he just had to read something once to remember it.' I asked him whether Rajneesh kept in touch with the family. 'Before his move to Poona, even after he was a god-man in Bombay, he would return to Gadarwara twice a year, for Diwali and Rakhi.' He didn't have much else to add.

The family settled here in 1940, he told me. It was his grandfather who had come here from the town of Timarni, hence the name of the shop – Timarniwala & Sons, followed for good measure by the title Osho dham. Perhaps the shops really were a stop on some Osho pilgrimage. They certainly should be. Talking to his cousin, I felt some stirring of sympathy for the man who had sought to leave all this behind.

The cousin spoke of a diamond watch presented to him by Osho. Rolls Royces and expensive watches were among Rajneesh's obsession with luxury, an obsession that seemed to make sense in the context of the shop I was sitting in. The cousin did not offer to show me the watch. I then went to the adjacent shop owned by another cousin who was older, closer in age to Rajneesh. I was hoping to learn something more personal about Osho, but all I got were terse monosyllables. I was told later he was sulking because I had failed to go to him first.

Among relatives such as these, Rajneesh would have stood out. Perhaps those first eight years of keeping his own company made the difference, but by the time he came to Gadarwara, he was no easy child to deal with, at least according to his own testimony.

His rebelliousness had a certain streak of perverse intelligence. Shortly after he arrived in Gadarwara, his father, in an attempt to impose his authority, ordered his son to get his hair cut. When his son refused, he snipped off a lock of hair. Rajneesh promptly went and got his head shaved, an act undertaken by an Indian son only at his father's death. At this stage, Rajneesh claimed, his father gave up.

Portions of his autobiography are exaggerations, some just untrue. He spoke of running sixteen miles each day, and boasted of swimming the floodwaters of the Narmada, a feat unbelievable to anyone who has seen the river in spate. But that he was at odds with authority was clear, and on his own testimony he would lie and cheat to get his way. His intelligence made it easy for him to step outside the bounds of whatever the town could present to him in the form of conventional morality.

His constant challenge to authority, or so he related, left his grandparents' Jain guru and then his teachers unable to deal with him. He would question all he was told, he would insist on pursuing an idea to its end, logical or illogical. In this little town, like in most small towns in India, where conformity and conventions were everything, he would have soon gained a certain reputation, as indeed he did.

It was no different in Jabalpur. The transition from a rebellious and questioning young man to a new-age guru was not easy to capture, but Rajneesh managed to do it with some honesty.

In my youth I was known in the university as an atheist, irreligious, against all moral systems. That was my stand, and that is still my stand. I have not changed even an inch; my position is exactly the same. But being known as an atheist, irreligious, amoral, became a problem. It was difficult to communicate with people, almost impossible to bridge any kind of relationship with people ….

I became aware that, strangely, the people who were interested in the search for truth had got involved in religions. Because they thought me irreligious, I could not commune with them; and they were the people who would be really interested to know ….

Then it was obvious to me that I would have to play the game of being religious; there was no other way. Only then could I find people who were authentic seekers.

It took a few years for me to change my image in people's eyes. But people only listen to words, they don't understand meanings: people only understand what you say; they don't understand what is conveyed unsaid. So I used their own weapons against themselves. I commented on religious books, and gave a meaning that was totally mine ….

An atheistic search for meaning was not a contradiction outside the Semitic world view. Genuine human experiences cannot be wished away; whether they lead anywhere is another matter altogether.

In his case, it was not clear where they led to, or if they led anywhere at all. The problem with Rajneesh was hardly one of intellect, but he was a product of small-town India of the mid-twentieth century. In the end, he never could escape Gadarwara.

~

The West came to know him in the 1960s. The children of parents who had lived through a world war wanted no part of the old answers. With their disdain for everything their parents stood for, they also acquired a disdain for their entire intellectual tradition. Unable to reason for themselves, they searched for easy answers elsewhere. Among those offering such answers was this man named Rajneesh.

Like the new maths this generation would engender, these children were looking for a new sexuality.

Rajneesh's notoriety predated his Western disciples. In 1964, he had delivered a series of lectures in Bombay. The lectures became a book: *From Sex to Superconsciousness*. Given the prudery of the India of his time, it was a shocking title. Little heed was paid to what he had actually written; here was an Indian guru putting his whole heritage to shame. A nation struggling for respectability felt the shame, a tradition used to shore up their view of themselves was being sullied.

Strangely enough, in the compilation of 1,500 pages devoted to himself, not once does Rajneesh speak of a romantic attraction or a sexual experience. In over half a million words, from the servant at his grandparents' house to a professor in his college, he takes up every interaction that matters to him. There is no hint of a woman. The Rajneesh who delivered these lectures in 1965, at the age of thirty-four, was in all likelihood a sexual novice. The book that first evoked sex in the public consciousness of modern India was written by a virgin.

It is only such naivety that would allow a man to imagine a sexuality devoid of jealousy and betrayal. Rajneesh never seemed to have realized that to think beyond the weight of these emotions was to think beyond sex. Or that sex was not a reasoned act, its very essence lay in these emotions. It was almost as if the man writing about removing jealousy from relationships, of sexuality unburdened with guilt, was hoping to create an ideal world removed from the constraints of his surroundings. In a town such as Gadarwara, it was precisely the fear of these emotions and the disruptions they bring in their wake that had forced sexuality into spaces closed to Rajneesh. He wanted the sex, but he thought he could do away with the attendant emotions. Only a man who had lusted in the abstract could think so.

In him the children of the 1960s found a match for all the wrong reasons. For a few brief years, sweeping aside their heritage, they learnt the mechanisms of the act and came to believe that the associated 'hang ups' were burdens imposed by society. They believed in an innocent state of nature free from such burdens. The prudery that Rajneesh faced and the promiscuity they had experienced led them to the same conclusions. In this virgin guru these promiscuous naifs found their guide.

Yet, the virgin guru's prescriptions of freedom seemed to have originated where so many of his other ideas did, from books.

A day after meeting Rajneesh's cousin, I had gone to the Gadarwara library to look for the jawbones of a dinosaur recently found in the library compound. A few workers had been digging to shift the swings and slides meant for children to another part of the compound when they came upon this jawbone. A few years later, it was still lying in the library; no further exploration had ever been undertaken around the site.

The librarian, keen to stress the significance of his town, said this was one of two things of 'world importance' in his library, the other was the collection of books donated by Rajneesh.

A separate shelf had been devoted to the collection. Each book was inscribed Rajneesh Chandra Mohan, B.A. Previous, D.N. Jain College, Jubblepore. I noted down a few names. *This Believing World* by Lewis Browne; *A Naval Venture – The War Story of an Armoured Cruiser* by Fleet Surgeon T.T. Jean, *1649: a novel of a year* by Jack Lindsay; and then, what for me was a surprise – *Phulmat of the Hills* by Verrier Elwin.

I really hadn't expected Elwin to appear in the Rajneesh story. I thought I had left the Gonds behind in Mandla. And then a few months later, back in Delhi, as I read through Rajneesh's autobiography, I came upon a section titled Aboriginals, where he talked of Bastar, the vast Gond territory that lay to the south of Amarkantak.

The setting of the section, like so many others in the book, seems fabricated. As a ten-year-old, he claims to have met Gandhi in a train compartment. When he writes of Gandhi again as an adult, he makes no mention of the chance encounter he had earlier conjured up. The unlikeliest of people surface in his accounts, among them the communist, M.N. Roy, who had spent time in Mexico. On another train journey, he befriends the raja of Bastar. At his invitation he travels to Bastar and writes about the people there:

Nobody goes into those deep forests. They live in caves; nobody goes there. And they have such beautiful caves.

And they are such beautiful people. You will not find anybody fat, you will not find anybody thin – they all look alike. They live long, and they live very naturally. Even about sex they are very natural, perhaps the only natural people left in India.

And exactly what they do, has to be done all over the world if you want people not to be perverted. Behind all kinds of mental sicknesses is sexual perversion. In Bastar I found for the first time, people totally natural.

After a girl and a boy come of age – that is thirteen and fourteen ... They have in their villages, in the middle of the village, a small hall just made of bamboos, as their huts are made. The moment a girl starts having periods, she has to stay in the central hall. By the time a boy is fourteen, sexually potent, he has to live ... All the girls and the boys who have become sexually mature, they start living together, sleeping together, with one condition – and that is a beautiful condition – that no boy should sleep with a girl for more than three days. So you have to become acquainted with every girl of the village, and every girl has to become acquainted with every boy of the village.

Before you decide to marry someone, you must know every woman of the village, so there is no question arising afterwards that you start feeling lustful for some woman. You have lived with all the women of your age, and it is your choice after the experiment with all the women.

And there is no jealousy at all, because from the very beginning everybody is living with every girl. Every boy has the chance to be acquainted with every girl of the village, and every girl has the chance to be acquainted with every boy of the village.

So there is no question of any jealousy, there is no competitive spirit at all. It is just an experiment, an opportunity for every child to know sex with different people, and then find out who suits you, and with whom you were the most happy, with whom you settle harmoniously, with whom you felt your heart. Perhaps this is the only scientific way to find a soul mate.

The description of Bastar and its people was borrowed from his reading. Some of the facts stated were just wrong – the Gonds do not live in caves – and then there was the astounding claim that the aboriginal children do not have dreams at all. But, beyond the facts, in these aboriginals he found his noble savages, unspoiled by civilization – the very same innocent state of nature that his flower-children followers reposed so much faith in.

The key to Rajneesh's communes lay here. He had said as much. 'And exactly what they do, has to be done all over the world if you want people not to be perverted. Behind all kinds of mental sicknesses is sexual perversion.'

The Gond institution he described in some detail is the ghotul of the Muria Gonds. Not all Gonds follow the same traditions as far as the ghotul is concerned. Certainly not all the Gonds of Bastar.

The Muria ghotul became well known to the outside world only because of a book written by Elwin. It was a book discussed widely in India, and the idea of 'free sex' had much to do with it. Rajneesh could not have escaped hearing of it. He was already a reader of Elwin's books, and the aboriginals he describes are aboriginals that seem to be imagined from Elwin's book. The ghotul of Bastar was eventually transformed into a commune in Oregon.

It would not matter so much now, but even years after Rajneesh's death, his ideas continue to impact people from Nepal to Latvia. Knowing my interest in Rajneesh, a friend forwarded me a 2008 news report from Latvia. 'It is hard to walk into a bookstore in Riga without seeing Osho's name. Prominent displays featuring his books abound – offering customers a little bit of Far East spiritualism in hard cover or paperback. A quick glance through the bookshelves in most Latvian's homes will reveal why the stores have him on display – the man sells. His works have become the most popular self-help books around.'

This is reason enough to remember what Rajneesh was not. Despite the words, and they often are words of some depth, he himself seemed adrift. His own tentative beginnings would explain some of what he later stood accused of by his devotees. One woman complained of an unwanted pregnancy, others accused him of fondling them in the name of arousing their 'chakras'. For a man born in Gadarwara, whatever the quality of his mind, the temptations of the body were impossible to resist. The red-headed mannequin outside the family cloth shop still speaks of a longing that remains part of growing up in Gadarwara, or for that matter, anywhere in small-town India.

In the end, even Rajneesh's mind could find little to hold on to. The ravages of age saw him turn to nitrous oxide for relief. He ordered a dentist's chair especially for his use. Most of his later works were dictated from this chair under the influence of the gas. His sense of himself was always exalted, but towards the end it seemed to have gone out of control.

Even the damage he did to himself could be forgiven. He did far more. As the guru sat high on laughing gas, his devotees were trying to poison an entire town in Oregon. Beyond this farce lay a greater tragedy, little written about.

Institutions do not transfer so easily from one context to another. The adults seem to have survived the ghotuls Rajneesh put in place in Poona and Oregon; the children were another matter. British journalist Tim Guest has written of his childhood in Rajneesh's communes where his mother was a sanyasin. It is not difficult to sense the echoes of Rajneesh's own childhood in what the children experienced.

'Bhagwan's attitude to the practicalities of schooling was simple: teach the important subjects, English and maths. On no account, he said, were we to be taught the useless subjects, especially politics or history ... For the rest of the time, Bhagwan said, the children should be allowed to play and to learn from each other and the adults around them.'

The children belonged to the commune. Rajneesh wanted to save them from the embrace of the nuclear family, the same embrace he felt he had been saved from. But what he forgot was that children learn by imitation from the adults around them. The village he lived in till the age of eight and the small town of Gadarwara where he did his schooling were environments very different from the commune.

The Muria Gonds had taken generations to create an institution without parallel. The very difficulty they had to guard against, their constant caution against attachment and jealousy in adolescents, was a reminder of how natural these feelings were. When adults and children imitated the model in an entirely alien setting without the generations of preparation that had gone into the ghotul, the result was something else entirely. In a chilling passage, Guest writes about the children from one of the communes named Medina, 'That year, the summer of 1984 at the Ranch, many of the Medina kids lost their virginity; boys and girls, ten years old, eight years old, in sweaty tents and A-frames, late at night and mid-afternoon, with adults and other children. I remember some of the kids – eight, nine, ten years old – arguing about who had fucked whom, who would or wouldn't fuck them.'

VII

E ven Rajneesh in his iconoclasm seemed far removed from the energy and intellect that marked the Sramanic ideal. It would be difficult to believe that such a period ever existed in our past, but for the textual evidence that supports it. The evidence also suggests that even as Sramanic ideas were finding a home in the Roman and the Christian world, they were being challenged at home. *The Laws of Manu*, compiled in about the first century AD, bears this out. The book today is the standard guide to Hindu rituals and practices, so much so that legal decisions relating to the Hindu way of life refer to this text.

An entire chapter of the *Laws* is dedicated to the idea of renunciation, but renunciation in a context that manages to deny the Sramana's radical rejection of ordinary life. Renunciation in this text becomes a necessary stage of life, an adjunct to the study of the Vedas, to be adopted only after a man has fulfilled certain obligations in this world:

> 36. Having studied the Vedas in accordance with the rule, having begat sons according to the sacred law, and having offered sacrifices according to his ability, he may direct his mind to (the attainment of) final liberation ...
>
> 41. Departing from his house fully provided with the means of purification (Pavitra), let him wander about absolutely silent,

and caring nothing for enjoyments that may be offered (to him).

42. Let him always wander alone, without any companion, in order to attain (final liberation), fully understanding that the solitary (man, who) neither forsakes nor is forsaken, gains his end.

43. He shall neither possess a fire, nor a dwelling, he may go to a village for his food, (he shall be) indifferent to everything, firm of purpose, meditating (and) concentrating his mind on Brahman ....

The Sramana idea of renunciation, in contrast, involved no sense of orderly progression of a human life. It involved the complete rejection of this life. The idea of the world as an illusion was not a Vedic but a Sramanic idea. The Brahmins made this idea their own by taming it, making it an adjunct to the duties of the householder.

This theoretical appropriation of renunciation did not suffice to end the tension between the Vedic world of sacrifice embodied in the Brahmins and the Sramanic world of the renunciates. What was required was a philosophical reconciliation between Sramanic and Brahminical belief.

～

The word 'philosophy' is a problematic one in the Indian context. Its counterpart in several Indian languages is the word Darshana – vision, a far more accurate rendering of what the quest meant on the subcontinent. The Indic philosopher was primarily a seer and his vision was never other than a totality, a system that was complete in itself. Philosophy was never an external game, removed from the self, played only in the mind. India's greatest philosopher, certainly the one who had the most impact on Indian thought, was Sankara.

He was not just the secular philosopher of the West, though his work stands its ground even on this circumscribed turf; he was also the founder of a religious order. Around the essential details of his life have accrued myths and legends only a little less elaborate than those that make up the life of the Buddha or Christ.

According to the legend, Sankara was born a Nambudiri Brahmin in Kerala in the deep south of the subcontinent. Despite opposition from his mother, he took sanyas early in life, well before he became a householder. So, even at the very beginning, he was both a Brahmin and a Sramana. He gained enlightenment on the banks of the Narmada, on the island of Omkara Mandhata. His guru was a Vedantin, a scholar of the Upanishads, and thus it was this view that Sankara was to refine and champion.

A Vedantin strives towards the realization that there is nothing that separates him from the eternal. Tat tvam asi – You are that – the Upanishads say, but the reason this truth is not perceptible has to do with the world. The world is maya, an illusion born out of ignorance of the true reality. Unable to sense this illusion, man is caught in the trap of the apparent.

In his bid to unite various schools of Vedic thought, Sankara debated and vanquished representatives of some of the major schools. His most formidable opponents though were the Mimamsiks. Finally, he headed to Kashi to seek out Kumarila Bhatt, the foremost Mimamsik of the times. He found him seated by a pyre, about to immolate himself. Clearly, the Sramanic tradition that the Romans had witnessed in the first century AD was still prevalent seven centuries later. Kumarila Bhatt told Sankara that it was too late for him to enter into a debate but suggested that Sankara should head to Mahishmati on the banks of the Narmada to challenge his foremost student, Mandana Mishra.

~

Mandana Mishra was a Mimamsik. Actually, I should say Purva Mimamsik, but to add a prefix to a term now devoid of meaning is of no help. Mimamsa is the name given to the study of the Vedas, and Purva Mimamsa is the study of the earlier portion of the Vedas. What we know as Vedanta – the study of the end of the Vedas or the Upanishads – is also known as Uttara Mimamsa.

It would seem natural to assume that the two fields of study complement each other, and so indeed is the case today. The study of the earlier portion of the Vedas is a necessary preparation for a Vedantin in search of liberation. But this was not always so. In roughly the eighth century AD, the two schools of thought stood in direct opposition.

The Purva Mimamsik did not see the world as an illusion, he took its existence as a given. This stemmed from a system of knowledge where observations and the inferences that followed were taken to be true unless there was reason to believe otherwise. It was a system that left no room for a Supreme Deity. It was an atheistic, realist school that is at odds with the Hindu vision of life today.

At the core of the Mimamsik's system lay a belief that was in common with the Vedantins: the Vedas are eternal. This might seem as problematic as prescribing a deity, but not quite. After all, the existence of the Vedas is not in doubt. You can see, read and hear them. Moreover, as far as anyone can make out, the Vedas cannot be attributed to any human author; thus there is no reason to deny their eternality.

The Mimamsik believed that the correct performance of sacrifices as enjoined in the Vedas is what earned merit for each individual soul in this world. Indeed, the Purva Mimamsik believed in the multitude of souls. It did seem a matter of observation that something not entirely of the flesh animated each individual.

How then did this soul accrue merit or demerit? The Purva Mimamsik prescribed a mysterious entity called the Apurva. Perhaps it is best to think of this Apurva not as a creative, willing or active power but rather as a vast memory bank that stores the merits and demerits that each individual soul earns.

The Apurva was forced on the Mimamsik simply because he accepted the existence of the soul and asserted that the proper performance of Vedic rites earned merit. Surely, this accrual of merit and demerit had to be noted somewhere because it came into effect much after the act that was performed. Again, the parsimony of the

Purva Mimamsik was exemplary, he assumed no more than was necessary to explain what he had observed. The Apurva was well short of a deity, because the system of the Mimamsik required no more than this.

It was a system that became whole when another tenet that is common to all Vedic schools – that of karma – was included. Again, this was almost forced by observation, for what else could explain the fate that befalls us, the circumstances that surround us, the tragedies that strike us. Karma, though, was not fatalism. It determined circumstances, not actions. There was a prescribed duty, the dharma of the Vedas, and merit or demerit accrued only to the degree that actions were in consonance with dharma.

Mimamsa then was a philosophy of action, not contemplation. Liberation was possible only through the proper performance of enjoined acts, not through contemplation, meditation or mystic realization. It went so far as to say that the Vedas were nothing but prescriptive texts for the proper performance of sacrifices and every statement in the Vedas that did not directly prescribe an act only explained or described such acts. The Mimamsik refused to give credence to the fact that parts of the Upanishads were purely contemplative.

Within the bounds of Vedic orthodoxy, Indic philosophy had never conjured up a more pragmatic viewpoint, one that had no wish to go beyond this world or seek beyond a self that was the soul. Given the speculative thrust of Indic philosophical systems that flowered from the sixth to the first century BC, this retreat to a pragmatic position seems bewildering. There seems to be only one plausible explanation – the rise of Buddhism.

~

The way of the Buddha was born in the ferment of the Sramanic world. Enshrined within Buddhism is this very culture of debate and dispute. The skill of monks at debate may have been one reason for its rapid spread. Perhaps no other sect refined the rules of logic or a skill at debate to the extent the Buddhists did through their striving to make sense of the Buddha's non-answers. In the face of this honed skill, the speculative thrust of the Upanishads was not easy to defend.

The effort to describe the mystic experience often results in a contradictory outpouring of words, seeking to limit or circumscribe an experience that seems to remain beyond words. Even here Buddhism traversed the path from Buddha's non-assertion to a climactic triumph of negation born out of an unsparing logic, a negation so absolute that Nagarjuna could even deny negation and liberation, illusion and non-illusion, and through this perpetually shifting mode of thought arrive in some measure back at the Buddha's original non-assertion. Less firmly fought out doctrines would have receded in the face of this challenge.

Purva Mimamsa seems to be Vedic thought putting up barricades, retreating to a minimally defensible position. It is almost as if Purva Mimamsa was designed to face Buddhism head-on in debate. Its challenge was straightforward. Error resides not in language but in human beings; words themselves are eternal. This assertion of the eternality of the word resulted in disputations that gave rise to works in linguistics that predate modern attempts by over a thousand years. These works argue over the very source of meaning. Does it reside in a letter, a word or the entire sentence? Are words but transitory phenomena, or is the transitory quality born out of their manifestation as sound? Various Indian philosophers and schools of philosophy have taken varying stances, but the Mimamsiks were firm in the belief that words, which are the unit of meaning, are eternal.

For them, it then followed that the Vedas were eternal and free of error. Error resides in human beings and the Vedas are not human creations, and if we need confirmation, a Mimamsik would argue, it comes from the fact that the Vedas have never been found to be in error. The Buddhist could not turn around and make equivalent claims about their own texts. The Buddha was human and the Buddhist argued for the transitoriness of all things, for the momentary nature of all existence. How then could a Buddhist be sure that the words he uttered carried unchanged the message of the Buddha? His own arguments led him to the conclusion that he could not be sure that the words he read or heard, given their transitory quality, were the words the Buddha uttered. Could he even be sure that what he believed or espoused was indeed what the Buddha preached?

This more or less was the position espoused by Kumarila Bhatt. His text on Mimamsa is still considered authoritative. It is divided into three parts, of which the second part is devoted to arguing the case against Buddhism. No other school or sect is treated in the same detail. Within a few decades, Sankara was to see the battle against Mimamsa as far more important than the battle against Buddhism. Perhaps this is an indication that by the time Sankara is reputed to have met the aged Kumarila Bhatt, the Mimamsik had already done enough to ensure the retreat of Buddhism on the subcontinent.

~

It was the most important debate of Sankara's life, and perhaps one of the most important in the development of modern Hinduism. If Vedic orthodoxy was to be Vedantic, the Purva Mimamsa position of Kumarila Bhatt had to be destroyed. As far as Sankara was concerned, the retreat of the Mimamsiks from Upanishadic knowledge had taken away the very core of Vedic teaching.

The Mimamsik saw renunciation of the world as a flawed idea. If the world was all that was, what did it mean to renounce it? The Mimamsik goal was liberation from the karmic cycle through prescribed acts, but in doing so the soul did not forsake its individuality. Nothing could be further from the Vedantic idea of a mystic unity through right knowledge. Action and knowledge as paths to liberation are not easy to reconcile.

In Mahishmati, it was not difficult for Sankara to locate the house of Mandana Mishra. A resident of this ancient city said that he would know he had found it when he saw a house where even the parrots recited the Vedas.

Mandana Mishra was not happy to be interrupted in the proper performance of sacrifice by an itinerant sanyasi. But after hearing Sankara relate his encounter with Kumarila Bhatt, he agreed to the debate. It was decided that Mandana Mishra's wife Sharda, herself a scholar of repute, would judge the debate. The two bare-bodied men sat facing each other, a garland of flowers around their necks. Sharda had decreed the wilting of the flowers would indicate defeat in the debate.

For over a fortnight the two argued. There was much about which they were in agreement – the eternality of the Vedas and the performance of sacrifices in the prescribed manner. But, for Sankara the proper performance of the sacrifice was only a preparation for the supreme knowledge hinted at in the Upanishads.

The debate slowly narrowed down to those very sentences of the Upanishads that the Mimasiks held were of little value. Tat tvam asi, Sankara argued, was neither a prescription for sacrifice nor even an exegesis or commentary on any such act. It was a form of knowledge that could only be reached through an inner realization. This, he claimed, was the ultimate vision of the Vedas, a vision in which the human and the divine came together in a transcendental reality, shedding the illusion that was the world. And as Sankara spoke of the world as a figment of the imagination born out of ignorance, the smile of the Buddha must have lingered somewhere. An earlier debate may have been lost, the eightfold path may have been in retreat, but in the end the spirit of Buddhism did not entirely disappear from India.

On the seventeenth day of the debate, the flowers adorning Mandana Mishra started to wilt, but victory still did not come to Sankara. Sharda told him that to be the victor in the debate, he would need to defeat her as well.

As the arguments commenced again, Sharda wanted to know something fundamental: how should a man live his life? And so a man versed in the Vedas found himself debating a subject that he had not even begun to master. What did a man who had renounced the world in his youth know of conjugal love?

In the retellings of this debate that have come filtered to us through the popular imagination, it is still possible to glimpse a vision of the world that left nothing out. It was a vision rooted in experience, and in the absence of experience, Sankara was lost. Admitting his ignorance, he sought a month's time to return to the debate.

As he travelled along the Narmada he came across courtiers mourning the death of their king. The body of a man suddenly struck down in his youth lay on a pyre awaiting the burning torch.

Seeing the dead king, Sankara entered the dense jungle that lay along the river. In a secluded cave his soul left his body, which lay there safe from wild animals and inclement weather, and entered the body of the dead king. To the shock of the courtiers, the king suddenly came to life on the pyre. The Mimamsiks had no patience for miracles but the Vedantins were not so constrained. This was, after all, a legend told by the winners.

The story does not speak of the queen's reaction to the return of her dead husband. Of her knowledge of a body that she had known so well that now sought her with a renewed but fumbling desire. How did she respond to his swift progress in the art of love? Within the month, Sankara was ready to return to the debate.

The story does speak of other responses. It did not take the courtiers very long to sense that a wisdom beyond the ordinary now inhabited the body that sat in court. The affairs of the kingdom had never been better handled. Soon they suspected the truth and sent their retainers to search the jungles for an abandoned body. The jungle was dense and the cave remote, but the kingdom had ample resources. News got back to the courtiers of the discovery of the miraculously preserved body of a young man with a calm countenance.

A king well versed in the affairs of his kingdom soon learns what his courtiers know. Before they could think of destroying the body, Sankara came to life in the cave and headed back to the arena of the debate.

The legend leaves the queen and the kingdom behind. Sharda

soon accepts defeat and along with her husband, she adopts the Vedantin view.

~

Consider the reconciliations Sankara brings about. Mimamsa is a Brahminical philosophy, it does not believe in renunciation, which is why Mandana Mishra was a householder. Kumarila Bhatt seems to be an exception, but legend has its own explanation. He is said to have adopted the life of a Sramana to better understand Buddhism in order to be able to triumph over it in debate. According to at least one version of the legend, his death on the pyre in Kashi is a form of penance for this deception.

In this philosophical defeat Brahminism actually won a great practical victory. The philosophical concession resulted in the unification of a very diverse set of practices, but with the Brahmins retaining and extending their supremacy. Today, no Brahmin subscribes to the Mimamsik position in its entirety. With the Vedic corpus united, the Vedantin position is the default option in Hinduism. Of course, there are divisions and subdivisions. There are various forms of the Vedantic vision which differ from Sankara's views, asserting the duality of the self and universal spirit, other schools of thought which believe in a formless god or in the worship of idols, but these are digressions on a theme. The Sramanic world before Sankara was far more diverse.

Even when innovations arose after Sankara from men such as Nanak, who founded Sikhism and questioned the validity of the Vedas, they lay within the ambit of Sankara's vision. Nanak rejected the Vedas, and so Sikhism is a religion that lies outside the Brahminical consensus, but in its approach it still remains Vedantic – the world is an illusion and unity with the one reality is what a disciple seeks. Sikhism is also a comprehensive defence of the life of the householder, and renunciation in the Sramanic sense is considered wrong.

In this victory through defeat of Brahminism, the Sramanic way of life did not disappear; its philosophical thrust changed. Rather than stand in opposition, it became part of a larger tradition. Sankara set up four peeths headed by priests who would henceforth be called the Sankaracharyas. In some measure they would become the high priests of Hinduism. Owing allegiance to each peeth were various akhadas of sadhus. Some versions of the legend say Mandana Mishra became his foremost disciple and the first head of the order of sadhus that Sankara founded in the south.

My attempt to seek a continuity of the Sramanic tradition among the sadhus was a mistake. The sadhus are and have probably been since Sankara the strongest defenders of Hinduism; the dullness I found in them a result of generations of unchallenged acceptance of a doctrine. By taming and codifying renunciation, Sankara seems to have deprived Indic thought of one of its essential elements, its boldest heretics and innovators, but he also ensured that what we call Hinduism today, or perhaps to use the proper term – Sanatan Dharma – was born 1,200 years ago on the banks of the Narmada.

VIII

Mahismati, the city where the debate between Sankara and Mandana Mishra took place, remains elusive today. Despite several references that crop up in classical Sanskrit literature, it is difficult to pin down its exact location. This has given rise to a host of claimants along the Narmada, the debate almost as intense as the original event that each town wants to lay claim to, leaving nothing aside — myths, fanciful notions, borrowings from questionable sources, notions that historians of repute would never touch.

Assembled before me, as I write these words, are two books that examine the evidence, and by no means dispassionately. The very first line of *Mandla: Ancient Mahishmati, Arguments, Evidence and Proof* by Girija Shankar Agrawal, M.A., head of the Mahishmati Studies Institute, declares, 'Mandla is indeed ancient Mahishmati.' On the contrary, *A Historical and Archaeological Guide to Maheshwar* by Babulal Sen asserts, 'Yes, this present day town of Maheswar was renowned in ancient times as Mahishmati.'

It is from these books that I came to know of the reference to the river in Sanskrit poetry. In Kalidasa's *Raghuvansha*, a princess who desires to see the Narmada from the balconies of a palace is told to marry the ruler of Mahishmati. Rajeshekhar, the court poet of the Kalachuri rulers, describes their capital city Mahishmati, surrounded by the Narmada. From such fragments, Mahishmati emerges as the foremost of the city states that came into being in central India after the breakdown of Mauryan rule in the second century BC.

It continued to exist as an important city for at least a thousand years. In AD 672, the Chinese pilgrim I-tsing mentions his visit to Mahishmati. Certainly, judging by Rajeshekhar's composition, there would have been no confusion about its location till the end of the Kalachuri rule in the twelfth century AD. Then, over the course of the next 600 years Mahishmati disappears, and two claimants emerge – Mandla, the capital of a Gond dynasty, and Maheshwar, the capital of the Maratha Holkar dynasty.

The claims arise in myth, the facts follow later. The ruins of the Mandla Fort have kept intact a few structures within its walls, most prominent of them a temple. In a rectangular gallery enclosing the sanctum sanctorum is an array of statues such as Garuda, Surya and Laxman that predate the temple. They range from the Gupta to the medieval period, each an exquisite specimen. But they are finally accoutrements for the main statue at the heart of the temple, the thousand-armed patron deity Sahastrarjun.

This king, a story in the Ramayana goes, was invincible in war. Once, Ravana sat meditating on the banks of the Narmada when the river suddenly flooded over, disturbing his concentration. He sent his courtiers to find out the cause for this outrage. They came back and reported that a man with a thousand arms had held the river at bay till it burst its banks. Enraged, Ravana fought Sahastrarjun in battle but was defeated and imprisoned.

A few kilometres from Mandla, an outcropping of rocks splits the course of the river into a thousand rivulets. It is the Sahastradhara, the river split into a thousand by the arms of the thousand-armed king who founded the city. More than five hundred kilometres west of Mandla, there is a similar outcropping of rocks along the course of the Narmada. It is also called the Sahastradhara. It lies a few kilometres west of Maheshwar.

In their setting on the banks of the river, the two towns could not be more different. At Mandla, the river encircles the town on three sides, still bearing the impress of the hills in its flow, answering to Rajeshekhar's description of a city surrounded by the river. At Maheshwar it is vast, placidly following a course as straight as an arrow. In Mandla, the sal forests are never far away. Maheshwar seems to be a land where agriculture has much deeper roots and the forests are but a distant presence. Yet, the two towns lay claim to the same Puranic geography. At different times and places in my journey, I sought the authors of the two books, hoping to find some resolution.

In Maheshwar, I was told to go to the barber shop in the town square and ask for Babulal Sen. I had thought of him as part of the Bengali diaspora that had accompanied the expansion of British rule, bringing in its wake the knowledge of English. But in this region Sen was the name for the traditional barber caste, and my expectations changed as I searched for a historian whose son was the town barber.

Following his son's instructions, I had little difficulty locating Babulal Sen's house. I stopped once to ask a woman. It was a Brahmin household, and she disdainfully pointed to the end of the street to where the Sens lived. The house was screened from the street by wooden slats criss-crossing each other diagonally. From the paved streets steps climbed over an open gutter into the house. An old bespectacled man sat on a fraying sofa, a woman lay on a bed placed along a wall. Across the room from her, a TV stood on a tin trunk.

Babulal Sen was eager to talk. His wife, he said, was suffering from an acute case of diabetes and always needed someone to keep an eye on her. He was over eighty and not so well himself, and so he sat by her side while he read and wrote. He was long retired from his government job and he said he was now paying his dues for what had come his way. In some way, he said, he was a gift of the Narmada. His father, also the town barber, had invoked the river and asked for a son to look after the shop so that he could head out on the parikrama. He was blessed with not one but two sons, Babulal was the elder.

He studied till the fourth standard and then his father set him to work. Once he was sure that his son could earn for the family, the father set off on the parikrama. He died somewhere near Amarkantak. Over the next twenty years, even as Babulal continued to cut hair for a living, he did not give up on his love for learning. In 1947 India became independent and his years spent reading writers such as Premchand at the local library paid off. He passed a national Hindi examination and got employed as a teacher in 1953. Government jobs were prized and his unlikely success would have provoked envy. Someone complained that he did not possess the educational qualifications for the post. He decided to clear his matriculation. In four months he feverishly acquired enough knowledge of English and other subjects to catch up with eight years of schooling. He went on to obtain an MA degree.

He said that for him to work on the history of Maheshwar was a natural choice, simply because this was where he was born. In the end, his case for Maheshwar as Mahishmati rests on archaeological excavations carried out in 1952-53 on the far bank in the village of Navdatoli. The archaeologists found evidence of human settlement in the area dating back more than four thousand years. Among the objects found in the digs were some coins from Mahishmati.

It was not difficult to locate Girija Shankar Agrawal in Mandla. I spoke to him on the phone and he asked me to wait for him at the shop now run by his son. I found myself seated among farmers who were haggling over the price of agricultural implements, water pumps, spare parts for the pumps and pipes of varying diameters that would carry the Narmada water to their fields. From time to time, the son would turn to tell me about a museum run by his father.

Girija Shankar arrived dressed in white, a fountain pen neatly clipped to his shirt pocket. His receding hair and the pencil-thin moustache that ran the length of his upper lip were both carefully trimmed and combed into place. Occasionally, he would speak a few sentences of English, just enough to let me guess at the extent of his knowledge and education.

As we drove to the museum, he spoke about the Gondi Public

Trust that had been set up by his uncle Rambharos Agrawal, who had once worked with Elwin. It seemed there was no getting away from Elwin along the river. In the prefaces to some of his books, Elwin has thanked Rambharos for helping with fieldwork in this area but from the evidence of the book I have lying before me – *A Social and Cultural Study of the Gond Tribe* by Rambharos Agrawal – their falling out seems to have been decisive.

The book itself is fascinating. It is encyclopaedic in the old sense, a reflection of the range and diversity of interests of its author, including his biases and idiosyncrasies. There is no other more comprehensive book on the Gonds, from their mythology to their dynastic history, from the vegetation that supports them to Rambharos's views on the inappropriateness of a policy of prohibition of alcohol for the tribals.

The entry on Elwin stands out from the rest of the book, or, perhaps, it has something to do with another entry that speaks with indignation about foreign missionaries. The section on Elwin is over eight pages long and begins by stating, 'Dr Verrier Elwin is now dead. I know many a thing about his conduct. We were friends. We became enemies. After his death to speak of his conduct would be unbecoming. I can describe his lack of knowledge.'

He begins by listing some mistakes in translation by Elwin. There do seem to be a few; Elwin should have known that ganja is smoked and not drunk and opium is drunk rather than smoked, but they do little to justify the indignation. Then he complains about Elwin's anti-India stance, but for Elwin to write that none of the Gond tales end with a moral in the approved copybook style is hardly anti-Indian.

The last charge against Elwin is one of obscenity. Rambharos does not dispute the truth of the statements he lists. Instead, he cites them as evidence of Elwin's depravity. It is an interesting list drawn mainly from Elwin's book on the *Folk Tales of Mahakoshal* and from *The Baiga*:

> The child simply picks up its knowledge in the ordinary casual way. "The penis and the vagina are our two teachers." Sometimes, I

was told in Kawardha, "an old woman gets a boy; she teaches him." I have been astonished by the number of people whose first sex experience was with old and unattractive women who seduced them.

The genitals should be well developed and regularly shaped. A large penis is admired in men and a small vagina in a woman. The Baigas distinguish between a vagina that is tip-tip or small and tight and one that is gus-gus, enlarged by frequent intercourse and child bearing.

The list goes on and on but it does nothing to separate the Baiga from the rest of humanity. Certainly Rambharos read Elwin with care but in the end the only case he makes is for a friendship gone sour.

His own interest in the Gonds led him to found the trust that runs the museum. Girija Shankar, with the help of a few others, had constructed the building that stands on the banks of the Narmada. He let us have our fill of the maps of the parikrama and the charts that list the history of Mandla, before he showed us the pride of his collection, more than 200 handwritten illustrated Sanskrit manuscripts. These manuscripts date back to the eighteenth and nineteenth century and had all been written in and around Mandla. Among them, he said, were some extraordinary finds such as the one written in palindromic verse 150 years ago by a Brahmin in a nearby village, another that read straight through extols the virtues of Ram and read back to front sings the praise of Krishna.

The feats were no surprise in themselves. The formal play with language, the virtuosity with words, and verses that allow several readings depending on how compound words are deciphered are all part of the larger Sanskritic tradition. The language allows great leeway for the kind of literary experiments that would later so delight the Oulipo. The surprise was in finding out how recent and widespread the tradition was in this region.

The Gond dynasty, over the centuries, seems to have become a patron of Indian music, art and writing. A large number of Brahmins from the Mithila region of Bihar, which was also Mandana Mishra's ancestral home, had become a part of the court. At a time when much of north India was under Mughal and Afghan rule, the Gond kingdom even as a feudatory seemed to have provided a safe haven. The high tradition of classical Hinduism may have finally found refuge in this tribal kingdom.

In part due to the arguments I heard, and my own readings on the subject, I was inclined to believe Mahishmati would have stood more or less at the site of modern-day Mandla. It is a conclusion based as much on my desire to place the emergence of the modern Hindu consensus in the heart of the Gond kingdom as it is on the evidence. Whatever the truth, the encounter with Babulal Sen and Girija Shankar Agrawal led to a chain of acquaintances, both in time and place, which guided me along the Narmada. In their passion for their past, in their interest in their surroundings, I could begin to believe something that a traveller always finds hard to digest, that there is a way of moving in time that can substitute for the lure of distant places.

~

Mahishmati was not the only classical city of antiquity along the Narmada. Many of these cities date back to Ashoka, who united the subcontinent into an empire whose extent was never again to be matched in the history of India. The emperor ruled from Pataliputra in the heart of Magadh but the spread of his empire made it inevitable that there would be other centres of administration. It was carved into four provinces. After Magadh, the most important of these was Avanti with its capital Ujjain. Along the highway connecting the two capitals, a number of cities came up and prospered, including some on the banks of the Narmada.

A coup by a Brahmin commander-in-chief, who in all likelihood could not tolerate the ascendance of Buddhism, brought down the Mauryan Empire. In the aftermath, Pataliputra could no longer exercise control over the unwieldy empire and the cities soon went their own ways. Each minted its own coinage, which in some cases is the only evidence left that such a city ever existed. Coins dating as far back as the third century BC have been recovered in such abundance from the Narmada Valley that the subject now forms a separate field of study.

We can guess at the existence of cities such as Bhagila, Kurara and Madavika only through the markings on their coins. The coins do not differ much in size from the modern coin, though square shapes appear to have been preferred. They are often crowded with symbols. A single square coin, no larger than the modern 25 paisa coin, could accommodate as many as five symbols on each face. Some of these symbols were in use across the subcontinent, such as the swastika; others, such as the Ujjain symbol resembling the iron cross, demarcated a region.

About a hundred kilometres further west of Mandla, along the river, the village of Nadner may well have been settled over the remains of one such city. The son of the village headman showed me around. An old fort wall surrounded the village and on its outskirts large earthen mounds overlooked the river. Brick shards stuck out from the eroded mudbanks of the mounds. Along the path leading to the top of the mounds, each footstep dislodged broken pieces of pottery. He didn't even bother to look down. For him these shards were commonplace.

Urad grew atop the mounds, which had been encroached upon by the local farmers. The Archaeological Survey of India, after a season of excavation here a few years ago, had covered up the site and left. He told me that each monsoon, he and his friends walked around looking for coins washed up by the rains. It was the same each time the farmers ploughed their fields. Scampering along the slopes of the mounds, the boy showed me a huge stone tablet projecting out of the earth. He pointed to another toppled over on its side that had slid down the slope. The script, at least to my eyes, was illegible.

We were on our own as we walked along the mound. The river flowed slowly, the water reflected the blue of the sky, wisps of cloud drifted by. Nothing was hurried, not even the wind blowing through the lentil fields. In this one moment everything coalesced, the months of wandering, the search for a narrative, the long journey from the mouth to its source. I could almost imagine the city walls; inside, a citizenry well versed in Sanskrit would have gone about its business; outside, on the river, boats would have travelled down this navigable stretch. Would this have been one of the cities Kalidas knew in his youth? No one really knows. The digs were inconclusive, some artifacts and coins were recovered. The ASI has too much of the past on its hands, it can only do so much. When we know so little of ancient Ujjain, what is one small feudatory city state along the Narmada?

The boy asked if we could return to the village. We walked back in silence. Others then insisted on showing me around. We walked to the main entrance to the village, where two stone pillars stood guard by the stairs that led down from the rampart of the fort. Huts had come up outside the fort walls. We descended the stairs, turned to the right and came to a halt outside a shack selling chai and biscuits. They pointed to some statues that had surfaced recently. Half-buried in the earth, they stood like fresh crop from the soil, ready for some collector to harvest.

I could not help but stare. Among the headless torsos and decayed forms, a Buddha seemed complete down to the waist. Implanted in the earth, it was exquisite. Sandalwood paste had been anointed on its forehead, but even the transformation into a village deity could not take away the serenity sculpted into its form. The sarpanch finally joined us. Thinking I was from the government, he made his excuses, taking refuge in the chikungunya epidemic that had recently hit the village. He complained that people kept coming here to buy statues. He had been offered Rs 5,000 for the one we had just seen. Little did he know the price it would command in the international market.

On the outskirts of the village, headed back to Jabalpur, I was waved down by a man who introduced himself as Akhilesh. He had seen me walking around the mound. He offered me two Mauryan coins and a few beads for Rs 100. I hesitated; to pay was to encourage the trade but the trade would go on with or without me. If nothing else, I could settle a debt I had incurred to a man who had just a few days earlier opened my eyes to the coins of the Narmada.

~

I had been told Ajay Jaiswal was interested in the antiquities of the Narmada Valley. I called him up and he asked me to meet him at home, next to his hotel, the Ajanta in Gadarwara, the town where Rajneesh had once dwelt. It seemed an unlikely combination, the antiquities and the hotel. In such towns, what passed for a hotel was usually a large grimy room lit up by fluroscent tubelights, two rows of wooden tables and chairs, a counter of tin and glass housing stale sweets and samosas, and a man in attendance who would hopefully wipe the tables clean with a cloth that left the surface dirtier than before.

I was used to such places. The food was usually palatable and at times delicious. I had a weakness for kachoris, pooha or jalebis washed down with sweet milky tea, and I had long grown impervious to the dirt. If anything, the absence of grime always aroused suspicion in my mind. My surprise at the Ajanta had little to do with the place. The kachoris were delicious; it was just that I had never associated a love for antiquities with the owner of such a hotel.

Ajay Jaiswal turned out to be a stout man, expected in his profession, and a Ph.D. in journalism, which was not. The hotel was a family business that paid the bills. His real interest lay elsewhere. He came from a family of collectors and the passion ran in his blood. Both his maternal and paternal grandfathers were collectors and he had inherited their inclinations, but he had built up his collection largely on his own.

It took an afternoon of talking, as I told him about my stay in Sonpuri, my trips to Amarkantak, the days in Mandla before he came to believe that my interest in the river was genuine. He slowly let me into his collection – a chillum of ashtadhatu with silver inlay, a body scrubber, several objects in bronze – but he was just whetting my appetite.

He had 25,000 coins in his collection, 200 coins from the Mauryan era alone; it was probably the largest such private collection in the country, hidden in this remote town by the Narmada. He told me all that I now know about city states and Mauryan coinage. As he pulled out a magnifying glass and made me peer at an album he had set to one side, the markings came alive. These, he told me, were one-eighth the size of coins currently believed to be the smallest in the world.

When I took out the two coins I had purchased from Nadner, he took a look at them. One of them was a cast copper coin from the first or second century BC, quite commonly found here. The other was from the city state of Kurara, now lost to us. Was Nadner Kurara? It was difficult to say, coins were currency and they would have travelled.

As I glanced through Ajay's collection, he made me stop and stare at a particular coin. He asked if I noticed anything in particular about it, but I couldn't see what he was trying to point out. Then he showed me where the gold plating had eroded, revealing the inferior metal below. It was a counterfeit medieval coin, one of the many in his collection.

It was a subject of particular fascination for him, and for the moment, it caught my fancy. Counterfeit coinage dates back to at least 400 BC on the subcontinent, closely following the introduction of actual coinage. Ajay pointed me to the *Arthashastra*, the compendium of ancient Indian statecraft that dates to the first century AD. It prescribed an office of the examiner of coins who could impose a cash penalty for circulating counterfeit coins; the penalty for actually depositing counterfeit currency in the treasury was death.

Today, in some cases, a counterfeit coin from that era is worth far more than the original. With no official around to impose a penalty for a lack of authenticity, the very objects that set the measure on value in a society become open to other forms of estimation. The idea of the original and the counterfeit and the precedence that we grant to one over the other appear to be a measure of time. Why then do we remain so sure of passing judgement on fakes? Who is to say what value they will eventually come to acquire? And does it not seem appropriate then to let both Mandla and Maheshwar lay claim to Mahishmati?

IX

Located less than fifty kilometres along the river from Rajneesh's hometown is the town of Hoshangabad. It is named after Hoshang Shah, once ruler of the Malwa plateau that lies further westward along the course of the river. The Malwa sultans had wrested control of the area from a long line of Hindu kingdoms, but their movement further eastwards had been halted by the Gonds. The BJP, affronted by a history they do not particularly like, are now campaigning to erase the name. They want to rename it Narmadapuram, the city on the Narmada.

Those afflicted with certainty do not realize how difficult it is to manufacture a history of their choice on banks where civilizations and cultures have settled and been displaced several times over. There is indeed evidence of a settlement called Narmadapur where the town of Hoshangabad stands today, but then there is also evidence of other much older and longer-lived settlements.

On the outskirts of Hoshangabad, heading south from the river, a rock face rises at a thirty-degree angle from the earth, clearly visible for miles around. It is known as Adamgarh, Adam's fort. The term, just one of the many day-to-day instances of the presence of Islam in this land, is often used to refer to the distant past, the time of Baba Aadam. The baba is a reference to a venerable elder. At the cave shelters of Adamgarh, there once dwelt men from the time of Baba Aadam.

The rock face is pockmarked with cave shelters. The Vindhya ranges that line the Narmada are made of sandstone that weathers easily. Over millennia, rain has carved out caverns in the rocks. Where a layer of a rock face has weathered faster than the others, it has given rise to giant open-air shelters with the roof sloping gently down to the floor. At many places, the roof is within an arm's length of a standing or crouching man, a perfect canvas for the Stone Age artists who reached out to depict scenes of hunting and battle.

The presence of Stone Age man in the Narmada Valley has been with me through my travels. At Sonpuri, walking along paths that slope down from the village to the wells and ponds below, my shoe kicked aside a pebble to reveal something gleaming in the sunlight. It was a piece of quartz, abundant on the hillside. But as I bent down to pick it up, a stone lying beside it caught my attention. Half the length of a finger, it had clearly been worked to a sharp edge. When I asked around, I was told such stones could be found in numbers anywhere on the hillside.

The day I first visited the Adamgarh shelter, there were no other visitors around. Empty liquor bottles lay strewn around on the floor of a cave shelter, abandoned by young men from the town. In many of the shelters, the constant flow of water had erased the paintings; in others a black moss had taken note of the moisture. The very weather that had made the shelters possible in the first place had also ensured that there was little of interest to the untrained eye. These were not the spectacular cave paintings of Europe, safely preserved from rain and wind in a cave in the interiors of a mountain.

It takes repeated visits to such shelters, abundant as they are in the Narmada Valley, to gain some sense of what is on view. The Adamgarh shelters are by no means the most spectacular rock formations in the region. Just off the road from Hoshangabad to Bhopal, forty kilometres from the Narmada, lies Bhimbetka. From a distance, on a vast flat hilltop, a few mushroom-shaped projections stand out. Up close, they are immense, enclosing space like cathedrals, echoing an infinite silence. Some open up like vast funnels to the sky, others are cavernous shelters overlooking the plain below. In comparison, Adamgarh may be more muted, but for neither would the term sacred be out of place.

Over a period of ten thousand years, men would have sought shelter here, as is evident from the art. In some caves paintings from several eras overlay each other, much as civilizations do along the river. Often it is difficult to discern any pattern in the whirling maze of lines, but where different colours have been used at different times, it is possible to glimpse the very beginning.

The colours used in the earliest cave shelters, ochre, yellow and white, seem to suggest those favoured by the Gonds in their day-to-day life for their traditional floor patterns. This could simply be a matter of the availability of natural pigments, the soil along the Narmada easily providing material for all three colours, or it could point to a continuity between the Stone Age cultures and the tribal inhabitants of the vast region between the Narmada and the Godavari.

Whatever may be the case, it is the earliest paintings that astound the most. The strict geometry of a triangle and a rectangle combined with a few curved lines easily evoke humans in motion. With such grace is movement captured in a single frame that everything that follows seems stilted, more realistic but burdened with effort. Gazing at these figures, it seems we have come very far from that primordial moment when art began. A beginning born of an insight far removed from reality, yet completely true to it.

～

The earliest paintings date back to well before 7,000 BC. Archaeological digs at the cave shelters reveal that they have been inhabited almost continuously over the past ten to fifteen thousand years.

By the last millennium BC, towns had spread on the plains below. The trade routes that connected these towns during Ashokan times ran along the Narmada. One would have passed not far from Bhimbetka, on the plains below, onward to Hoshangabad, connecting the river to the great Buddhist centre of Sanchi, which lay less than fifty kilometres to the north.

The same trade routes would have opened up the subcontinent to Buddhism after Ashoka's conversion. Certainly, under Ashoka, a great number of the laity in these towns was Buddhist and its support made possible a vast network of Buddhist viharas where monks resided.

They had inherited the traditions of the Sramanas, wandering through the year and halting only during the four months of the monsoon, the chaturmas, when torrential rain and flooding would have made travel impossible. The pilgrims following the traditional ways are walking much as the Sramanas once would have. They carry nothing with them, they depend on the residents of the villages and towns that they pass through for succour and they do not stay anywhere for longer than they have to, except when the monsoon arrives, and then they choose a dry, safe spot to pass the months of the rain.

For many of the Buddhist monks who travelled the trade routes, the cave shelters would have been an obvious choice of residence during the chaturmas. It was a phenomenon that was all too evident in and around the Narmada Valley. Across the Narmada from Hoshangabad, along the route from Bhimbetka, lies the town of Budhni, the name itself in all probability derived from the Buddha. The evidence seems to suggest that this crossroads on the trade routes was once a thriving Buddhist centre.

My guide to this region, Gopikant Ghosh, bestowed to me by the same chain of connections along the river, had been told of two Buddhist complexes that lay along the hills west of the town. As the vehicle left the main road and headed to the hills, the road progressively deteriorated. We eventually parked at the base and walked up to the Talpur stupas. The Gond chowkidar at the site soon caught up with us. He had seen us climbing, and had stirred out of the village below where he had been sitting sipping chai. His name was Damdami Lal and he had been here for the past eight years, working this job for a salary of Rs 1,100 a month.

Few visitors came this way, he said, and he had not had people from the department visit for the past five years. He was not even sure why he had been assigned the task of watching over the shelters. The question answered itself at the cave shelter that opened up before us halfway up the hill. It was enormous. The paintings were a dizzying profusion of the same fading ochre, yellow and white. Stairs carved in the rocks led up past the rock shelters to two Buddhist stupas. Their roofs had caved in. The river was clearly visible in the distance as it would have been even when the stupas were in use.

As we walked back to our vehicle, a cowherd joined us. His cattle were grazing on the slope and he had time to kill. Leopards are often seen here, he said, and he recently saw a bear by the cave. Once every other month or so, a tiger that inhabits the forest reserve north of the hill can be spotted along the ridge above and behind us, he said. True or not, such stories helped keep away vandals. But they did suggest that the job the chowkidar was paid to do, incomprehensible to him, was not easy.

We had to stop often and ask for directions to the next site at Panguradia village. The local people referred to it as Saru-Maru. A wrong turn led to a dead end before we hit a rocky road that took us to another hill further along the same range.

There was an enormous stone grinder at the base. With yoked oxen circling its periphery, it must have once provided grain for the monastic complex on the hill. A ramp led up past two stupas which had either been excavated or ransacked. It opened up to a clearing where we saw the inevitable rock shelters. Caves led into the mountain, bats lunged overhead. The cave paintings had faded with time, but enough traces remained to tell of their extent.

An Ashokan edict in the Brahmi script had been carved into the walls of the shelter. A translation I came across later read: 'Ashoka visited Upnith Vihar two years, five months and six days after his coronation at Ujjain. He also instructed Kumar Shava, the then Raja of Malwa, to maintain the place well.'

The term Upnith Vihar seemed to refer to the elaborate Budddhist complex that lay above the rock shelter. What we had just seen at

Talpur was dwarfed by this complex that seemed to cover an entire hillside. Remains of several stupas were scattered through the complex. The ruins also suggested vast rectangular halls; some may have housed the monks, others may well have been meant for study and meditation.

Through this region, the phenomenon of rock shelters used as a Buddhist complex was repeated over and over again. Occasionally, the Buddhists were more enterprising.

In 1857, the nineteen-year-old James Forsyth first reached Pachmarhi, the highest point in central India, located just off the Narmada Valley. In 1862, after the inducement of a hunt, plentiful mahua and grain from the plains, Forsyth was able to persuade the Gonds and Korkus in the neighbouring villages to occasionally lend a hand in building a lodge that still stands as a museum. The journal of his 1862 journey, *The Highlands of Central India*, was published in 1871, a year after his death at the age of thirty-two. Forsyth's book, marked by the unexpected insights of an intelligent young man, describes a prominent Buddhist centre:

> A remarkable feature in the configuration of the plateau is the vast and unexpected ravines or rather clefts in the solid rock, which seam the edges of the scarp, some of them reaching in sheer descent almost to the level of the plains. You come on them during a ramble in almost any direction, opening suddenly at your feet in the middle of some grassy glade. The most remarkable is the Andeh-Koh ... Looking over its edge, the vision loses itself in the vast profundity. A few dark indigo-coloured specks at the bottom represent wild mango trees of sixty or eighty feet in height. A faint sound of running water rises on the ... wind from the abyss.
>
> ... Legend has made the Andeh-Koh the retreat of a monstrous serpent, which formally inhabited a lake on the plateau, and vexed the worshippers of Mahadeo till the god dried up the serpent's lake, and imprisoned the snake himself in this rift, formed by a stroke of his trident in the solid rock. It needs no

very ingenious interpreter of legend to see in this wild story an allusion to the former settlements of Buddhists (referred to as snakes in Brahminical writings) on the Puchmurree hill, and their extinction on the revival of Brahmanism in the sixth or seventh century. Certain it is that there once was a considerable lake in the centre of the plateau, formed by a dam thrown across a narrow gorge, and that on its banks are still found numbers of the large flat bricks used in ancient buildings, while in the overhanging rocks are cut five caves (whence the name of Puchmurree), of the character usually attributed to the Buddhists. Beneath the lower end of the lake lies a considerable stretch of almost level land, on which are still traceable the signs of ancient tillage, in the form of embankments and watercourses. Looking from the portico of the rock-cut caves, it is not difficult for the imagination to travel back to the time when the lower margin of the lake was surrounded by the dwellings of a small, perhaps an exiled and persecuted, colony of Buddhists, practising for their subsistence the art, strange in these wilds, of civilised cultivation of the earth, and to hear ... the sound of the evening bell in their little monastery floating away up the placid surface of the winding lake.

As we walked down from Upnith Vihar, Forsyth's words running through my mind, I recalled something I had read in a news report in a Bhopal newspaper. I went looking for the chowkidar's hut. He was away, but just as the news report had said, lying inside, unprotected, were a stone Hermika (umbrella) and a Yashti (the pillar that supports the umbrella) donated by Emperor Askoka's daughter Sanghamitra for the main Stupa at Upnith Vihar. The local name Saru-Maru indicated that what these ruins housed 2,250 years ago was no ordinary monastery. Emperor Ashoka had travelled here, as had his daughter, who was to carry Buddhism to Sri Lanka.

~

The stupas at the site are believed to have contained the relics of Sariputra (Saru) and Maha Moggallana (Maru), two of the most important disciples of the Buddha. Sariputra is often shown sitting on his right, an embodiment of wisdom, and Moggallana to his left, master of that more sinister aspect of divinity, the supernatural.

No records seemed to exist of any excavations at the Upnith Vihar but during the excavations at Sanchi, as described by a Buddhist scholar, in one of these, the now famous Third Stupa,

> Sir Alexander Cunningham discovered the sacred Body Relics of the Buddha's Chief Disciples, Sariputta and Maha Moggallana, in 1851 …
>
> On sinking a shaft in the centre of the stupa on Sanchi Hill, Cunningham came upon a large stone slab, upwards of five feet in length, lying in a direction from north to south. Beneath the slab were found two boxes of gray sandstone, each with a brief inscription in Brahmi characters on the lid. The box to the south was inscribed *'Sariputtasa'* '[Relics] of Sariputta', while that to the north bore the legend *'Maha-Mogalanasa'*. '[Relics] of Maha Moggallana.'
>
> The southernmost box contained a large flat casket of white steatite, rather more than six inches broad and three inches in height. The surface was hard and polished and the box, which had been turned on a lathe, was a beautiful piece of workmanship. Around this casket were some fragments of sandalwood believed to have been from the funeral pyre, while inside it, besides the Relic, various precious stones were found. This casket contained a single bone relic of the Venerable Sariputta, not quite one inch in length.
>
> The stone box to the north enclosed another steatite casket, similar to that of Sariputta but slightly smaller and with a softer surface. Inside it were two bone relics of the Venerable Maha Moggallana, the larger of them being something less than half an inch in length.
>
> Each of the two steatite caskets had a single ink letter inscribed on the inner surface of the lid: 'Sa' for Sariputta on the southern and 'Ma' for Maha Moggallana on that to the north. In Cunningham's words, 'Sariputta and Maha Moggallana were the principal followers of the Buddha, and were usually styled

his right and left hand disciples. Their ashes thus preserved after death the same positions to the right and left of Buddha which they had themselves occupied in life.' This is explained by the fact that the Buddha customarily sat facing east.

According to tradition, Sariputra and Moggallana were Brahmins born on the same day in neighbouring villages. Their families were known to each other, and the boys grew up as close friends. Their quest for enlightenment began at a fair in Rajgir, the capital of Magadh province, home to the Mauryans.

After they had spent two days at the festival, they were both struck by the same thought – the men who performed before them would be dead within a few decades, what then was to be gained from such distraction? Pursued to its logical end, the question did not seem to allow for an easy answer. The two friends decided they would look for a teacher who could deliver them from this affliction of the human condition. Their first teacher was Sanjaya the agnostic, the best known of the ascetics of Rajgir.

Like the Charvaka, little has survived of Sanjaya but for the criticisms of his opponents. In the *Digha Nikaya* No. 2, the king Ajatashatru tells the Buddha:

> One day I went to Sanjaya of the Belattha clan and I asked him: 'Can you, sir, declare to me an immediate fruit, visible in this very world, of the life of a recluse?' Being thus asked, Sanjaya said: 'If you asked me whether there is another world – well, if I thought there were, I would say so. But I don't say so. And I don't think it is thus or thus. And I don't think it is otherwise. And I don't deny it. And I don't say there neither is nor is not, another world. And if you asked me about the beings produced spontaneously; or whether there is any fruit, any result, of good or bad actions; or whether a Tathagata continues or not after death – to each or any of these questions do I give the same reply.

This admirable and sceptical approach could hardly lead to deliverance. In contrast, the Buddha's answers went to the very heart of their question. It is understandable that the two friends left Sanjaya to seek their answers with the Buddha, but two millennia later, there is little to suggest that Sanjaya was wrong and the Buddha right.

~

Some days later, we headed to one of the lesser-known rock shelters in Budhni that lay less than 500 yards off the road from Hoshangabad to Bhopal. The dirt track from the road to the shelter took a much longer route, winding its way past hillsides blasted apart by quarrying. A few dumper trucks headed back to the main road, carrying their illegal load. Among the hillsides scarred by the deep gashes running along their length, a hillock stood miraculously unscathed. A temple stood at the very top and some shepherds nearby spoke of shelters dotted with paintings.

It was an easy walk up to the top. Even from a distance, the tiny white shrine to Banjari Mai was clearly visible. Behind the temple, at the very summit, was a cave shelter. Its walls had been whitewashed and then painted red. A sadhu had recently moved in, his name was Hirananda, and Gulab Singh, a disciple from a nearby village, kept him company. They were settled in for the chaturmas when we met them.

Hirananda told us he was originally from Betul and pulled out an album of photographs from his ashram there. The devi, he claimed, had appeared to him in a dream and directed him to this exact spot. He then pointed to the Narmada placidly winding its way past Hoshangabad to the fertile plains of the Nimar. 'You see the temple in the river,' and indeed it was visible in the distance, a small speck on the river, 'that is the tail of the Sheshnag, and this spot where we sit is the head.' He pulled out a small booklet, which he claimed gave the Puranic description of this hillock. His story expanded into an explanation vast enough to include the love that brought Shiva and Parvati together.

I could see the assimilative power of such thinking. Diana L. Eck, in her book *India: A Sacred Geography*, makes a vivid distinction between the India of the modern map-makers, and the India constantly re-imagined in the manner of the sadhu I had met. 'In a range of Hindu traditions,' she writes, 'imaginative "mapmaking" became the domain of both cosmologists and mythmakers. It is arguable that the imagined landscape they created is far more culturally powerful than that displayed on today's most geographically precise digital map of India. The imagined landscape bears imprints of meaning: the self-manifest eruptions of the gods, the footprints of the heroes, the divine origins of the rivers, the body of the Goddess. In this mental map, geography is overlaid with layer upon layer of story and connected in a storied landscape. In a broad sense, each village, river and hillock has a story. Some of these stories are local, but some places are linked through their stories to several other regional shrines, and some are linked through their stories to a network of shrines all over India.'

The difference between the maps is vivid. One is an ordinary map on paper, the other is dynamic, much the way the web is. Towns, villages and shrines are linked to one another in invisible ways spelt out by stories, distances are shortened by myths. New links are forever coming into being.

As Hirananda showed us around his hillside, he went out of his way to exaggerate the importance of his new domain. The caves extend to the bowels of the earth, he told us, and the peace at this spot was beyond the worldly. And indeed, if I ignored the gouged out remains of the illegally quarried hillsides nearby, I could see the Narmada winding around Budhni, and in the north, away from the river, fields stretching out to the mill complex near the Talpur shelters.

He was planning a set of steps that would be carved into the hillside, leading up directly from the fields to the shrine. He expected thousands of devotees to be clambering up for a darshan of the deity. He could probably glimpse visions of a bhandara larger than the one he had organized in Betul.

He told Gulab Singh to take us to another rock shelter located less than a hundred yards down the slope from the summit. It was still possible to see a few deer painted in white and human figures in red. When we walked back to Hirananda, he told us, 'This is why the devi brought me here. Men have painted such scenes in blood; now it is time for something new.' In his telling, the ochre had turned into dried blood.

He took us back to the main shelter and pointed to the large smooth rock face painted white which served as a backdrop to the idol he had placed there. 'The painting here was spectacular. Two hundred men wielding shields and spears stood there, two armies facing each other. I had it painted over.'

Shocked into silence, we descended quietly to our waiting car. It seemed to me that like history, mythology could be wielded in many ways. Even if the BJP had not yet managed to erase the history of this region, this baba, who shared their belief that new myths could be used to lay stake to old territory, had shown that the past could indeed be painted over for the sake of a more convenient present.

His sacred geography may have assimilated the hillock but his map had no space for Talpur or Upnith Vihar, and the presence of the rock shelters was being layered over.

In places as far removed from each other as Israel and Punjab, some people, whether Jews or Sikhs, have come to believe that they have exclusive rights to a geography sacred to them. Others, who may have lived there as long, if not longer, are being excluded. In much the same manner, the proponents of Hindutva are attempting to use an older and at one time inclusive sacred geography of the subcontinent to lay exclusive claim to the land.

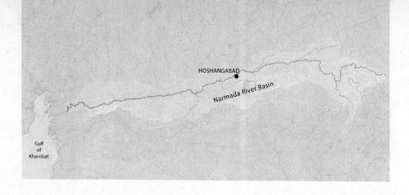

HOSHANGABAD

Narmada River Basin

Gulf of Khambat

X

Hindu ascetics were not the only religious wanderers drawn to the Narmada.

At a small stall tucked away in one corner of the Delhi Book Fair of 1994, I came across a slim blue paperback, simply but elegantly produced: *Narmada: The Life of a River*, by Geoffrey Waring Maw. It was published by the Friends Rural Centre and had been edited by Marjorie Sykes. The names may have been unfamiliar but I was just back from a trip to Amarkantak, I could not help but buy the book.

Maw turned out to be an English Quaker who had spent a considerable period of time living in the Narmada Valley during the first half of the twentieth century. After his death, his papers had been deposited at the Central Library of the Selly Oak College in Birmingham. This is where Marjorie Sykes, a prominent English Quaker who had spent the last years of her life putting together a history of the Quakers in India found them in 1990. In these papers, she came across 'a good deal of material about the traditions and pilgrimages associated with the Narmada' which became the basis for the book.

In her own book, Sykes devotes a chapter to 'Sadhus and Pilgrims'. It brings together three extraordinary characters. Sundar Singh, a Sikh convert to Christianity, was a mystic who donned the garb of a sadhu at the time of his conversion and later seemed to have found solace in Swedenborg. Samuel Evans Stokes was a Quaker who lived out the life of a sadhu for a period of time before following a trajectory that inverted Sundar Singh's life, proceeding from Christianity to Gandhian thought to the Arya Samaji version of Hinduism in 1932 when he took the name Satyanand. Somewhere in between, he found the time to set up the apple industry that sustains Himachal Pradesh today. Another of those influenced enough to consider the idea was C.F. Andrews, who was later to become one of the closest associates of Mahatma Gandhi. In 1909 the three of them came together to consider a Christian brotherhood that would follow the way of the sadhus. A name was proposed – *Brotherhood of the Imitation of Christ* but it was finally Sundar Singh who expressed an inability to belong to any organized order.

Maw came to India in 1910 to work at the Hoshangabad Quaker Mission on the banks of the Narmada. He was heavily influenced by Stokes's description of life as a sadhu, and he had met Sundar Singh who had visited the Hoshangabad Mission. In 1943, on a visit to the island of Omkara Mandhata or Omkareshwar, Maw noted, 'The more I talked with the pilgrims I met ... the more I listened to their stories, the more I longed to see it all: the temples and sacred places, the forts and palaces whose crumbling walls had known so much of India's history, the hidden hermitages of those who had renounced the world's prizes to "realize God". I too longed to turn my back on the rush and worry and set out on pilgrimage.'

In bits and pieces, he slowly managed to see the course of the Narmada, much as I was doing now. There is a traditional term for our lack of method, the bandar parikrama, the monkey pilgrimage, which does not tie down the pilgrim to the usual norms, leaving him free to cross the river as he wills or even to pick and chose his route along the parikrama. In 1949, six years after his visit to Omkareshwar, Maw, in his version of the bandar parikrama, made it to Amarkantak, ending where I had begun. He arrived by train at Pendra Road and then travelled the twenty miles to Amarkantak. He covered the first eleven miles by bullock cart before halting for the night at a village.

'Next morning I hired a chamar (a worker of leather) with a pony to carry my luggage up the last eight miles of forest track to Amarkantak. It was mid-January, the air was cold, jungle birds sang a morning chorus, the palas, "flame of the forest", glowed with its pointed flame-red flowers. Without a guide I should soon have been lost, for the track was steep and rough and often divided. We were not alone; from time to time parties of men, women and children, traveling in long single file, passed us by. They swung quickly along, singing as they went. For them the hills were home, they belonged to the local forest tribes, Gonds and Kurkus. We met another man alone, sadly driving some cattle, a tiger, he said, had killed two of his bullocks in the night. A little further on a sadhu was living in a tiny hut by a stream, protected from the tigers by a stockade; he gave me a warm welcome and some flowers from his garden.'

Maw left India shortly after, but the Quakers lingered on in the Narmada Valley.

~

It was in 1869 that Elkanah and Irena Beard responded to a call by their fellow Quakers in India to help run a girls' school in Benares. The Quakers – or to give them the name they prefer, The Religious Society of Friends – began as a religious movement in England almost 350 years ago when George Fox bore witness to the living Christ within him. The revelation that God dwells within comes with the realization that his presence requires no ritual, ceremony or clergy. A few centuries earlier in medieval India, the entire sant tradition sang a similar revelation. 'Seek him in the depth of your heart,' Kabir had insisted.

The Quakers, given the name because some of them would literally quake in God's presence, have stayed true to that initial revelation. In the same way that the sant tradition spoke against caste, the Quakers stood up to slavery in the US. In 1864, the Quakers of Indiana had appointed Elkanah Beard to go south and work among those recently released from slavery with 'three mandates: to inspect the condition of contraband camps, hospitals, and black settlements; to set up a network for distributing clothing; and to establish schools at such points as may be deemed advisable.'

In 1868, after his work in the South, Elkanah and his wife obtained permission to head to India. En route, the couple stopped in England, only to be left perplexed by the attitude of the English Quakers who did not lay the same stress on the word of the Bible as they did. Over the course of this journey, Beard kept a diary, which I was able to track down to Earlham College in Indiana. The library was generous enough to send me a digitalized copy. The excerpts describe the bewilderment that seemed to have doomed his years in India:

12 mo, 18th, 1868
Today met with our Foreign Mission Association at Richmond which was organized at our last yearly meeting. I laid before them a prospect which has for some years dwelt more or less with myself and dear wife to engage as soon as way opens for it in religious service in southern Asia. For a time to make our home in Benares, India, and labor as ability may be given to bring the people who are heathen to Christ.

5 mo 17, 1869
We were however encouraged to proceed in any gospel service we might find ourselves drawn to whilst remaining in England. The liberty given and sympathy manifested is comfortin but we are so weighed down with our prospects in India that we cannot enjoy or enter into other matters with that life we really desire ...

25th
Today some objections were made by certain friends to my ministry on first day at Devonshire House because I said "ye must come to Christ if ye will have your sins forgiven." This they said was not the first step in religious doctrine according to the Friends. I could but pray that the Lord might have mercy on them and show them that man of himself could not find peace or forgiveness until he comes to Jesus. It grieved me to find

such strange and foreign views to the gospel plan of salvation. Truly I am thankful there are not many called friends who are of this belief.

16th
Early this morning came in sight of the Indian coast which produces in my mind great thankfulness to God for his many mercies. During the past week nothing of particular interest occurred until last night a lady was delivered of a child. Which the father informs us today has received the name of our ship "Orissa". At dinner the crew and passengers drank to the health of various persons, a practice that is productive of much evil. The speeches made on such occasions are often immoral and tend only to vanity. 8 pm – Set our feet on shore at Bombay. Lodged at the Hope Hall Hotel. O how still everything seems – no rattle of machinery, no vibration of the vessel, no rolling waves of the mighty ocean to disturb the quiet. Surely the contrast is great.

10 mo 23
Arrived at Benares very much worn from our long and tedious land journey. 160 miles by Dak carriage and over 800 by rail. Irena was very ill one day and night on the way. We are now comfortably cared for by R. Metcalfe who has taken a house and fitted it up for our home. The place is known as 39, Sudder Bazaar. Evening was greatly blessed in prayer, W. Moody Blake called to bid us welcome. From what we see of our surroundings I am not pleased with our location for mission work. Our compound is large, pleasant and healthy but we are too far from the city. May the Lord show us what to do.

6 mo 1 st
...
For three mos. the weather has been very hot and oppressive, so much so that I really wonder how the English keep up so well and we are now having rain. The miasma in many parts of the city is most offensive. Cholera and smallpox is prevailing in certain districts. Every day a great many dead corpses float past our house. The poorer class of Hindoos not "being able to buy

sufficient wood to burn their dead, they cast into the river and are eaten by both birds and beasts of prey. I have seen vultures, hawks, crows, hogs and dogs fighting over the remains of little children. Babies are mostly devoured by crockdiles, alligators and large fish which abound in the river here. These are sickening and loathsome sights and I often turn from them really heartsick and cry unto the Lord for grace to run with patience and bear with fortitude all that may come upon us in this heathen land.

Disgusting as the afore mentioned sights are, I am more shocked at seeing young and old wholly given to idolatry. I have seen the old grey headed father and mother bow before gods of stone or wood and of brass. I have seen them after they are too feeble to walk carried by their children and set on the rivers brink and left to die. One case of this kind occurred just before our door. I have seen little boys and girls kneel before the idols and kiss the feet of the officiating Brahman priest, then arise and make their offerings first to the god and then to the priest. Once a week a man passes by our house, who as he walks along in a loud voice declares, "God is everything and everything is God, hence it is our duty to worship everything we see and loudly to praise those from whom we derive the greatest benefit." This mans favorites are the peepul tree and the river. He often stands and bows and sings and prays before one of these trees. When he goes to the river to bathe he bows seven times then walks into the water and dips up with his hand three times and pours it out as a drink offering for the Sun, moon and stars each, or either of which, or all, just as we *may* imagine are God and should have our reverential worship.

This he says "no man but a fool will deny". The poor people generally regard this as one of their wisest and best of men, hence it is not uncommon for groups of children to follow him to listen as they say to his sweet words – O when will this people know, love and fear the God of heaven and earth. When will they worship the true and living God. When will they cease to make themselves gods of every specie of things whether animate or inanimate.

Our feelings are from these and various other causes

constantly wounded and we cry night and day for wisdom and strength to put before our fellowmen the plan of salvation through Christ as set forth in the gospel.

8 mo 1st

...

Notwithstanding our poor health we are getting on in the language and I feel a great desire to see a friends mission established in the country. There is a right place as well as a right time and we have been asking the Lord to show us where we should attempt to locate for a permanent mission station. Ever since we came to Benares our minds have been turned toward the Nerbudda Valley, central India but we must wait the Lords time – No doubt it is in mercy that He chastens us.

10th mo 15, 1871

My dear Irena is very poorly. She is suffering less pain but on the whole I fear she is gradually declining. Entirely confined to the house and mostly to her bedroom. I have lost all hope of ever seeing her well again. Day before yesterday I drove out five miles to a village on the Nerbudda River. I took a good supply of tracts in Hindi. After I had been there a little time the people came in great companies begging for my books. They said they had no Shastras that read like mine did. Several Brahmans wished a copy of the New Testament. I was very sorry I had none with me. They promised to come and see me soon. Should they keep their word it may be better for them and the cause of Christ that I had none to give at the time.

One old Brahman priest who sat on the river bank with twenty four little pods of stone and brass in front of him after hearing a part of one of the tracks said "your heart must be very good or you could not drew such words as them out of it."

Another priest said "that man is like God" at which a fellow priest said explain yourself.

He replied, "because his heart is full of love."

After considerable talk on various matters I left the Ghat for home. To my great surprise when I was nearly through the village a company of near fifty persons were sitting under a tree waiting my return and the cry for tracts and hymns was at first almost deafening. I supplied all that could read and their expressions of gladness and thankfulness that I had come to see them etc. was very striking.

I bade them adieu and after going several hundred yards I heard some one hollow and looking out of my gari I see a man and boy running at full speed to overtake me. They soon came up saying, "please give me some of your good words" and bowing themselves to the earth. I supplied them and was soon on my way again rejoicing that my way among them had been made so easy. May God bless the good seed scattered among them to His own praise and glory.

12 mo 1st 1871

...

Last first and second days I attended a large melee or Hindoo festival which is held yearly at the Marble Rocks. There was probably near twenty thousand persons present and I should think fully three fourths of them women. My heart was grieved to see the people bowing before the images and making their offerings to gods made of stone.

In one place on a high hill there is a collection of about one thousand images nearly all of which have been more or less broken by the Musselmen nevertheless they are gods still and held in great reverance by thousands.

I distributed about 500 tracts which I hope may under Gods blessing turn the minds of some of the poor heathen from darkness to light and from the power of satan unto the true and loving God.

About 50 persons out of the many thousands applied for tracts, which I presume is a pretty fair representation of those who are seeking something more soul satisfying than they find in idoltry.

New Years –

0 how changed: our prospect now to sail in a few days from this dark and berefit land for England. Irena is quite helpless and being urged by the best physicians to retire from the mission

field for a season. We have concluded to yield. It is however the greatest mortification of my life but for her sake and we trust it may also be for the furtherance of the gospel in some way we intend going to Bombay next week having already engaged our passage to Southampton via Red Sea and Mediterranean in one of the P. & O. Steamships.

1st 15th 1872
Now in Bombay, the Rail road journey from Jubbalpore here was very trying on my dear wife and it looks very uncertain as to her ever reaching home again. We can only say the Lords will be done. Our work in India brought to a close, It has been attended with great privation and hardship but we have done what we could and wait for further developments. Perhaps our God may make way for one or both of us to return. Any way the seed sown will in time bring forth a harvest to the glory of the great husbandman. We are happy in a Saviors love come life or death. All is well – the Lord be praised.

Elkanah and Irena made it safely back to the US, where she went on to live for another four decades, outliving her husband by fifteen years. For all their fervour, or perhaps because of it, there seemed to be something self-serving about their faith. Bound by the dogma they had made of Jesus, a dogma the British Quakers did not seem to share, it never seems to have occurred to them that there were things they could have learnt from the people they felt they had so devotedly served.

～

Among the men in London who had met Elkanah was twenty-seven-year-old Charles Gayford who volunteered to replace the couple in India. In October 1873 he set out on a journey of his own. Majorie Sykes writes, 'From the Mandla district he followed the Narmada river westward, from close under the Satpura ranges on the south to the foot of the Vindhya hills on the north bank opposite Hoshangabad. He travelled on foot, remembering the robust prescription given him by his mentor before he left London: "*No* beefsteak or brandy, and *plenty* of physical exercise!" He took a servant to help him, and a pony for possible emergencies, and carried a tent, and a supply of simple medicines, in a bullock cart. On the road he met many friendly villagers, and talked with them as farmer to farmer about their growing crops; he slept in the open air, among people of such simple honesty that the whole police "circle" of 63 villages was guarded by *one* Head Constable with seven men.' When he reached Jabalpur in 1874, he reported that Hoshangabad would be a 'fine center for Quaker witness to spiritual truth, which should include both healing of the body and enlightenment of the mind'.

~

The road from Bhopal runs along a high embankment skirting the edge of Hoshangabad before it descends and turns left into town. Few people in town today are aware of it, but the embankment is a reminder of the great famine of 1896. By the time it was over, more than a million people had died. Marjorie Sykes writes, '... it was not until November 1896 that the Friends there realized how serious the situation was. No one had dreamed that there could be famine in such a favoured district, and there was some delay in bringing the famine code into operation. Before it became effective, people were dying of starvation ... in Hoshangabad district relief was given on a "food-for-work." basis ... (one of the projects) was organized from Rasulia itself with Government cooperation and approval. This was the building of the 18-foot embankment which now carries the Hoshangabad-Itarsi road across the low marshes south of Hoshangabad railway station to the higher ground on which Rasulia village stands. The road here had been submerged in every rainy season, and was often impassable.'

Rasulia was a small village on the outskirts of Hoshangabad. 'In 1889, along with the first missionaries, came an English Friend named Fredrick Sessions ... Sessions took much interest in the orphans, and knew the importance of preparing the growing boys to earn a livelihood ... there was in town a mechanic named Shiv Dayal, who had the reputation of being able to tackle any job from blacksmithing to watch repairs – and even dentures! ... On being consulted, this mechanical genius made a most generous offer: he would contribute the goodwill of his own business and reputation, and for a modest salary train the apprentices himself ... Fredrick Sessions himself made the second greatest contribution. In his own building business he was employing ... Alfred (Taylor), who was a skilled carpenter and plumber. Alfred was interested in the scheme, and he and his wife reached Hoshangabad in the autumn of 1891. They bought a 10-acre plot of land from Rasulia village ... Shiv Dayal and his boys brought their sheds and re-erected them on ... the site ... In its first year the new "Industrial Works" employed 18 men and boys as its three or four first orphan apprentices.'

In 1896, by the time the famine hit Hoshangabad, the 'Industrial Works' was well established. 'The square, strongly built office of the Industrial Works had inside it a wooden gallery, reached by a hinged staircase which could be raised and lowered at will. Here, says a reliable local tradition, the daily wage of grain was distributed, the stairway being lowered or lifted to regulate the traffic. The small safe once used in that office is still in use. An attempt in 1987 to repair the nest of drawers it contains led to the discovery of a receipt relating to the relief work of 1897. Ninety years later its beautiful Hindi script was still legible, acknowledging payment for the bricks which were used to build the bridge which spans the central water channel below the new road.' In the 110 years since, not once has the road been closed.

~

Christians numbered 2,706 in 1901, of whom 303 were Europeans, 102 Eurasians and 2301 native Christians. The number of native Christians increased by 2000 during the preceding decade. The principal proselytizing agency is the Friends' Foreign Mission which has stations at Hoshangabad, Sohagpur, Seoni, Itarsi & Bankheri. The staff consists

of 36 European missionaries assisted by 368 native converts. Funds
are contributed principally by the members of the Society of Friends
in Great Britain, but a considerable amount is now raised locally.
At Rasulia near Hoshangabad workshops have been established
for training the boys in carpentry, and the building and repairing of
carriages, and excellent furniture is turned out. Carpet-weaving and
shoemaking is taught at Seoni, and a number of orphan boys are
employed at Itarsi and other places in weaving cotton materials. A
mission training farm is maintained at Iehi near Seoni. The mission
also supports 24 schools and four dispensaries. Its converts number
1200 persons.

Central Provinces District Gazeteer: Hoshangabad, 1908.

~

On my way from Bhopal, I crossed the Narmada on the old
Hoshangabad Bridge and headed up the embankment built a century
earlier. I turned right, away from the town, descending to a solitary
double-storey house. I parked the car outside, walked up to the gate
and knocked. No one answered for what seemed a long while and
I stood there looking around. Less than 100 metres from the road,
there was a quiet to the surroundings. Large trees surrounded the
house, and in the distance, there were more trees and fields that
appeared fallow. I looked at the house and remembered what my
fellow journalist Rakesh Dewan had told me in Bhopal when I had
spoken about the Quakers, 'Go meet Raju Titus,' and then he had
added in his precise fashion, 'Raju is a man who believes in letting
things be, letting nature take its course.'

Finally, a woman opened the door and asked me to come in. A
reclusive presence, she said she was Raju's daughter-in-law, seated
me down, switched on the fan and went looking for her father-in-law.
As I looked around, that same odd juxtaposition that I had sensed
outside, of lived-in decrepitude, struck me again. As the fan started
whirring, dustballs softly spiralled down to the floor. Raju entered

the room along with his daughter Rano. She had shoulder-length hair and striking eyes, and took over the conversation as soon as she stepped in. The mere mention of Rakesh's name was enough for her to speak with a degree of comfort. Straightaway, I was thrown into the local dissensions that still continued to split the small Quaker community left in town.

'We,' Rano said, referring to Raju's family, 'have been isolated. We are Gandhian Quakers, but the Friends Rural Centre,' and she pointed to the fields I had seen while standing outside the house, 'has been taken over by the Christo-Quakers.'

The battle between Gandhi and Christ, I gathered, had to do with the affirmation of Christ and the Bible that the Christo-Quakers insisted on, in contrast to the non-denominational Gandhian views that the Titus family preferred. This was the same battle Elkanah had waged in England on his way to India 150 years ago.

Her father sat there silently, strangely withdrawn as she spoke. Later in the evening, he told me that his wife, after years of trying, had finally convinced him to get his beard shorn, and he was feeling like a blindfolded man suddenly exposed to light. Once he confessed the sudden absence of a beard, he seemed on surer footing. The story of the family's faith, he began telling me, went back to his grandfather. The family then farmed land near the river on the far shore, surrounded by the dense jungle that once extended up to the banks. His grandfather's earliest memory was of a famine, perhaps the same famine that led to the embankment next to the house. People had died in great numbers and he found himself alone in the forest, after his mother succumbed to the famine and his sister to wild animals. The Quakers adopted him and brought him to Rasulia where he worked as a cook at the Friends Centre. He died, Raju recalls, attempting to cross the river in a boat lying unused at the centre, hoping to tend to his lands lying fallow on the far bank.

Over the years the Friends Rural Centre, as the 'Industrial Works' in Rasulia had come to be known, grew to become a pioneer in farm technology; new types of wells, farm implements and techniques were tried out, and farmers from the nearby villages would come here to see and learn. Raju's family bought some land adjacent to the centre, where the house now stands.

'I used to farm our own land according to the latest scientific techniques demonstrated at the farm, using pesticides and machinery such as a tractor. But I ran into losses. Then one day, Marjorie Sykes who had moved to the centre, came by to our house. I would rarely speak to her because I did not know English but she left a book with my mother. That's how I first came to know of Fukuoka.'

I knew nothing about Fukuoka, so I ventured a guess and asked him if it was a book about organic farming. He corrected me, 'It is not organic but natural farming. No tillage of the soil, no manure, only the natural cycle of nature.' The conversation moved on to other things. It was only the next evening, when I came back for dinner, that we picked up the thread. We were sitting on the first-floor verandah overlooking the trees and shrubs that grew pell-mell on the farm, the embankment rising behind us. The food was being cooked on an open chullah not far from where we sat. Given what he was telling me, I did not have to ask him about the open fire. 'I did away with the tractor and the pumps powered by electricity.' As he spoke, Rano looked at him with a weary indulgence. It was a story she must have heard many times, while her mother sat by the fire turning the rotis over on a tawa. The day I was to leave Hoshangabad, I stopped by again for breakfast. It was substantial, as was any meal at the house, but after we were done, I found Raju pulling out a very modern instrument to record his blood sugar. He was a diabetic and there were a few blessings of technology that even he could not dispense with. I walked out to his farm with him. To my eyes the farm looked run-down, neither wilderness nor farmland, somewhere in between, a place where trees had been allowed to grow wild. He then started pointing out a few things to dispel my belief. The knee-high grass that grows so easily during the monsoon had been cut down and left to mull in the soil where it would provide nourishment to the seeds which were to be scattered on the ground. In some places, babool trees had been chopped down.

He explained apologetically, 'I need to do that if fruit trees are to flourish. Fukuoka had no idea of such matters.'

As a compromise he had let the branches lie where they had fallen, letting them slowly rot away into the soil. He admitted he'd had to keep dairy cows to provide a model for other farmers.

'They,' he said, 'will only emulate a model that they can see working. So far it does not work in their eyes.'

Nothing that he showed me seemed likely to convince the farmers, now or, for that matter, any time in the future. We moved deeper into what he insisted on calling a farm, where the undergrowth was more overgrown as the trees had taken over the land, and sat down on a log that he had set aside for this very purpose. It was quiet and green here, difficult to believe that a town lay on the other side of the embankment. After a stretch of silence, he started speaking.

'I came to understand Gandhi and Sykes through natural farming. When a belief in God arises within you, it is all you need. You need not go to anyone or any place. This is what the Quakers say. This is the meaning of the silent prayer that dwells on his presence and the shared partaking of that experience that follows. What does Fukuoka say? Nature is God. And when we are in nature, we need not close ourselves to the world. Looking at what you saw today [I had told him about a stroll along the river in the morning] is to meditate on God. It depends on where you are for you to decide how much to see, how much to hear.

'There was a time when I was in great distress. My mother was very ill and a close friend suffered a paralytic stroke. He was doing badly and I asked for him to be shifted here from the hospital because I did not like the treatment. The doctor said it would kill him. As is my wont, I stepped out to the world of nature that is my farm and as I sat there, a thought came to me: who can explain the mystery of the seed and the tree, of the profusion of life around me and who can hope to know everything? A weight lifted off my shoulders and when I returned to the house, my friend was on his way to recovery. '

~

The distance from Raju's house to the main gate of the Friends Rural Centre was less than a kilometre. The gate was locked. I parked the car by the side of the road, and walked in through the unlatched entrance for pedestrians. I couldn't see anyone around as I walked to the nearest building. The crop in the fields had been hit hard by a recent storm, the stalks of rice had been trampled into the ground by the rain and wind. As I reached the visitors' centre I saw a figure walking towards me, even from a distance marked out by his clothes and demeanour. I sat down on a wooden bench and waited. The bench fit in well with the building, sturdy and functional without any decorative elements. Both seemed to have been made at the Centre, and both took me back a decade and a half, to a cycling trip to Ohio across Amish territory.

As he approached, I got up to have a word with him. He put his hand out, perhaps the first time on my journey along the Narmada that I had been greeted by a handshake. He introduced himself as Daniel Yakub Masih, literally Daniel Jacob Messiah, treasurer of the Centre. When I told him about my journey along the river, he offered to show me around.

I had read a lot about the Centre, a lot of people had spoken to me about it. I knew Elwin had once been a visitor and during the Independence movement, Indians opposed to British rule had free access to the Centre. Many took shelter here even when they were wanted by the government, among them Dr Rajendra Prasad, India's first president. Soon after Independence, the American Quakers displaced the English as the major funders. The changes that came along with this ensured that it moved from its Gandhian leanings to the kind of technology that formed the heart of the Green Revolution – fertilizers, hybrid crops and irrigation. Then, in the 1970s, Marjorie Sykes came to live here and helped bring in a director who changed course back to the Gandhian way.

The day before I visited the Centre, I had met Suresh Dewan who was head of the Gram Seva Samiti that was founded in 1952. He lived in a village named Nitaya, less than an hour's drive from Hoshangabad.

The Rasulia Centre, he had said 'was an umbrella, which let others flourish under it'. He recalled that when he first came to Hoshangabad, the movement against the Tawa Dam that was finally built in the 1970s had just started. 'We feared waterlogging because of the way the project had been planned. The drainage was improper and the land consolidation was left half done. In many ways the ideological centre for the Narmada Bachao Andolan (NBA) lies here, many of their methods and ideas date back to the Tawa movement.'

The suggestion made me pause. The connection between the Quakers and the movement against the dams on the Narmada was not far-fetched. The NBA had been supported by a loose coalition of NGOs in this region, many of whom owed their origins to the Rasulia Centre. Far from this Centre, the Quakers had already contributed greatly to the modern environmental movement. In 1958, the former US navy commander, Albert Bigelow, who had become a Friend in 1955, had sailed a thirty-foot sailboat with four others towards an American nuclear testing site in the Marshall Islands. The boat was stopped and the crew detained. The journey eventually gave birth to Greenpeace in 1970.

But walking through the Centre, it was difficult to connect its present state with any intimations of past glory. The chain that went from the Quakers to the anti-dam movement along the Narmada may well have passed through Rasulia, but I could see little evidence of it. Daniel walked with me through the Centre. He saw me looking at the decimated crop in the fields and seemed to discern my thoughts. He said he was trying to revive the Centre. 'The rice is Pakistani Basmati, we thought we'd give it a try. We've also got tuar and urad growing but both have been hit hard by the storm.'

I mentioned that I had met Raju. 'Yes, I know what he would have said. But we tried no tillage, we sowed in quintals and reaped in kilos. It just doesn't work.'

I asked him about the Quaker families in town, and he said they were now down to no more than a handful. I did not find that surprising. The lack of religious exuberance among the Quakers would not have sat easily in this land, where even the more demonstrative forms of Christianity such as Catholicism had trouble finding a hold. Perhaps this decline explained the incongruity of the situation. As the numbers shrunk into nothingness, each matter of doctrine became an issue of life and death. The battle between the British Quakers and the Americans, the battle between Gandhi and Jesus, or rather between Gandhi and the organized church, was actually a battle of attitudes. It had even impacted the choice of farm techniques at this Centre.

We walked past a few compactly built structures: two rooms, a tiled roof and a verandah. They were in a state of disrepair, the red tiles broken or missing.

'We have to make do with what we earn from the Centre, there is no money coming in. We have not gone back to the old days of pesticides, we still do organic farming, but we till the land. We may not use fertilizers, but we do not farm the way Raju does,' he said, again bringing up Raju in the conversation. In his mind the decay of the Centre and Raju's criticism seemed inseparable.

Perhaps to emphasize his point, he abruptly veered away from the tour and the fields, and took me to the dairy. He introduced me to Daya Ram. 'This man has been here looking after the dairy for decades.'

Daya Ram showed me the half a dozen or so cows they still had, before echoing Daniel's lament, 'I have seen the days when we produced 600 litres of milk a day. Name the breed, Holsteins, Thapakars, we had them. I have milked them all with my hands. Who knows what sort of thinking led them to give it all away? People used to come to us because we ran a school, a dispensary; now we have lost everything. All that remains is this shell you see around you, and a few old men to help Daniel Masih keep it going.'

We continued walking through the farm. Daniel showed me the quarters where Marjorie Sykes lived. To my eyes they were not very different from the others I had seen. An old man sat nearby on a verandah, reading. We walked over to meet him. Jagdish Mishra turned out to be an old associate of Jayaprakash Narayan, who had met Sykes when she was involved with Vinoba Bhave's Sarvodaya movement.

'I first came here in 1970, thanks to her. At the time, Rasulia led the country in science education, sixteen schools were affiliated to the Centre, and after Arjun Singh authorized the project, professors from Delhi University and the Tata Institute of Fundamental Research used to visit us. With Sudarshan Kapoor in charge, the farming also took a scientific turn, using a lot of fertilizer. There were eighty cattle breeds, Jerseys, Holsteins, Sahiwal. This supported a hospital, the schools. Then Pratap Aggarwal came by in 1978 at Sykes' insistence and wound up the agriculture and the dairy, said cross-bred cows were a bad idea and sold Rs 6 lakh worth of animals. This was then! And he implemented rishikheti.'

His words added to the melancholy that I had felt the moment I entered the Centre. Everything was old and decaying. Perhaps I had come on the wrong day, but the flattened fields seemed to fit the general mood. The wizened old man and his desultory cows, JP's associate and his recollection of Marjorie Sykes's temper, Daniel's weariness with Raju's ideas. Perhaps this is how all Utopias ended, not with a bang but a whimper, decaying away into a semblance of nothingness.

XI

From the Sramanas to the Quakers to the anti-dam movement, there was a world view in common. It was not simply about turning away from modernity, or renouncing materialism. Each of these quests sought an alternative form of organization, something that stood against the established social order, the church or a technological society.

I, on the other hand, had no reason to disbelieve the rhetoric about dams. I was perhaps ten or twelve years old when I first saw Bhakra. Nothing I had read or heard had prepared me for the size of the dam or the reservoir. I do not recall that day in its entirety but I can recall parts of it very vividly: the long descent into the depths of the dam, the roar of the water rushing through the enormous turbines, the knowledge of the enormous store of water pressing down on the walls which shielded us and the damp that seemed to hang in the air. It is easy today to mock Nehru's invocation of dams as temples, but what I felt then is perhaps the closest I will get to the Semitic God, awesome and terrifying.

It was due to my maternal grandfather that I could see the dam in such detail and with such ease. He had trained as a civil engineer in England in the 1920s and come back and joined the irrigation department. In 1960, he took over as the first Indian chief engineer of the construction of Bhakra. The dam was completed three years later.

My memory of my grandfather dates to a much later period of his life, when he had retired to his Chandigarh house. He was an Anglophile, with a British sense of reserve even with his grandchildren. Occasionally, he would sit down with me over a game of chess. These were the only times that he would reminisce about his love for poetry, his travels to the US when few of us knew what it was to travel abroad, and much more rarely, about his own life.

I remember him talk of being a boy in his teens, watching the fields being irrigated in his village in Punjab. 'A boy no older than me was driving two bullocks around in circles. They were tethered to a log that turned a Persian wheel. The monotony of the task, the drudgery of the boy and the animal's life made me feel there has to be a better way of doing this. It is a feeling that has never gone away.' And then he fell quiet, and we went back to our game of chess.

I had no reason to believe that many of the engineers or technocrats who worked on the dams along with him did not have a similar approach to their work. But the sense of mission that drove that first generation after Independence could not be invoked with the same ease in our times. Our knowledge of the world and what technology can engender had changed a great deal over the past few decades.

As we have slowly come to realize, building a dam is a task that can be formulated and executed in a much more precise fashion than assessing its impact and trying to plan for it. The calculations involved in the construction are reasonably precise and the methods are well studied. As for the impact, from seismicity to the nature of soil, from the problems of distributing water to the social anthropology of the people affected, from the effect on wildlife above and below the dam to the ability of the bureaucracy to honestly cope with the demands of rehabilitation, there are a vast number of indeterminate issues, and simplifying assumptions lead to grave errors. A training in building and designing a dam is of little help in coping with such complexity.

The surety with which I speak of the dams as a mistake came to me only after years of reporting. From 2002 to 2004, I was based in Bhopal as the Madhya Pradesh correspondent of *The Indian Express*. The newspaper's own editorial stance was vehemently in favour of the dam.

With some regularity, protests organized by the Narmada Bachao Andolan would take place in Bhopal. Like the protests over the Bhopal gas tragedy, these merited no space in any newspaper in Delhi. It does not matter how important an issue is, there is only a limited amount of time people will expend on a tragedy. Once it loses its novelty, it is difficult to interest anyone in the story. This is not a problem with the media, it is a fact of human nature. Only occasionally, an event out of the ordinary directs attention towards old tragedies.

On the morning of 21 May 2003, I left home a little earlier than usual. I had just heard that a meeting of the Narmada Bachao Andolan activists with Congress deputy chief minister Subhash Yadav at his house had escalated into a confrontation. The NBA activists led by Medha Patkar were protesting the decision to raise the height of one of the Narmada dams by another five metres. Yadav, who was in charge of the Narmada Valley Development Authority, had allowed them to come into his huge government residence but had brushed off their questions. Medha and her associates were now sitting in protest on the tarmac within the bungalow compound, outside the verandah.

I was waved in by the guards at the gate. It was just past nine in the morning but the May sun was already blazing hot and the temperature was soon touching 40 degrees Celsius. Yadav had lined up chairs for journalists in a room adjacent to the verandah, from where he could look out at the protesters sitting barely a few yards away in the sun.

Every half-hour or so, a couple of the activists would get up and attempt to hold an umbrella over Medha but she would brush them away. Refusing food and water, her lips already parched, her voice hoarse, she looked incredibly frail. I knew her appearance was deceptive. The greying hair and the khadi sari draped over her slender frame may have led some politicians to misjudge her in the past, but by now they had learnt otherwise.

It was much cooler inside, where Yadav, who would have been a large man anywhere but seemed enormous in Madhya Pradesh, was seated in an armchair. Attired in the trademark Congress white kurta-pyjama, he was leaning back and talking to the journalists as his attendants emerged at regular intervals from the kitchen, offering water, coke and cucumber sandwiches.

Many of the journalists, as scathing of the NBA as he was, were prompting him as he spoke. 'These people are responsible for the power problem in the state.' Elections were due later that year, and the power situation was threatening his party's chances. The truth about the power failures had nothing to do with the dams, which in any case wouldn't have been generating much power in May when most reservoirs are at their lowest.

'She is only interested in publicity and international awards. She wants to build her international image, show that no one is a bigger environmentalist than her.' I told him I couldn't see a foreign journalist around, so he changed tack, 'They think *akele thekedar yahin hain* (they believe they are the only spokespersons). *Ye bolti jab hai, jab media ka focus hota hai* (She speaks only when the media focuses on her). *Nau saal se jhel rahan hun* (I have been putting up with it for nine years).' He turned and joked, with the cameras pointing at him, '*Ise paani pila kaun raha hai* (Who in any case is offering her water)?' But for all his bluster, Medha's presence in the sun was beginning to bother him.

Late in the afternoon, with the TV cameras having ensured the news had now gone national, he agreed to meet some of the activists. It was a mistake. They could cite the situation in a specific village, name each person who had been denied compensation. Yadav hated dealing with specifics. After half an hour he called off the interrogation and waved the cameras away. Within the hour the police had picked up Medha and taken her to a hospital to 'safeguard her health'.

～

Two months later, brushing aside my news editor's objection, my friend Prakash Hatvalne and I were headed to Jalsindhi. The drive from Bhopal followed the course of the river. We drove past Barwani into the Bhil tracts of Jhabua. In the summer, the bare surfaces of the hillocks that pockmarked the landscape verged on the desert. Now the hillocks were green, water flowed down the slope in irrigation channels carved over the years, joining a stream flowing by the roadside. Even in a country where the transformation of a parched, brown landscape to a green soaked by the monsoon rain was commonplace, it was a breathtaking change.

Dusk had descended by the time we made it into Gujarat, eight hours out of Bhopal. It didn't require a sign at the border to alert us; within minutes the landscape had changed. We were only a year away from the violence against Muslims in Gujarat and the signs were everywhere. Singed habitations, abandoned and gutted shops, and then a large cupola that lay toppled by the side of a mosque.

We stopped for dinner and by the time we reached the edge of the reservoir created by the Sardar Sarovar Dam, night had descended. We parked the car and wandered down to the water's edge where the man by the boat told us we'd have to wait till the morning. In the distance, by a flickering light, the Bhil watchman was sitting on the ledge of his one-room accommodation, sipping mahua with his wife. We walked over and offered to buy some. He refused, saying mahua was never meant to be sold, but we were welcome to drink as much as we wanted, sitting in their company.

He didn't say much, neither did his wife, as we sat with them and sipped mahua in containers shaped out of sal leaves. It was rare outside the tribal areas of India to have women sit with us and drink. Two little children wandered in and out. An hour or so later, we bid them goodbye. They gave us more mahua to carry with us as we headed to the car. Sleep came to us easily after that. Early in the morning, we were ready to leave for Jalsindhi.

The NBA motor boat had been refuelled and as we headed out into the water for an hour-long ride, we looked back to the watchman's house. The family seemed to be asleep, and the hut drifted away as the boat started riding the waves headed out to shore.

Telephone poles jutted out of the water, the lines skimming low over the surface before dipping in. Trees stood half-submerged, and as we started moving further away from shore, only an occasional branch made it to the surface. The landscape signalled that water was a recent intrusion here. Only a boatman who knew the perils that lurked close to the surface could make his way through. We passed the Hapeshwar temple, partially submerged only a year or so earlier. The boatman bowed as we passed the temple, slowing down to let us have a look.

Soon the distance to the shore widened and we were travelling through a vast reservoir. The slopes of thickly forested hills rose in the distance. We were headed to villages that had been cut off from this shore by the waters of the dam. A landscape that was once jungle and villages connected by forest paths winding their way through these hills had given way to this immense loneliness. Somewhere below us lay the old parikrama path. Almost an hour later, we could see a few huts clinging to a low hill by the edge of the water. A few larger peaks looked down on the settlement which was relatively new. Many of the residents had moved up to this height from their dwellings which now lay below us, underwater.

The boat was tethered as we approached the bank and we were asked to step directly to the shore. The water's edge was a precarious place, laden with silt, a death trap for the unwary. A path led through small plots of maize to a nearby hut where we deposited our backpacks and waited. Medha had already left early in the morning for a nearby village. Till she returned, we were free to wander around the village.

The children were following us around, amused by Prakash's camera even though it was not a complete novelty. The remoteness of Jalsindhi and the annual ritual of the jal samadhi, where Medha, acccompanied by a number of NBA activists, would stand in the waters of the Narmada as they rose with the fury of the rains, had attracted their own share of visitors. The ritual always ended in Medha's arrest by waiting policemen, as the cameras rolled.

The visitors here, in their own way, were purveyors of the other: the other media, the alternative vision, the green life. It was easy and often reasonable to be cynical about these efforts, as it was to be about the Jal samadhi. I did not subscribe so easily to their enthusiasm, but somewhere along the line, the reality of what was happening here had begun to erase my cynicism.

We went with the children to a nearby hut, larger than the rest. It was a school run by the NBA. The government considered these villages resettled, these people were not supposed to be where they were. A young man was teaching a handful of students lined up on the floor when we walked in. He greeted us, as did the students, who seemed to range in age from five to ten. He stopped to talk to us, telling us that the number of students had steadily dwindled, as some of the villagers had chosen to move away. Now, since the numbers were small, he could deal with each student individually.

Medha joined us at the school. There was a gentleness and vulnerability about her that was not so apparent when she spoke in public. It was the kind of vulnerability that often makes men feel they need to come to the aid of a woman. It is usually a misplaced feeling; in this case, certainly so.

Our first stop, as for so many others who came here, was at the house of Luhariya Shankaria and his wife Bulgi. He was one of the most articulate of the residents of Jalsindhi. Tall and slender by the standards of central India, he had a bearing that marked him out. Years later, I was to see him in the documentary on the anti-dam movement, 'Drowned Out', and suddenly the elegant gestures of his hand that mirrored his speech came back to life.

Luhariya commanded respect as the healer of the community. It was knowledge that had been passed down to him through generations and it depended on an intimate acquaintance with the local vegetation. For the people here, the government was a remote entity; their world consisted of their community, spread over the surrounding hills. The extent of their kinship ties and their knowledge was confined to this area.

Luhariya and Bulgi and their three sons largely depended on the crop from their plots of maize, the milk from their cows which grazed freely on the hillsides and the little that the jungle provided. His brothers, Gulabia and Gulalia, lived not far from them. Through some bureaucratic sleight of hand which no one here understood, Gulabia had been awarded 5 acres at a resettlement site in MP some 50 km away, which he found was unfit for cultivation, while Luhariya had only been awarded a plot for a house and Gulalia had been offered land in Gujarat.

In a country where, for the vast majority of the people, kinship and community ties are the very basis of life, the rehabilitation effort had taken refuge in the idea of the autonomy of the individual. It had happened by default, simply because no one had considered rehabilitation as a task that required resettling a community. It also reflected the manner in which the bureaucracy had approached the problem. The whole process was seen as a legal requirement that had to be fulfilled because of some court directives, which is why all that mattered was the paperwork.

Bavajia's hut lay not far from Luhariya's home. He had a son who was the father of four children. He had brothers whose children had children in turn. Yet, going by the land records, there was only one landholding in the name of Bavajia's father, who had been dead for years. As far as the government was concerned, 5 acres of land had been granted in Bavajia's name, which now had to take care of the resettlement of the entire extended family.

Again, this was possible because the survey work for the resettlement was not actually carried out by going from village to village, house to house, nor did anyone bring a degree of empathy to the task. It was an exercise in ensuring the paperwork was complete. All that mattered was for Jalsindhi, and every other village being displaced, to be resettled on paper.

We walked further up the slopes with Medha. After a slow and steady climb along a forest path, we met a group of men from the surrounding villages who had been waiting for us. Medha had sent word to them and now they were assembled, each with a typed piece of paper in hand. Some of these pieces were torn, others were fraying, a lucky few had managed to obtain plastic folders to shield them from the vagaries of the weather.

Each of them wanted to make sure I noted down the details of the injustice that was being done to them. I had come with Medha, and this was reason enough for them to believe something could happen, despite the fact that they had told the same story to several people who had come to see them, with little or no result. Medha knew each case personally, and as they spoke, she filled in many of the details that they left out from their account.

In theory, each of their problems could be remedied by a body set up precisely to deal with such complaints. It was called the Grievance Redressal Authority and was staffed by senior bureaucrats who had recently retired. It was a sinecure that came with a bungalow in Bhopal and a staff car. Again, the intention was to do the right thing on paper, for most of the men here were like Bavajia, for whom the local patwari was a remote official, sitting in a distant place wielding enormous power. The idea that they could make a trip to Bhopal, stay there for a few days, stand before men even the patwari feared, and make a cogent case for a re-examination of their award was not even conceivable, but what mattered was that the redressal authority existed as a recourse, on paper.

The next day, we took a donga, a boat carved out of a single tree trunk which could seat two to three people, to another village that lay across a stretch of water from Jalsindhi. The story there was much the same. On the way back Medha, pointing to the nearby hills and islands, described the landscape as it had been once. The slightest movement would set the little boat rocking. The enormity of the muddy water around us, laden with silt, and my feeble knowledge of swimming weighed on me. I registered very little of what she was telling me, but I could sense the courage it had taken for a young woman from Bombay to come here more than fifteen years ago and start this movement. It is this image of Medha that I try and keep in my mind when I see her speaking on prime-time television. Even Gandhi would have seemed a far less impressive figure if he had taken to regularly appearing on prime-time talk shows.

A day later, we were headed back on the hour-long boat ride to our car. The sky was dark, overcast with thick monsoon clouds that dipped down to touch the forlorn villages that clung to the steep slopes of former mountains. It was the loneliest, the most haunting place I had seen in my life.

~

On the drive back to Bhopal, near Barwani, a structure glinting in the sun caught my eye. We asked the driver of our Ambassador to stop the car by the roadside and trudged through the fallow field to the structure. There was no one around. It was made of sheet metal propped up over a hastily put together wooden skeleton. There was nothing stored inside. It didn't seem strong enough to shelter any animals. It seemed to have no other purpose than to enclose space.

We looked around for someone to speak to, but we couldn't see anyone. Further along the fields, away from the road, we spotted another such structure. As we walked up to it, we saw there was not one but a number of such structures, each longer than the other, some reaching 500 ft in length. A ghost town seemed to have been constructed out of wood and sheet metal, awaiting a film crew.

Out of nowhere, a few young children appeared to follow us around. We called out to them. They stepped back, hesitant, staring at us. Prakash rummaged through his photographer's jacket and pulled out a handful of sweets. They came running over, and sweets in hand, they told us, 'The people in the village think you are the survey wallahs'.

The camera, the white Ambassador, our city clothes, it was no surprise. But eventually an adult made his way over from the village. It took us some time to explain that we were journalists.

'It's for the compensation,' he said when he finally believed us. I told him I didn't understand.

'They say only our fields will be submerged, not our village. The compensation for submerged houses is much more than for land that gets submerged for part of the year. So people have built these structures on the fields.'

'But these sheds are enormous?'

'We've been told the compensation depends on the size of the house; the bigger it is, the more you get.'

~

At the rehabilitation sites they will have more and better amenities than which they enjoyed at their tribal hamlets: Supreme Court majority judgment.

I came back and filed what I thought would be the first of a series of stories on rehabilitation. I waited a few weeks for it to appear, but when it did, I barely recognized it. Some of the details had been retained, but it had been shorn of any context.

I decided against filing any other story. But soon enough, in the summer of 2004, Harsud was a story that was too big to be ignored. Over the next few months of the monsoon, this town of 25,000 was meant to disappear as water rose to fill the dam. My earlier visit had taken me to areas affected by the Sardar Sarovar Dam; Harsud would be drowned by the reservoir of the Indira Sagar Dam. These were the two biggest of a chain of dams on the river, which were meant to reduce the river to a series of artificial lakes cascading down from the source to the Sardar Sarovar.

The town of Harsud was not meant to disappear overnight, but the Indira Sagar Dam had finally reached a height which made submergence only a matter of time. The construction of both the Indira Sagar Dam and the Sardar Sarovar Dam had proceeded in fits and starts. The courts were forced to pass a judgment stating the obvious, that each increase in the height had to be preceded by the rehabilitation of those likely to be affected by that increase. In practice, this involved considerable exaggeration of the rehabilitation work by the state administration to ensure the courts did not halt the construction of the dam.

By the time I travelled to Harsud, the Narmada Valley Development Authority had already declared that everyone in the town had been resettled, on paper. This was news to the residents of the town, which was why the same state administration that had made the claim was now busy setting up temporary shelters for 7,000 persons just outside the zone of submergence.

Harsud was a town marked by schizophrenia. The bazaars were functioning as if nothing had happened, people stood sipping chai and gossiping, while around them others were at work purposefully, hammers in hand, demolishing the roofs and walls of homes where their families had lived for generations.

The government was compensating only those who could show that they had demolished their home. It was one way of ensuring that the residents of the town would move. The rather hopefully named township of Naya Harsud (new Harsud) near the village of Chhanera some 20 km away was part of the 'largest rehabilitation package in India's history'. The package entitled a resident to a 18x25 sq. m plot in what was no more than a shanty town.

The only people who had moved here were those who had no other option. They had hurriedly piled up bricks to construct walls that were no more than waist-high, and used wooden poles to prop up a sheet metal roof to keep the rain out. Others made do with a tarpaulin shelter, amounting to no more than the most basic of tents.

Roads were still being constructed, schools had not been set up, there were no sewage facilities. Kusam Bai, her four young children ensconced under the tarpaulin, her labourer husband away looking for food, had just a brief moment to speak to us. 'In the morning, we have to go use the fields surreptitiously, otherwise the farmers chase us away. What are we supposed to do, shit in our tents? Naya

Harsud indeed!' Then she waved us away, indicating she had better things to do than talk to us.

I spoke to I.K. Khatri, the civil engineer of the new township, who told me it would be months before basic facilities could be provided.

The residents of Harsud had heard these stories, seen the township, and most were unwilling to move. I went back and wrote the story. I was not the only one. Others travelled to Harsud, many stories made it to print, TV cameras hovered around the town, waiting for its end. The submergence was staved off, but only by a year.

SAKAD
SENDHWA
Narmada River Basin
Gulf of Khambat

XII

On the road to Sendhwa, a rock sent spinning by the tyre of a passing truck had shattered my windshield. A gentle push sent the glass crumbling onto the bonnet. When I arrived at the Aadharshila School run by Jayashree and Amit in Sakkad village, I felt as if I had driven the entire distance on a motorcycle. If nothing else, it earned me the approval of the students even before I met them.

I owed my introduction to Amit to a friend from school, Gaurav Bhatnagar. We had both ended up going to the US for a Ph.D. in mathematics. I didn't finish my degree, Gaurav did, but we kept in touch. Occasionally, I would hear of his older brother Amit, a student of architecture who had dropped out midway to go work in Madhya Pradesh with the Narmada Bachao Andolan, but this was the first time I would be meeting him.

Amit turned out to be a bespectacled man in a kurta, with a beard. Jayashree, dressed in a sari with her hair pulled back tight, allowing a few stray strands to escape, resembled Medha in her dress and demeanour.

The school they ran was set on a hillock — a building for the classrooms, another for the students who boarded here, and next to a large garden, the building where Amit, Jayashree, their two children and the occasional guest would sleep.

Its setting was reminiscent of Sonpuri, taking me back almost to my journey's beginnings. But it was a Sonpuri denuded, with a bare beauty of its own, and each morning and evening we were witness to some spectacular sunrises and sunsets.

Our conversations took place over household errands which were shared among the family, with their daughter Revati and son Sarang lending a hand. Chopping vegetables for the evening meal, watering the garden or walking around the classrooms while the school was in session, they told me about their journey to Sakkad.

In 1983 Amit had come to Jhabua, to work among the Bhils of the local hills, organizing them under the banner of the Khedut Mazdoor Chetna Sangh (The Peasants and Workers Consciousness Union). 'I had first gone to work with Bunker Roy at Tilonia but I felt the approach there had its limitations. A friend was working in Jhabua and I joined him. We wanted to work with the adivasis. This was the work we really wanted to do, which is why we are sure about what we were doing and why we were doing it.'

For several decades the Bhils had been harassed by forest officials who extorted money for letting them farm their nevad or new fields. They had lost their traditional rights over the forest as the British colonial state declared large tracts of forest state property, to be used for extracting commercial value from forest produce. The Indian state inherited this structure, and even when attempts were made to update land settlement records, their fields in forested tracts of the hills were the last to be recorded, if at all. Even those families who had farmed such plots for several generations were now, as far as the law was concerned, encroaching on forest land.

'We went among them, lived with them. We knew the people we worked with, and what people they were. Full of spunk, bow and arrow in hand, always ready to stake everything. Once, one of them shot a havaldar on a motorcycle. When we asked why, he said someone had bet him that he could not hit a moving target with a bow and arrow. Even a ten-year-old would hold up someone returning from the haat. Who could argue with an arrow from a bow stretched taut? Quick-tempered, they were ready to kill. A guest at dinner drunk to the hilt could take umbrage at being asked if he would eat more. After all, he was a guest, why the need to ask! Whenever we found a new blanket in one of the villages by the Narmada, we knew it had come from a parikramawasi, but we also knew that these people owned even less than the pilgrims.'

'We convinced them not to yield their rights. We picked our battles,' Amit recounted, 'and we only took on the forest officials, making use of the antagonism between the police and the forest department. My friend once had an inspector visit him. Decked in a banyan, he ordered chicken at our expense while he wrote out the desired FIR. Two havaldars cooked the chicken, charging us even for the masalas.

'All this was so far removed from the culture of NGOs, driven by funding agencies who have the same idea of development that we stand against, the tamasha of meetings in Brazil. All we say is you make the laws you want, what we will do is make sure we only allow what is right at the level the laws are implemented.

'Today young people are not taking up such issues. They are not ready to shed their way of living and adopt another which would allow them to live and see for themselves. The NGOs provide a safe halfway house. It allows them to do the right thing, yet maintain a lifestyle no different from anyone else. When we came to Jhabua, the need to do so was very much in the air, but even then there were very few who were willing to do what we did.'

In the midst of this long-term work, the dams were a more immediate threat. In the hills of Jhabua, most of the villages likely to be submerged were inhabited by the Bhils. Even those willing to make their peace with the dam would suffer; having lost out on rights to their land, they would lose out on the right to claim compensation. As I heard this, the inexplicable confusion over compensation I had encountered at Jalsindhi made much more sense.

As the movement against the dam gathered strength, a number of activists such as Jayashree came to the region along with Medha Patkar. This is how she met Amit and soon they were married.

'The first time we went to a rally, we found that the Nimaris working with the NBA were employing hundreds of Adivasis and Dalits themselves at well below minimum wage. A few among us even felt that the NBA was a hindrance in the way of real change, but it exposed us to larger issues. Without it there would have been no rehabilitation at all. One by one, senior people in the NBA like Sylvie and Sripat fell out with Medha, now all of them are working on their own.'

Moving away from the immediacy of the NBA, Amit and Jayashree started working together with the Adivasi Mukti Sangathan in the neighbouring Barwani district. Their attention turned to issues that needed more prolonged attention. With children of their own, the state of the government schools was an obvious focus. The schools barely functioned, teachers rarely if ever taught, and in the happy circumstances where these problems did not exist, the Bhil students were repeatedly tested on a curriculum that had no relevance to their lives.

They decided to set up a school that stemmed from a way of seeing and acting in the world very different from what they had left behind. In the years since it was set up, thay had managed to implement several of the ideas they had in mind. A curriculum had been designed with local needs in mind, built around a history that meant something to the Bhil students. The learning was interactive. Students tried out science projects and mathematical problems on their own rather than through rote learning. Even something as simple as tending to the garden with its organically grown vegetables ensured these children of farmers carried a new knowledge home.

This would stand out in any of India's large cities, leave alone this corner of tribal India where a functional school was a small miracle in itself. But there were no teachers in the region who could teach what was required. The solution was obvious in hindsight: the older students, who had already learnt the material through their interaction with Amit and Jayashree, knew what to teach. The timings for the classes were staggered, and the older students acted as guides on the same journey they had already undertaken. Education and stay for them was free; the school sustained itself on the fee the parents of the younger students could afford to pay, as well as the money from friends and well-wishers.

As I sat through some of these interactive sessions with the students, I could see them being guided, with some vehemence, to an understanding of the issues that had driven people like Amit to the struggle against the dams. But with this guidance came a world view that was not shaped by their thinking or understanding. It was inculcated much in the same way religion would be elsewhere. At times the stridency of the students' belief in the aims of the anti-dam struggle, the assertion of their traditional rights, struck me as being at odds with an attitude that claimed to look at issues critically and sceptically. But I also knew far too well that knowledge does not come from nowhere.

A name was invoked in our conversation, one that I was not familiar with, Paolo Friere. It was only when I went back and read about the author of *The Pedagogy of the Oppressed* that I gained a better sense of what Amit and Jayashree were trying to do in Sakkad. It is difficult to summarize the Brazilian educationist other than in his own words:

> It doesn't hurt to repeat here the statement, still rejected by many people in spite of its obviousness, that education is a political act.
>
> No pedagogy which is truly liberating can remain distant from the oppressed by treating them as unfortunates and by presenting for their emulation models from among the oppressors. The oppressed must be their own example in the struggle for their redemption.

While I did not accept many of the beliefs that were central to how Amit and Jayashree saw the world, in these circumstances, with their experience, among the students they were teaching, I may perhaps have also come to believe what they hold true.

My first evening at Aadharshila, I was formally introduced to the students. I told them about the slow, punctuated journey along the river that had brought me to their school. The students talked of the villages they had come from, of the dam and the submergence. Some sang, others asked me for a song. I tried explaining what tone deafness was, and Amit intervened to spare me the agony of trying to sing.

They asked what I did for a living. I didn't have a ready answer. I had quit my last job over another disagreement with another employer. The money I had saved, under a lakh of rupees, and this seems difficult to believe today, had seen me through the months of the journey, thanks to the kindness of acquaintances and the inexpensive economy that existed along the river. But it seemed like an indulgence that was difficult to explain to these students. Amit came to my help again, 'He is a writer, like the person who was here last night, Arundhati.'

Under the circumstances, it did seem futile to claim that I'd never seen myself as anything other than a journalist. More to the point, there was little I could say to express my reservations about the comparison. In the valley, among the activists, Arundhati Roy had come to occupy iconic status, next only to Medha.

It was easy to see why this should be so. With the Supreme Court verdict in 2000 upholding the construction of the dam, it seemed as if the years of struggle had been a failure. When Arundhati Roy travelled to the Narmada Valley and wrote her critique of the judgment and the paradigm of development it reflected, the impact was enormous.

The article also saw the media and documentary film-makers outside the country pay attention to the struggle in a way they had never done before. A Booker Prize winner, a critique of development and progress, big dams, displacement – suddenly the Narmada story was sexy.

I was not so sure. Even in agreement, I was taken aback by the easy generalizations and overdose of capitalized words that marked her piece, *The Greater Common Good*. On a closer reading, it seemed to me, though, that the real problems with her writing went much deeper, and these became apparent only once the breathlessness of the prose was set aside.

In a crucial section of the essay, she had claimed:

> According to a detailed study of 54 Large Dams done by the Indian Institute of Public Administration, the average number of people displaced by a Large Dam is 44,182. Admittedly, 54 dams out of 3,300 is not a big enough sample. But since it's all we have, let's try and do some rough arithmetic. A first draft. To err on the side of caution, let's halve the number of people. Or, let's err on the side of abundant caution and take an average of just 10,000 people per Large Dam. It's an improbably low figure, I know, but ... never mind. Whip out your calculators. 3,300 x 10,000 = 33 million. That's what it works out to. Thirty-three million people. Displaced by big dams alone in the last fifty years. What about those that have been displaced by the thousands of other Development Projects? At a private lecture, N.C. Saxena, Secretary to the Planning Commission, said he thought the number was in the region of 50 million (of which 40 million were displaced by dams). We daren't say so, because it isn't official. It isn't official because we daren't say so. You have to murmur it for fear of being accused of hyperbole. You have to whisper it to yourself, because it really does sound unbelievable. It can't be, I've been telling myself. I must have got the zeroes muddled. It can't be true. I barely have the courage to say it aloud. To run the risk of sounding like a 'sixties hippie dropping acid ('It's the System, man!'), or a paranoid schizophrenic with a persecution complex. But it is the System, man. What else can it be?
>
> Fifty million people.
>
> Go on, Government, quibble. Bargain. Beat it down. Say something.
>
> I feel like someone who's just stumbled on a mass grave.

It was difficult to believe any intelligent person could make such a frivolous, if not deliberately dishonest argument.

The initial IIPA report Arundhati Roy had cited listed an average of

44,000 persons displaced per large dam. This is a figure that applied only to the very largest of the dams in India. Arundhati, however, applied it to all of India's 'large' dams, while condescending to reduce the number by a fourth to arrive at a figure of 10,000 per large dam.

She claimed, 'It's an improbably low figure, I know ...' Actually it was an improbably high figure. The term 'large' she used, applied to all dams whose height exceeded 15 metres. As far as displacement of people was concerned, what really mattered was the area submerged by a dam, not its height. The vast majority of her 'large' dams had a reservoir area of less than 5 sq. km, and to say each such dam displaced 10,000 people is a travesty.

The exaggeration involved in her claims becomes apparent once a serious attempt is made to arrive at the real figure. Consider the national register of dams compiled by the Central Water Commission registry, which lists sixty-one dams of 'national importance' with the largest reservoir areas in the country. The area submerged by these dams adds up to approximately 13,775 sq. km. Rounding up the IIPA figure to 45,000 displaced for each of these sixty-one very large dams leads to an estimate of 2.75 million displaced persons. This implies a density of 200 persons per sq. km for the submerged areas, which seems reasonably accurate given that the overall Indian population density is 364 per sq. km and dams are built away from urban centres in areas of low population density.

A rough estimate based on the national registry of dams shows the total reservoir area of all the 'large' dams in India to be under 40,000 sq. km. The earlier estimate of 200 persons per sq. km for the submerged areas gives a figure of 8 million people displaced by large dams in India. Every figure involved in the calculation is an overestimate, but even (rather unreasonably) assuming that the population density for the submerged areas is the same as the Indian average, the figure of the total displaced adds up to 14 million.

It is a staggering figure in itself, but to reach Arundhati's figure of 33 million, the area submerged by 'large' dams in India would have to be 165,000 sq. km. This is a figure equal to the area submerged by all waterbodies in the country, including all rivers and lakes. Another way to see the absurdity of her claim is to realize it requires a population density of over 1,000 per sq. km in the submerged areas, three times the Indian average!

Arundhati, while invoking mass graves, had conjured an imaginary army of 20 million displaced simply to bolster her case. She continues to cite this number. As far as I am concerned, this exaggeration, both rhetorical and factual, has done no favours to the movement or the argument against the dams on the Narmada. Especially given that the case for the dams on the Narmada was made through precisely this kind of numerical exaggeration. Roy certainly made a huge number of people aware of the problem and the movement, but she also angered as many. After her intervention, there was no middle ground, no space for discussion; there was just for or against.

This for or against was not restricted to the dams in the Narmada, it was about an entire paradigm of development. For Arundhati, the battle against the dams was only the foundation for a larger argument, and the tribals only an instrument in the larger battle against this paradigm.

The activists in the NBA went along, not only because they felt that she was strengthening the cause, but because they shared much the same views. It is another matter that the tribals themselves had no such understanding of the critique.

~

Yogesh Dewan was a Marxist who has been associated with the NBA for a considerable period of time. He was Rakesh's brother, hence one of the first persons I met in Hoshangabad. He had spent two years on a project studying self-help groups ranging from groups with Gandhian inspirations to modern NGOs. The result was a scathing book in Hindi – *Dastan-e-Swayamsevita* (The Story of Self-Help Groups), tracing the route from Gandhian movements to the modern NGOs and the differences in attitudes they represent.

The back cover, instead of the usual description of the book, carried a poem by Brecht:

A Bed for the Night

I hear that in New York
At the corner of 26th Street and Broadway
A man stands every evening during the winter months
And gets beds for the homeless there
By appealing to passers-by.

It won't change the world
It won't improve relations among men
It will not shorten the age of exploitation
But a few men have a bed for the night
For a night the wind is kept from them
The snow meant for them falls on the roadway.

Don't put down the book on reading this, man.

A few people have a bed for the night
For a night the wind is kept from them
The snow meant for them falls on the roadway
But it won't change the world
It won't improve relations among men
It will not shorten the age of exploitation.

Translated by George Rapp

The poem is a precise summation of Yogesh's critique of the NBA. Over a long evening, strolling along a ghat overlooking the Narmada, discussing among other things the culture of the modern NGO world, he told me that he kept returning to the question of what had happened to the people's movement in this country. Where had the spirit of such enterprises disappeared, what became of them?

It took me a while to understand the problem as he had framed it. As he tried to explain what he meant, he referred to Brecht again. 'Is it only about shelter and beds? We have educationists, we have environmentalists, but what is the larger vision that ties it all together?'

On the ghat, as he talked, I could see people bathing. On the far bank, men were quarrying sand, perhaps illegally, and to our right the temple bells were ringing. The question of NGOs and their culture seemed far too distant to me, but he was only leading up to the NBA.

'And I think that was the problem with the NBA. Across the Nimar, in the valley where the Patidar immigrants from Gujarat farmed fertile land, there is a close association between belief and culture. The BJP is strong in that area. So activists would turn up for the NBA meetings and ask why they were being told to keep away from the RSS shakhas. But no answers were ever given.'

I wondered if any answers were possible. The NBA was funded in the main by these very Patidar farmers and their agricultural practices which were far removed from any idea of organic farming. The NBA's sustenance as a viable organization was a direct result of the very modernity that Arundhati Roy wanted to dispense with, born out of intensive irrigation, fertilizers, high-yield crops.

This was not lost on Yogesh. 'No answers could be given. The NBA's own mobilization was based on the religious symbolism of the Nimar. The breaking of the nariyal, the sankalp of the sacred thread, became the norm for NBA meetings, for much of the NBA work. But where did the tribals fit into all this? As far as they are concerned, the Narmada is theirs. When she swells in flood, she is one of them, she is not the Ma Narmada of the plains.'

Amita Baviskar has examined in some detail in her book, *The Belly of the River*, how this dichotomy was built into the NBA. The Patidars needed to be mobilized but they could not be the face of a successful people's movement outside the region, hence a discourse couched in terms of the rights of indigenous people, their land, their forests, the sustainability of their lifestyle and its harmony with the surroundings. The discourse was not false, but it was an exaggeration even for the Bhils of the hills. The day modern medicine touched their lives, however tangentially, this sustainability was already in question, even without the shrinking of their forests.

There was also the question of the traditional interaction between the Bhils and the Patidar peasantry. Over the past five hundred years, as the Rajputs had moved into the Bhil territory, and the Bhils had retreated into the hills, communities such as the Patidars had been brought in by the new rulers to farm the land that had become available. The Bhils who had stayed back in the plains became landless labour to the Patidars. At the NBA gatherings in the plains, as Amit had earlier observed while speaking to me at his school, the Bhils from the hills were quick to notice this.

In practice, the NBA was a pragmatic movement, seeking to harness different constituencies towards the same aim, against the dams on the river. Such contradictions would always be part of large public mobilizations, and their temporary resolution was what lent such movements strength. It was as true of Gandhi and the Independence movement as it was of Medha Patkar's Narmada Bachao Andolan.

But Arundhati Roy and others like her wanted to impose an ideological purity on the NBA, which went beyond what the movement actually stood for. Like Brecht, she believed blankets had their place but they were unlikely to shorten the age of exploitation. Medha Patkar, on the other hand, understood the constraints of a popular movement even if ideologically she held the same position that Roy articulated. It was because she had to keep the movement going that her beliefs and actions often seemed to contradict each other. This pragmatism was a product of circumstances. In contrast, the educated young men and women who had come to the Narmada Valley to fight against the dams saw their own vision being articulated by Arundhati Roy. In private, like Yogesh and Amit, they were very critical of the compromises Medha had made, even when conceding the practical necessities behind her choices. However impractical or unreasonable this battle against modernity was, it was the battle they actually wanted to fight.

The Patidars, who formed the backbone of the movement in terms of numbers and finances, or the Bhils, who formed the public face of the movement, were against a particular dam in a particular place. And they would have been happy to win that battle. Instead they were made foot soldiers in a war they had not signed up for.

The activists would often argue with me that this critique of development was a necessary corollary of understanding and working with the Bhils. The problems they were facing were the direct result of a paradigm of development that did not understand who they were, that reduced everything to an economic calculation, a cost-benefit analysis in which individuals and communities were dispensable.

But few, if any, of the Bhils ever saw things in these terms. They could not have; this critique could only be constructed out of an actual experience of the modern world. The issue was not one of right or wrong but of enlisting the Bhils in a war they could not possibly comprehend. The question the activists in their certainty never stopped to ask was, what if their analysis was flawed, where would it leave the Bhils, and what did it impose on them? It was one thing to live by one's beliefs, it was quite another to burden others to live so. But then, they were not alone in being caught up in the power of their ideology. At much the same time, the Bhils were being besieged by others from the outside world who were as sure of themselves, as determined to lead them on the one true path.

XIII

A small jungle track leads from Amarkantak to Kabir Chabutra along the edge of the plateau overlooking Chhattisgarh. The steep cliff gives way to dense forest hundreds of metres below. It is not an easy walk. The main road descending rather more gently further away from the cliff makes for an easier but much longer route. The jungle track meets the road further down and the walk gets easier. Just where the road forks into two, one headed to Chhattisgarh, the other to Madhya Pradesh, a dirt path descends to a small complex of mud huts, their walls lined with lime.

A visitor takes off his shoes outside the largest of the huts, bends to enter through the small doorway and finds himself facing a pair of wooden clogs, believed to have been once worn by Kabir. Parikramawasis gather by the small pool out in the clearing in front of this Kabirpanthi ashram, where drops of milky water emerge periodically from the soil. They believe that this pond is the Narmada's homage to Kabir, and their belief adds a detour of a few kilometres along their long journey.

Almost five hundred miles along the river, on the northern bank, the parikramawasis make a similar, though much longer, detour to honour another myth of the river's manifestation. The story goes that in the time of Akbar, a beautiful young woman named Roopmati lived by the banks of the Narmada. Baaz Bahadur, the sultan of Malwa, while out riding along the river, heard her singing by the bank. He rode over to see who the singer was. He was smitten, but she said she could only live by the banks of the Narmada, his royal capital of Mandu lay far from the river.

He offered to build her a palace at the very edge of the plateau, from where she could see the Narmada gleaming in the sun as it wound its way through the plains. Roopmati agreed, but her longing was not assuaged by the daily sighting of the river. The strength of her devotion, the legend claims, forced the Narmada to manifest herself in a pool below the Roopmati pavilion in Mandu, much like the small pond at Kabir Chabutra.

From the Roopmati pavilion, on a clear day, it is possible to see the Narmada winding its way in the distance. The pilgrims on the parikrama believe that an underground stream leads from the Narmada to the pool called the Rewa Kund. At the very point they believe the underground stream originates, men and women who may have already walked a thousand kilometers, turn away from the riverbank towards Mandu. Paying heed to the requirement of the parikrama that forbids crossing the river, they walk up to the plateau, circle the Rewa Kund and walk back to the banks of the river, adding an extra fifty-odd kilometres to their long journey.

Perhaps this small detour to Kabir Chabutra is only a test for the much more tiring climb to Mandu. But for the pilgrims, the story of Kabir, the low-caste weaver claimed as their own by both Hindus and Muslims, who had spent his life telling them that the truth is not to be found in books — whether the Vedas or the Koran — is enough justification for the journey.

～

The ashram was my first encounter with the sect Kabir's followers had forged, little known in India despite millions of adherents drawn from the artisan castes and tribes such as the Gonds and the Bhils. I met the mahant of the shrine outside the hut. His name was Mehtu Das. He was from the neighbouring Durg district in Chhattisgarh, and very reluctant to talk to me after he came to know I was a Sikh. Only a mention of my early years of schooling in this region made him open up.

The long history of his sect of Kabirpanthis, he told me, goes back to 'a wealthy merchant whom we now know as Dharam Das of Mathura. He was then named Judaman and his wealth in those times amounted to Rs 56 crore. Devoted to Kabir, he went without food and water for seven days to convince Kabir to accept him as a disciple. Finally Kabir agreed. He came and stayed with Judaman at a Bandhavgarh ashram for twelve years. A satsang was held every day and food was fed to the people. It was only after Judaman spent all his wealth in this fashion that he came to be known as Dhani Dharam Das. For forty-two years he retained the Kabirpanthi gaddi. The current Vanshacharya – Prakash Muni – is the fifteenth in the line of succession.'

He pointed to the hut which I had just seen. 'In his lifetime Kabir visited this place several times, but the longest he stayed here was on his way to Jagannath Puri. He spent time here, held satsangs at this spot that we call Kabir Chabutra and rested under the banyan tree above the chabutra.'

He stopped talking as we wandered through the vast canopy of aerial roots, branches and leaves. The main trunk had disappeared but the tree continued to spread along a network of aerial roots thrust into the ground.

'This is where he met Guru Nanak. In our sakhi, it says it was Nanak's good fortune that he met a satguru like Kabir.'

The meeting between the founder of Sikhism and Kabir is often alluded to in popular mythology but historians seem to have arrived at the conclusion that their dates do not overlap. In their view, such a meeting would have been impossible. Reality though has little to do with the facts as the historians seek to understand them. The reverence for Kabir in the Sikh tradition and the inclusion of a great number of Kabir's compositions in the Granth Sahib seem to suggest that in any reasonable world, the two should have met.

Burdened by the duty of bringing order to a chaotic world, mythology has obliged.

Mehtu Das told me that he never spoke of the sakhi he had just recited 'to the Sikhs who come visiting. They create too much turmoil. It is okay if they want to pay obeisance or help out, but they want to possess, take charge. Some years ago they had gathered here in large numbers to build a gurdwara. *Sikhon mein ahankar aa gaya hai* [The Sikhs have become arrogant].'

He wanted to go on, but I already knew more than I cared to about my community. I steered the conversation back to his Kabirpanthi sect.

'I was born to the sect, but anyone can join after taking diksha from the Vanshacharya. I have now been here as a mahant for eleven months, but I first became a mahant in 1978. My Guru was the fourteenth Vanshacharya. I had to clear exams on scriptural matters and the proper ways of doing our pooja.'

He described the elaborate rituals that had become part of the panth over the centuries. The major aarti required the presence of the Vanshacharya, a hundred other mahants seated on their gaddis, a hundred aartis, a hundred kalashes. It seemed a burden on an ordinary disciple, and far removed from the idea of simplicity that lay at the heart of the panth.

The same evening after the return to Amarkantak, I headed along the river to a small Kabirpanthi ashram I had spotted on one of my walks past the town. Mahant Sewa Das was a more humble figure than the mahant I had just met at Kabir Chabutra. He had his own story of the origins of his sect of the panth, and in his telling Dharam Das was no longer a wealthy merchant but a pujari, a Vaishno bhakt.

He told me he belonged to the Kharsiya-based Nadvansh sect which had a guru-shishya tradition unlike the hereditary Vanshacharya tradition. With the relish for gossip that schisms in faith engender, he told me that the current Vanshacharya had two daughters and no son. A crisis was looming ahead, he said, and he did not need to add that a woman could not be given the position, or that such a crisis would never occur in his sect. His resentment had much to do with the Vanshacharya sect's recent takeover of Kabir Chabutra, which till then had been the common possession of the entire panth. Suddenly, Mehtu Das's worry about a Sikh takeover acquired an ironic hue.

As Sewa Das spoke, we were joined by Sadhvi Jamantri Sahib, the only other resident of this tiny ashram. She was the first sadhvi I had met in Amarkantak. She told me this was a practice common among her people. Her family had been Kabirpanthi for three generations. She married, had four children – two sons and two daughters. Kabirpanthi sants would often come and go at their home. When she first became a sadhvi, her husband supported her decisions. She lived as a sadhvi at home for thirteen years, and then eleven years ago she came here to Amarkantak.

Amidst this simplicity, Sewa Das could not restrain himself. Feeling the need to impress a visiting stranger, he told me his sect was exceedingly well off in Gujarat.

～

Along the Narmada, the message of Kabir had been spread by Kabirpanthis very similar to the ones I had met. It was that rare social movement in India that had managed to attract both Dalits and tribals in large numbers. But typically, as one moved towards Gujarat, the message of inclusion that Kabir had forged was slowly but radically transformed into an assertion of a political Hindu identity.

Well past the dam at Sardar Sarovar, some ten kilometres or so from Bharuch is the island of Kabirvad. A regular boat service runs from the north bank of the river, taking tourists and pilgrims to the island, whose main attraction is another vast banyan tree associated with the legend of Kabir.

Like the Buddha before him, Kabir's words and his compositions have come to us through the legends that involve some of his earliest followers such as Dharam Das. The legend of Kabirvad also goes back to two of his earliest disciples, the Brahmins Tatva and Jiva.

The legends matter because the historical Kabir is still a largely unknown figure. Vinay Dharwadker, in his study, *Kabir: The Weaver's Songs*, notes, 'After nearly two centuries of research on Kabir, we still cannot reconstruct the historical figure behind the name with much confidence. But if the composite portrait that emerges from all the circumstantial evidence is an index of historical fact, then we might conclude this poet lived in and around Banaras from about 1398 to 1448; that he belonged to the community of Muslim julahas in the region, either by birth or by adoption, and became a cotton weaver by occupation; that he was a poor artisan, a subaltern from the lowest socio-economic levels of fifteenth-century north Indian society, with no practical opportunity in his immediate environment for either education or spiritual initiation; that he nevertheless succeeded in composing and circulating poetry in the oral and musical mode, and in acquiring a reputation as a poet, critical thinker and religious practitioner; that he was perhaps persecuted for his outspoken and unorthodox views about religion and society, and was forced to flee from Banaras; and that he passed away in Magahar, in the vicinity of the monuments that constitute his Hindu-style *samadhi* and his Muslim-style *dargah* today.'

The myth of Kabirvad in Gujarat is far removed from this context. The brothers Tatva and Jiva were Brahmins who lived on the island now known as Kabirvad. Searching for a guru who had attained wisdom, they would invite holy men to their hut. After receiving them with due honour, they would wash their feet in a pail of water and pour the water over a dry stick implanted in the soil outside the hut. When they so welcomed Kabir, the stick sprouted leaves and grew into the banyan that today spans a large part of the island.

It is a strange story in the Kabir canon. The syncretic nature of the Kabir myth that invokes Hindus and Muslims is totally missing in this case. In the two tales I had heard at Amarkantak, Dharam Das was alternately a wealthy merchant or a humble pujari. In the case of Tatva and Jiva, their Brahmin origin was emphasized (as was the case with Saru-Maru and the Buddha). The names of the two brothers suggested a possible metaphorical explanation for this straightforward myth. In the Jain and Vaishnava traditions, the term Jiva-tattva is used to describe the essence of living beings which separates them from other tattvas that describe divine or non-sentient beings. The myth then is a story of how Kabir's learning allows the essence that distinguishes humans to flourish.

It was this Vaishnava manifestation of the Kabir tradition that established itself among a large number of Gujaratis as well as the Bhils. It was, perhaps, helped by the fact that Kabir used the term Rama for the One that/who shapes the universe. Kabir was clear he was not referring to the mythological or historical figure who went by the name, but if every faith were to subscribe to the vision of its founder, we would live in a very different world.

In 'The Ten Avatars', a composition from the Bijak translated by Dharwadker, Kabir says:

> My good men,
> what comes and goes,
> bustling about the world,
> is Maya.
>
> The One who's the True Guardian
> doesn't inflict
> death on anyone –
> He doesn't come and go
> He has never moved from place to place.
>
> ...
>
> The Guardian of the universe
> wasn't the one
> who married Sita,
> He didn't build the bridge across the sea
> with rocks and stones.
> That was merely
> The master of Raghu's clan,
> who's commemorated for such deeds –

anyone who memoralizes him
as though he were the Lord
is a blind man.

But as others before and after Kabir have realized, humanity cannot sustain such a vision. When it becomes part of an established order, it gives rise to rituals and ceremonies of its own, even if the idea of ritual and ceremony is what the vision challenges. It happened to Kabir with the Kabirpanthis, to Nanak with Sikhism. Their vision eventually became a new orthodoxy managed by mahants and granthis.

A large number of Bhils also became followers of Kabir over the centuries; they were termed 'bhagats'. Like followers of any other sect, their knowledge of the vision that founded their faith was limited, but through their faith they acquired a familiarity with the term Rama.

~

The Mahi Kantha Bhils speak a language in sound something between Hindi and Gujarati and very hard to understand. They eat almost all kinds of flesh, including that of the cow. They worship stones covered with red-lead and oil, and are firm believers in witchcraft and much given to the practice of witch swinging. During the last ten years on the north-east frontier some Bhils taking the name of bhagats have become the followers of a Bhil teacher Kheradi Surmal, a native of the village of Lusdia Tabe Kuski in the Idar state, about four miles from Samlaji. This teacher believes in the Hindu god Earn [sic but perhaps this is a corruption of Ram], and forbids the killing of animals, the drinking of liquor, and the committing of offences. Like a high caste Hindu the bhagat takes no meal without bathing, puts a red mark on the brow and ties a yellow strip of cloth round the turban. In 1871, during the Samlaji fair, Kheradi was visited by the Assistant Political Agent. He was living by himself and had, including the members of his family, about 400 followers. On account of their change of customs the Meywar and other Mahi Kantha Bhils treated

these bhagats as outcastes and caused them much annoyance. This
the authorities put a stop to. Since then two of Kheradi's disciples
have settled at Pahada and Oad in the Idar state, and have almost
doubled the strength of the sect. The bhagats live by tillage and are
better off than they were before. During the last ten years not one of
their number has been accused of any crime.

Gazetteer of the Bombay Presidency, Vol. V, Cutch, Palanpur and
Mahi Kantha, Government Central Press, Bombay 1880, p. 366.

~

I first met Vaibhav Surange in 2003, a month after the Assembly
elections in Gujarat, and several months before the elections in
Madhya Pradesh. He was the RSS zila sahkaryavahak for Jhabua, the
most important Sangh functionary in the district.

I was in Jhabua because of the violence against the Muslims that
had taken place a few kilometres away, across the border in Gujarat.
The Bhils had played an active part and almost as a corollary, their
votes had shifted from the Congress to the BJP. Men like Surange were
working to ensure much the same would be repeated in MP.

I landed up at the local RSS office without a phone call or an
appointment. Surange happened to be there, unprepared for
a journalist from Bhopal. He was very fair, and his pale colour
dramatically set off the saffron-red tilak on his forehead. Hesitant to
speak to the media, he could find no easy way to get rid of me. He
satisfied himself with the name of my newspaper and the knowledge
that I was a Sikh. Seated on a chatai on the floor, three other RSS
men seated beside and eagerly listening to him, he told me he was
an engineer from the Benares Hindu University but had felt that his
'life had another purpose'. Soon after leaving college, he became a
full-time member of the RSS.

It struck me that the NBA was not the only social movement
that had drawn the young and the educated looking for some other
'purpose'. When I asked him for a few more details about his early
years in the RSS, he said we should really not spend so much time

talking about him, rather we should talk about the work he was doing in Jhabua.

He began by mentioning the Sewa Bharti. I had done enough reporting not to be concerned about the nomenclature of the various Sangh organizations doing work in a region; their functionaries were as interchangeable as the work they did.

'We've seen hindutva grow among the vanvasis.' His words reflected a deliberate choice. For the Sangh, the usual term Adivasi (the original inhabitants) is unacceptable because of its implication that the rest of the inhabitants of India were later arrivals. It implied that even Hinduism was an import or a later creation, hence the use of the seemingly neutral term vanvasi or forest dweller, which had now acquired political overtones of its own.

Hindutva was, of course, the specific political and religious ideology that was propounded by men such as V.D. 'Veer' Savarkar. Savarkar was an atheist, and even for his ideological descendants in the RSS, the question of faith was far less important than the cultural reassertion of those they chose to term Hindu. Vaibhav was clear that his task, and one that he had been carrying out successfully, was to spread this hindutva among the Bhils. If Hinduism as he understood it was only 1,200 years old, the hindutva his organization propagated was a faith less than a hundred years old.

As he turned away from speaking about himself to the work he was doing, he became far more comfortable with the conversation. He spoke in the manner of a man caught up in something larger than himself.

'Dharam prachar is one of our aims. We have set up Dharma Raksha Samitis in every village. We have ensured there is a devalaya in almost every tribal home and we make sure Ganesh Utsav is observed in every village.'

The choice of Ganesh Utsav was in keeping with a past history of the festival's use for cultural mobilization. The god of good fortune had been taken up at the turn of the nineteenth century by

Bal Gangadhar Tilak and transformed from the family deity of the Peshwas, high-caste Brahmins who eventually gained control of the Maratha Empire, to a symbol of Marathi assertion. Tilak transformed the worship of this family deity into the now familiar ten-day street festival in western India.

In less than a century, it became central to the practice of Hinduism in Maharashtra and the politics of parties such as the Shiv Sena. The Sangh, through men like Vaibhav, unsurprisingly a Maratha, were hoping to repeat this success among the Bhils.

The day after I met Surange, I drove towards the Gujarat border in a taxi. Just short of the border, we took a road that ran along an arid plateau. Like the Gond villages, the Bhil hamlets were spread out over a large area, and within each village the huts were set apart from each other.

Unlike the reception at the RSS office in Jhabua, in these villages we were received with great ease. The reticence that came naturally to most RSS workers when they spoke to someone from the English media was missing here.

At Dundka, a small village set among rocky outcrops, we were taken to meet the sarpanchpati, the husband of the elected village head. The post had been reserved for a woman, but the power actually resided with her husband Basubhai Damor, a Congressman. 'Till two years ago we never observed Ganesh visarjan. Then, because of the Sewa Bharti work, some of the neighbouring villages took it up and we also started.'

In the beginning, people here did not see the connection of this work with politics. 'The Sewa Bharti workers are everywhere. Last year, before the Hindu Samagam, they distributed lockets and pictures of Hanuman. We all went for the function.'

Vaibhav had told us that in the lead up to the Samagam, several lakh lockets of Hanuman had been distributed and idols of Hanuman had been installed by 'dharamveers' who had gone and stayed in each village for a week at a time.

Damor took us to one such devalaya where an idol stood, mace in hand, one foot thrust forward. Hanuman, the devotee of Rama, cast in his most potently aggressive form.

The Samagam was addressed by the then RSS chief K.S. Sudarshan. The gathered crowd, said to number over a hundred thousand, was the first indication to the outside world that Jhabua was changing.

The men seated around Damor told us that after the Samagam, Dharma Raksha Samitis had been set up in each village. The samitis institutionalized the work the 'dharamveers' had started. Five people from each village were selected and trained to organize functions around religious themes as well as collect funds for the devalaya. It was only when they started organizing people for Sewa Bharti gatherings that the new political reality struck Damor. 'The Sewa Bharti is for the phool (the flower, referring to the BJP's lotus). They dress the same way, all of them wear the bhagua gamcha (a saffron neck-wrap) while in the case of Congressmen, it is white.'

At the nearby village of Piplia we met another Damor, Chaman Singh, who was a Sewa Bharti volunteer and the panchayat secretary for the village. He had attended an overnight camp where senior RSS leaders from Bhopal had come and spoken to the volunteers. 'We were taught that we tribals were Hindus and should not convert to Christianity. We were told to spread this message in our village.'

We headed back to the main road and then took the path to Amli Patthar, a village of Patlia Bhils where the Sewa Bharti was particularly strong.

The Patlia Bhils of the village were Kabirpanthis. Rai Singh Rathore was one among the small group that had gathered at the arrival of our car. When I asked him about how their perceptions of faith had changed, he said, 'We always considered ourselves Hindus. We used to invoke Ganesh before ploughing our fields but we never knew what he looked like. Now there is traffic jam on the way to the town of Meghnagar on the occasion of Ganesh visarjan.'

He was only affirming what Vaibhav had claimed, 'We tell people about Ganesh, about Hanuman. Everyone here says Rama, Rama, but they did not even know who Rama was. We tell them he is very powerful to counter what preachers here state about the power of Christ.'

The Rama of Kabir had become the master of Raghu's clan. The journey from mythology to the intricate vision of Kabir had been reversed among the Bhils. The nameless, unknowable One had been rendered in human form. In the elections a few months later, the Congress was decimated. If Rama could be so used, how were the NBA ideologues sure that Marx would meet a more benign fate?

Narmada River Basin

AMARKANTAK

Gulf of Khambat

XIV

The Amarkantak Express from Bhopal arrives at Pendra Road at four in the morning. Once again, I am headed back to Amarkantak, this time in the dead of winter. Outside, the January cold is less severe than I had expected. Even at this hour there is a large number of people milling around. A chaiwallah tells me today is makarsankranti, the day of a big fair at the source. For the past few years, he adds, the Gondwana Ganatantra Party has been organizing an annual gathering on the occasion.

A driver of one of the jeeps that ferry passengers to Amarkantak, carrying over twenty persons a trip, agrees to let me have the front seat to myself for an extra fifty rupees. The bargain falls through when a saffron-clad sadhu arrives with two chelas in tow, one of whom has his briefcase in hand. The sadhu gets the front seat, I share the back with the two chelas and the briefcase. The sadhu's presence ensures no more passengers join us.

The driver is a Brahmin, the sadhu addresses him as Shuklaji, and he in turn calls the sadhu, maharaj. Just at the outskirts of the town, we stop for diesel. Shuklaji asks the maharaj for Rs 400, I take out a hundred. They bargain, each reminds the other of old obligations, but despite his skill at inveigling funds from his disciples, the maharaj is in another man's domain.

Soon we start climbing. The sankrant moon shines through the sal, the Maikal Hills silhouetted against the horizon. The maharaj turns to Shuklaji. 'You know, if I had walked all the way, I would have earned thousands, instead you are fleecing me of hundreds.' It seems an old game, for Shuklaji parries, 'But maharaj, I have been waiting at the station all night, you know it is not the Gond samaj that will pay for my vehicle.'

There is a pause and I ask the sadhu, who I have gathered lives in an ashram at Amarkantak, about the Gondwana party. They are a tremendous force, he tells me. Shukla agrees. 'But they won't come to a good end. Like the BSP (Bahujan Samaj Party), soon they will also start talking of sabjan (everyone) rather than bahujan (the majority).' The maharaj adds, 'Yes, all this talk of doing away with the old gods, devas and devis, pandits and pujaris in the name of Bada Deo. What, after all, is Bada Deo but a ghost who can be aroused easily.'

We reach Amarkantak at dawn. I am staying at what the MP Tourism department calls a resort. Parts of it are still under construction, while the rest has already started coming apart. I sleep for hours. When I venture out, it is afternoon. The streets are crowded with pilgrims, the temple complex at the source is much as I remember it. For once, even the old Kalachuri temples are thronged by pilgrims, most of them Gonds headed to the GGP gathering.

The gathering has been organized in an open maidan past the Sankaracharya's folly. The mood is festive, like an enormous village fair. The stage is decorated with multicoloured festoons, banners proclaim the Gondwana slogan, 'Jai Sewa, Jai Bada Deo.' A huge crowd is gathered at the centre of the maidan to hear the speakers. At its periphery, people come and go to wander among the stalls set up around the maidan, which sell chai, pakoras and water chestnuts. A full meal of rice and bhaji costs barely Rs 5. Other stalls are doing brisk business, selling books, posters and cassettes. Some of the posters list out simple words in Gondi, others the chronology of the Gond kingdoms. There are books that connect the Gonds to the Indus Valley Civilization, others that relate the history of Gondwana. The tapes blare out renditions of Gond folk songs interspersed with the message of Gondwana.

Over the milling crowds, speaker after speaker returns to the same theme. 'We are the original inhabitants of this land, we have a language, a culture, a religion of our own. We once ruled this land, others came and took away what was ours.'

A speaker talks of ousting the state government in the next elections. In less than a decade, the GGP has gone on to change political equations in the entire Gond belt of Madhya Pradesh. Men who were once afraid to speak to the local police inspector sit in the state legislature.

~

Ganga Patta was the head of the Gondwana Ganatantra Party in the district of Dindori. His village lies barely a half-hour walk from Sonpuri. I had first met him at a weekly haat where he sat at a tea stall surrounded by the slightly obsequious men always present around political figures in India. Neither in his speech nor in his appearance was there anything to mark him out as a Gond; he could have been at ease anywhere in small-town India. We talked for a while and he asked me to come and see him the next morning.

We were late getting there, a delay that forced a rare awareness of the tyranny of an appointed time. In Sonpuri, time was measured in indefinite spans described by words such as soon, in a while, later. I needn't have worried. Ganga Patta was still waiting for us. He sent for some black tea that arrived in cracked porcelain cups.

In anticipation of our arrival, a few Hindi publications had been placed carefully on the table set out on a verandah. They were the kind that the district administration brings out with some regularity to list the progress of various developmental schemes. I was meant to ask the question, and he answered that he had been the head of the district mandi board – a position of some power, for the body deals with the purchase of agricultural commodities in this largely agricultural area. In Sonpuri, the mention of his name had always brought forth a statement about the lal battiwali gadi, the official Ambassador car with the privilege of a flashing red light on the roof.

The trappings of power seemed a world away from the hut where we were sitting. 'I was the first person from my family to go to college. An uncle of mine had studied till class X, but that was all. I had no one to guide me, but I had this desire to study, to achieve something. I never took tuition, but I had to compete against those who could afford to do so. I learnt everything on my own in Shahdol.'

The choice of Shahdol was curious, for there was a college closer by, in Dindori. 'They did not offer what I wanted to study. I enrolled in the BCom course at Shahdol. There were others from this region and we shared accommodation. The government provisions for the Scheduled Tribes meant that my room rent was paid for. It was in college that I first understood politics and its importance in how the country is run, but I never thought of joining political life. After college, I got a government job in the state excise department and was posted to Chhindwara. But eight months later, I quit because I wanted to study further and I felt I could do better.'

It was an act of courage in a country where such jobs are hard to come by. There was enough in his narrative to indicate an ambition out of the ordinary. It was evident in the choice of a commerce degree, the pride in doing as well as any other student, the belief that he could quit the job and end up doing better.

'I returned to finish my MCom in Shahdol and got a job as an irrigation supervisor. I was posted to a site near Shahdol. It was then that I became a member of Kanshi Ram's BAMSEF (Backward and Minority Communities Employees Federation).' It was an interesting connection. Kanshi Ram's move towards a Dalit reassertion in Indian politics had started with this employees' federation that wanted to bring together Dalits, tribals, minorities and other backward castes. In some measure, the GGP was hoping to achieve among the Gonds exactly what Kanshi Ram had managed among the Dalits.

'It was during this time that I realized the injustice that comes with hierarchy in a society. In our villages, I had never seen the oppression that was visible against Dalits and tribals in the Vindhya region around Shahdol. It affected me personally. The custom in the region was that a thakur had to be addressed as Lal Sahib irrespective of his rank in the department. This custom did not exist in our part of the world and I did not like it. There was a thakur at the worksite who was a bit of a goonda. He was big built and everyone was afraid of him. He threatened me verbally when I refused to address him in the required manner. I didn't pay attention, but it was through such incidents that I understood what BAMSEF stood for.

'In 1984 Indira Gandhi clamped down on BAMSEF. Kanshi Ram responded by dissolving the body and starting a political party, the Bahujan Samaj Party. I became active in the party without joining it because I was still working for the government. Among the employees, I continued to stress on the need to live with respect and dignity. Then I quit my job and returned to my village to establish the BSP's presence in this region. At the time, the party had no roots here. Soon some of my friends joined, mainly for my sake, and then a few others came along who genuinely believed in the idea. In 1993, I contested the MLA election from the Bijak constituency. The Congress cadres opposed my work because they used to take our Gond votes for granted.'

Till this point in his narrative, there was little sign that he thought in terms of a specifically Gond identity. It was another humiliation that led him there. Far too often, we learn that we are more than our individual selves when events mark us part of the collective assigned to us by birth. In his case, such a recognition seems to have transformed itself into a carefully thought out sense of identity.

'In 1998 I resigned from the BSP. I wasn't given a ticket, but that was not the reason I resigned. The state president and the secretary of the party conspired to help the Congress candidate win. When I raised the matter at the post-mortem on the party's performance in the elections, I was blamed for the defeat. Even Kanshi Ram paid me no heed. I realized I couldn't move ahead and decided to work in other ways. For over two years I stayed away from politics. The Congress and the BJP were both wooing me, and the GGP had just started emerging as a real force. Ministers and MLAs would come to persuade me, but I preferred to stay at home.'

He changed his mind after receiving a letter from Hira Singh Markam, the founder of the GGP. The letter seems to have had a strong impact for he could still recite it verbatim. 'Dada (as Hira Singh is often addressed) wrote to me:

> *Jis jaati mein janam liya,*
> *Jis jaati ka aap ne doodh piya,*
> *Us jaati ke godh mein pale badhe,*
> *Aur wohi jaati jo behan beti ke grahasti ki nirman karegi,*
> *Aur marne ke baad bhi arthi ko kandha degi,*
> *Us samaj ke tum karzdar ho,*
> *Main jaanta hun tum Gondwana ke saput ho,*
> *Is karz se chhootne ka ya hal karne ka ek hi madhyam hai,*
> *Us samaj ki sewa karna.*

> (The jaati you were born to; the jaati that nourished you;
> the jaati that raised you; the same jaati that will enable
> your daughters and sisters to establish a home;
> and after your death will lend a shoulder to your coffin;
> you are a debtor of that community; I know you are
> a son of Gondwana; there is only one way for you to
> repay or shed this debt; serve that community.)

It was striking how generic the letter was, how Ganga Patta's involvement with a specifically Gond identity went back to a letter that could well have been written within any Indian community, expressing sentiments that would be common to them all. I asked him where the sense of the Gonds as a community apart came from.

'From my childhood, I was interested in our tradition. There has always been a separate tribal religion, language and culture and there always will be. In our region, people have not spoken Gondi for generations, but there is one part of the district where the language is still spoken. Even in our dialect, the words that really matter to us come from Gondi. Our word for jungle is dongar, for deep, still water is dahar, these are Gondi words. Some attempts are being made to revive the language, some schools have been started by our allied institution, the Akhil Gondwana Mahasabha. It is to us what the RSS is to the BJP. As a party we do not speak of one people, one tribe, we want to carry everyone with us.'

Ganga Patta spoke Hindi fluently but it had taken me a few days to clearly comprehend the local dialect that is spoken by most people here. It was a variant of Hindi that had now been spoken in this region for several generations. His conversation about the revival of Gondi was just part of the reinvention underway here, born out of the ideas of nationalism that had created the Europe of today. Ganga Patta was working to ensure fewer and fewer Gond children would be named Ganga in the future. He was part of a conscious search for an identity that was attempting to sift the genuine from the acquired, but it was troubling for those who knew another way to live.

I told him of a conversation I had with an old Pardhan Gond from Garkamatha. The Pardhan had told me it was good that there was a party of the Gonds. His family and neighbours, he said, had voted for the Congress for generations but were ready to switch to the GGP. There was only one problem, the party wanted them to stop saying Ram, Ram. How could they? He told me there was a time when Ganga Patta was with the BSP, when he had gone around burning the Ramayana.

Ganga Patta's reaction was measured, it was as if he had been asked this question several times earlier. Subhash, my host at Sonpuri, later told me this was indeed so. Among the Gonds, each political question was settled the way the Pardhans told stories: questions were raised and the answers were debated before anyone could be convinced.

Ganga Patta told me, 'The objections this man raised can only be answered when he finds out for himself what is right. We are the original inhabitants of this land, all our forts and palaces are here.

As far as religion is concerned, compare our rituals. The Hindus say "Ram, Ram", the Muslims "Salaam", the Christians "Jai Issu", we say, "Jai Sewa". Our supreme deity is Bada Deo, he has no form, he is only energy, the energy manifest in the natural world.

'For us, animals are sacred. Unlike the Hindus or Muslims, we consider both the cow and pig sacred, and we offer both as sacrifice to the deity. As far as Ram is concerned, we think he is a man worthy of respect. Let people do what they believe. There is no question of coercion. For us, service is the main concern, Jai Sewa. When they come to understand this, they will face up to the world. At another level, you have to realize this is a dharamyudh.' It was interesting that the word he used for religious war goes back to the Gita.

'This is a battle for social change; they are saying what has been imposed. The time will come when they will see for themselves. Already you can see what is happening. According to the 2001 census, in Dindori alone, 100,000 people have declared Gondi as their religion. From none to 100,000 in just one district alone, you can see for yourself that things are changing. Ask people around you. Today a bus driver from outside the region does not show the contempt he would have had for a Gond only a decade back. The police listen to us. These are the things that make a difference.'

~

I found the two strains of my conversation with Ganga Patta at odds. His personal journey seemed true to his self. And the experiences of a few like him had brought a political sense learnt elsewhere to a party that needed it. But there was something rehearsed in his utterances about Gond identity and culture. Nothing in what he said was at a deviance from the GGP's avowed position, but in his years in the BSP, he may well have uttered the rhetoric of Dalit oppression with equal ease. What I had seen in Amarkantak and in the course of my travels in MP seemed to run much deeper.

Just days after I met Ganga Patta, I had travelled with my hosts to Baigachak. They had an agenda of their own: the wife of one of their relatives had run back to her parents' home in Baigachak. I had tagged along because of my curiousity about the Baigas, who in the Indian nomenclature were a 'primitive' tribe largely dependent on the jungle. Unlike the Gonds who have a long agricultural tradition, the Baiga were loath to plough the earth.

The government had pumped a huge amount of money into the area, only a little of which had made it to the Baigas. According to Ganga Patta, the government had spent 'Rs 73 lakh per Baiga, with little to show for it'. The results had a dreary predictability about them: school buildings that leaked from the very first day, hostels unfit to be occupied, housing that no Baiga would ever use. It was a short visit and it left me with the feeling that the spirit had ebbed out of the Baigas.

For the moment, as we travelled around Baigachak, I could sense a little of the apathy that Elwin had once detected in this entire region. Ramachandra Guha writes, 'In private letters and published essays Elwin drew a pointed comparison between the aboriginal situation in own Central Provinces (today the Dindori and Mandla districts of Madhya Pradesh) and in Bastar (today part of Chhattisgarh). In the CP, he noted, "hunting has been forbidden for decades, adventure has been wiped out by Law and Order, achievement has been dented by disease and hunger." There the tribesmen were oppressed by landlords and moneylenders, and subject to extortion by state officials. But the Bastar aboriginal retained control over his lands and forests, while an administration specially adapted to his needs had protected him from scheming politicians and corrupt officials. The "vigorous and healthy" life of tribal society in Bastar contrasted with the "decay and inertia" elsewhere in aboriginal India. He found it "most refreshing to go to Bastar from the reform-stricken and barren districts of the Central Provinces". Every time he entered the state from British territory he seemed to hear the whole countryside bursting into song around him.'

But in these very 'reform stricken' areas of the Central Provinces, something very interesting was unfolding. It was brought home to me once again in the strongest possible manner at a tea shop in the heart of Baigachak. Another vehicle had stopped at the shop. Over tea, I started talking to Shankar Lal Dwivedi, a Brahmin now residing in the town of Samnapur, 55 km away. Dwivedi said, 'I know this entire region rather well. I used to live here, as did my father before me. I used to be the pandit for several of the villages here. I have walked from village to village in this entire belt. Just from a single tribal village I would earn Rs 15,000 to 20,000 a year for presiding over pooja and other ceremonies. All this changed over the last decade since the GGP became active. My income dropped to less than Rs 1,000 a year from each village. My children had no future here. I have moved to the town to make ends meet and secure their future. There, at least, there is a demand for my services. Here, when I now go to a household where I was received with great reverence, they do not even say namaskar, they expect me to say Jai Sewa.'

There was certainly something stronger at work here, something in addition to the modern political ideas that Ganga Patta brought to the party. The ideas Ganga Patta embodied had linked up with the perception of several of those who still commanded respect within the Gond cultural framework, who wielded enough power to take along people like the Garkamatha Pardhan, who were not always convinced by the rhetoric of a Ganga Patta.

~

Almost a kilometre from the source of the Narmada at Amarkantak, Thunnu Singh Markam lives in a solitary hut by one of its tributaries, the Kapila. He is a vaid, a healer, who also heads the local unit of the GGP. For him, the annual convention at Amarkantak is also about keeping this tradition alive. 'Last year at the Gondwana function I instructed over thirty to forty men, this year they were back. They need to recognize the trees, the herbs. In my family the gift passes from generation to generation. When someone is ill, I dream of where I will find the herb to cure him. Illness comes about when some tat (element) is no longer present in the body. The herbs reintroduce that tat and the person is cured. This is a gift that will pass on to some descendant of mine when I die, as it came to me from my father and to him from his father before him.'

He is wizened and looks older than his sixty-eight years. 'We had begun to forget our traditions. According to our ways, everything is done by the naths (in-laws) and it is reciprocal, we do everything for them. At a birth, the cleansing of the house, the sprinkling of haldi paani, the singing of songs, everything. In return, new clothes are given to them, and instead of feeding Brahmins, the entire family is fed. At the time of death, it is the same thing. For three days after the death the naths visit our home, console us, bring food for us. Now about 25 per cent of the Gonds have returned to their own tradition, but for the others, the Brahmins still matter.'

'We are trying to tell people, forget the Brahmins, they come from UP and make chutiyas out of us. The main difference is, they do not observe rajo sulaha. In our families, a woman during her periods stays separately, even the food is cooked by the man. If we violate this tradition our crops fail, evil descends on us. The Brahmins do not observe this rite with any strictness, this is important. Our people have also forgotten, which is why today, when they call to their ancestral deity, sometimes he does not answer. I remember fifty years ago, even the Narmada temple would be shut when the maiya was in this state. Even the water would be a polluted red during this time and when the periods ended, the water would be sparkling clean. It was only then that the temple would open.'

The isolation of women during their periods was strictly observed, as I was to find out for myself. Strangely, this attitude went hand in hand with a relative equality for women, unmatched in much of Indian society. These were among the few districts in all of central and northern India where the sex ratio was biased in favour of women. There was also something ironic in the fact that the very idea of purity and pollution, so central to the Brahmins' position in the caste system, was now being used to drive them out.

'I recall when I was young, there were no pandits. In this whole region there was no idol worship, only the Narmada temples existed. I have seen ten years of British rule. Each followed his own tradition, there were not so many "gyanis" around. Soon the idols of Durga, Kali and Ganesh were introduced and worshipped. During my childhood, I saw none of this. If there was an utsav, our "bada raja" would come and our own men would be there. I can speak of this region. Once Gondi was spoken here, a few men still speak it, but in the main it has been forgotten; I do not speak it.'

I was later to read some accounts of Amarkantak written before Independence. Some details were at odds with what Thunnu Singh had recounted, but it seemed to me that his memory of the past meshed perfectly with the modern assertion of identity that Ganga Patta represented. Here, the GGP was traversing a trajectory that was in complete contrast to what the RSS was attempting in Jhabua. Rama was slowly being diminished to a historical personage, pandits and idols were being evicted. I had the feeling that among the range of possible identities available to the Mandla Gonds today, a few would disappear. An effort was being made to define what was genuinely Gond, and what was not. It had happened frequently in this country, at different times in different places, but in the absence of a sense of history, it was a process that was often ignored. Even change that was recent, once it took shape, was consigned to a forgotten past. Among the Sikhs, the particular identity that so categorically identified them through the turban, beard and the external symbols of the faith became predominant only in the first decade of the twentieth century. When the GGP attained the success it was seeking, it would come to define the one way of being Gond.

This change was born out of the engagement of the GGP with democracy, an engagement that was akin to the Pardhan painters' negotiation of the market. A reinvented authenticity was profitable in both cases. For the painters, this was obvious; for the GGP, it represented a clear mobilization of people who would stand behind the party.

The 'authenticity' that was likely to emerge out of the present churning would be very different from the pre-modern authenticity that Elwin thought he had found in Bastar. Perhaps, to get to this stage, the very acculturation that Elwin had bemoaned may have been necessary, but as I could see among the Bhils, there was a limit to how far this acculturation could progress before the possibility of a response disappeared. Which is, perhaps, why what was happening among the Gonds of Mandla was so rare; it depends on change coming at a particular stage of acculturation, neither too early nor too late.

XV

Usually when outsiders stride in and look to create someone else's world anew, they are marked by a lack of self-doubt and scepticism. However, the activists and outsiders who came to the Narmada Valley to work with the NBA have had considerable time to introspect. Many, like Amit and Jayashree, have come to believe in more modest and longer-lasting interventions which build the Bhils' capacity to speak for themselves, as the Gonds in Mandla have begun to do. Others have continued to painstakingly work on the day-to-day task of ensuring rehabilitation for many who even today continue to be afflicted by the dams still coming up along the river.

Yet, most seem to retain faith in the vision Arundhati Roy articulates: 'Big Dams are to a Nation's "Development" what Nuclear Bombs are to its Military Arsenal. They're both weapons of mass destruction. They're both weapons Governments use to control their own people. Both Twentieth Century emblems that mark a point in time when human intelligence has outstripped its own instinct for survival. They're both malignant indications of civilisation turning upon itself. They represent the severing of the link, not just the link – the *understanding* – between human beings and the planet they live on. They scramble the intelligence that connects eggs to hens, milk to cows, food to forests, water to rivers, air to life and the earth to human existence.'

When Arundhati speaks of big dams as 'weapons Governments use to control their own people', she tells us nothing about the term 'Government' and how it controls people through dams. She, I believe, assumes that her readers share the view that the 'Government' is a superstructure with a logic of its own, controlled and directed by big corporates, a giant bureaucracy at the service of a military-industrial complex that is as capable of using dictatorship or democracy for its purposes.

As a journalist I know there is considerable truth to the fact that large corporates exercise influence over decision making, that the bureaucracy has a life and trajectory of its own, but even so, Arundhati's rhetoric only leads to a dead end, a rage against a conspiracy perpetrated by an entity that operates independently of the persons who happen to constitute it at any given point of time. But this conspiracy is a reality born out of the consent of the many.

~

Marshall Berman's book on modernity – *All That Is Solid Melts into Air* – begins with a description of how Jewish and Irish neighbourhoods in the Bronx of his youth were torn down to build 'an immense expressway, unprecedented in scale, expense and difficulty of construction'. This was done in the name of the values of progress 'that we ourselves embraced'.

It is to make sense of this embrace that Berman's first chapter, 'Goethe's Faust: The Tragedy of Development', turns to the very inception of modernity. Almost 300 years ago, long before technology had made the transformation of the world possible, Goethe had embodied the desire to ceaselessly create the world anew in *Faust*.

In part II of Goethe's work, far less studied and commented upon than the first book, Faust turns from his inner turmoil, from the personal quest for fulfilment through love and desire to the external world and its transformation. Magic is the power that is at his disposal thanks to Mephistopheles, but it is a magic that can achieve much that technology does today.

In Act IV Scene I of Book II, Faust stares at the sea, and laments:

> If anything makes me despair, of my intent,
> It's the aimless force of that wild element!
> Then my spirit dared to soar high above:
> Here I must fight, and this I must remove.
> And it's possible! – However tides may flow,
> At last they nestle round the hills below:
> So they are tamed in their exuberance,
> A modest height tops their proud advance,
> A modest depth draws them forcefully on.
> Quick, through my mind, leapt plan after plan:
> Let rich enjoyment be mine for evermore,
> To keep the noble ocean from the shore,
> To channel all the wide and watery waste,
> And urge it backwards to its own deep place.
> Step by step I know how to design it:
> That's my desire, so be brave and promote it!

Mephistopheles tells him that his dream of rolling back the ocean and developing the land is easily done. Timely aid to the emperor in a war secures Faust a royal decree. In the next Act, which takes place several years later, an old couple, their names Philemon and Baucis derived from Greek myth, living at the edge of the land reclaimed from the sea, describe the magic that has been wrought around them.

Philemon

> He wants to comprehend the gift:
> Tell him, freely then speak out.

Baucis

> Well! It was a marvel, really!
> It troubles me to this day:

Then its whole nature, surely,
Was peculiar, in its way.

Philemon

Is the Emperor, then, at fault,
Who granted him the land?
Didn't a herald make his halt,
Crying out what was planned?
Not far away there, on the dunes,
The first bold step was made,
Tents, huts! – And on the downs,
A palace, quickly raised.

Baucis

For days, work rumbled on in vain,
Pick and shovel, blow on blow:
Where the night's fires flamed,
Next day a dam would follow.
Human blood was forced to flow,
At night, rose the sound of pain:
The seaward floating fiery glow
Was a canal, come dawn again.
He's a godless man: he'd steal
Our hut, and our few acres:
But like subjects we must kneel,
When we boast such neighbours.

Philemon

Yet he's offered us another
Holding, on his new-won land!

But they remain steadfast in their attachment to their land. Their refusal to move irks Faust.

Faust

Such obstinacy and opposition
Diminishes the noblest position,
Until in endless pain, one must
Grow deeply weary of being just.

Mephistopheles

Why bother yourself so much about them?
Shouldn't you long ago have colonised them?

Faust

Then go and push them aside for me! –
You know the land, with my approval,
Set aside for the old folks removal.

Mephistopheles

We'll take them up, and set them down,
They'll stand, once more: I'll be bound:
When they've survived a little force,
They'll be reconciled to it, of course.

The couple does not survive Mephistopheles's 'little force'. The change that modernity promises could only come about with the death of those who live in the traditional way.

Goethe's *Faust* was a premonition born centuries before the gigantic acts of transformation conceived by Faust even became remotely possible. But at least in Goethe's fiction, Faust had little reason to doubt the efficacy of Mephistopheles's magic. The sea was rolled back, new lands were opened up, the canals did flow.

Centuries after Goethe's work, technological projects have provided many of the benefits Faust envisaged. We often forget that long before large dams, the Suez and the Panama Canal were projects undertaken on a gigantic scale. The dams, far more ambiguous today, were only one among the many technological feats that transformed us. Highways, railroads, high-rises, aeroplanes, the technological apparatus of modern medicine and thermal plants are just a few instances.

Such successes have given rise to another category of projects which are imitative. Societies which want to claim the mantle of modernity have undertaken such projects just to be able to show they are also capable of conceiving and building them. They seek to emulate only the gigantism, not the analysis and planning that goes into completing a successful project.

Berman prefers to call such projects pseudo-Faustian, simply because, unlike Faust's projects, 'they do not work'. He traces the peculiar history of such projects to the Soviet example. Stalin dreamed up the White Sea Canal, connecting the White Sea to the Baltic Sea, but the final depth of the canal constructed using Gulag labour (at least 10,000 died building it) was too shallow to allow most seagoing vessels to use it.

What makes the Soviet case so depressing, Berman argues, 'is that its pseudo-Faustian enormities have been enormously influential in the Third World … millions of people have been victimized by disastrous development policies, megalomaniacally conceived, shoddily and insensitively executed ….'

In many countries, it is easy to blame a select ruling class. In India, the belief in technology has far greater legitimacy and has been easily used as justification for projects that do not meet simple tests of rational planning. We see such attention to detail as the meaningless mantras that go with any ritual. We have started believing technology is magic, not subject to the questioning rationality that brings it into being. Nowhere is this truth more evident than in the enormous project of which the Narmada dams are only a part.

~

I had long debated with myself the possible course of my journey past the Sardar Sarovar Dam. I did travel the entire length of the river to its mouth at Bharuch, but I came away thinking that only a century from now, when the dams would have disappeared and the river would again flow unhindered to the sea, would it make sense to tell the story of the parikrama as it once was. For now, in our times, I decided I would abandon the old pilgrimage path, and follow the river through the canals of the Sardar Sarovar Project.

Driving along the Rajpur sub-branch of the main canal in Gujarat, I stopped at Vikram Kanobhai's custard apple and guava orchard in the village of Chaloda in Ahmedabad district. It was mid-morning and he was preparing to irrigate the orchard from the overhead tanks filled with water from the borewell installed at his farm. For nearly a decade, water from the Narmada had been flowing past his farm, but he had never been able to make use of it. As he took me for a stroll through his orchard, our shoes sloshing in the mud, he told me that the canal carried water from July to March every year, but none of the minor canals which are actually meant to take water to the surroundings fields had been built. Like most farmers living adjacent to the canal, he was pumping groundwater for irrigation.

The canal, he admitted, had brought an indirect benefit. The groundwater was constantly being recharged. But that was little compensation for the damage done every year. For the last six to seven years, he said, no repairs had been carried out along the canals. Each year there would be a breach and his farm would get flooded. No compensation had ever been awarded for this annual deluge.

After meeting Kanobhai, I covered over a hundred kilometres along the canal system in these two districts and spoke to dozens of farmers living by the canals. Kanobhai seemed to be speaking for almost all of them. Some had attempted to pump water directly from the canal. This would be tolerated for a year or two and then perfunctorily, after complaints would be received from those living downstream who depended on the canal for drinking water, the police would crack down, seizing pumps at random.

The figures told a dismal story. The canal network was supposed to have been completed by 2010. At the time I travelled along the canals, less than a third of the work had been completed. Of the proposed 74,626 km of canals, only 19,500 km had been built. In the three years since my visit, the Gujarat government has added a further 289.22 km to the network.

Much of the network to be completed consists of the minor canals and sub-branches that actually take water to the farmers, so the state cannot use a large part of the water flowing through these canals. To be precise, 93 per cent of the water share of Gujarat flows out to the sea, and in the process the network is suffering extensive damage because no repairs are being carried out.

Before setting out along the canals, I had met the chairman of the Sardar Sarovar Narmada Nigam Limited (SSNNL), N.V. Patel. The SSNNL was overseeing the entire project in Gujarat and his office was like any senior bureaucrat's anywhere in the country. He was seated behind a massive desk, the list of the names of his predecessors hanging on the wall behind going back well over a decade, in itself a sign of the project's slow drift.

Like a supplicant, I sat before him. It was only the notebook in my hand that restored the balance somewhat. Long decades of being surrounded by subservient men, the fate of all senior bureaucrats, had ensured he was not used to being questioned.

I asked him about the repeated breaches in the existing canal system. The problem was so acute that the area irrigated by water from the Narmada canal network in Gujarat has actually declined year by year from 2004–05 onwards, going down from 133,155 hectares to 72,000 hectares in 2008–09. He was already beginning to get annoyed. 'The canals will break time after time. Only a lining of 3 to 4 inches is being laid on the earthen canals. This is like pappad. Breaches will keep happening, we have to live with them.'

I finally asked him about the 2010 deadline for completion. No one should expect miracles, he said, but in another two to three years the project should be complete (in that time, as I have noted above, less than 300 km of the remaining 55,000 km of canals have been constructed). When I suggested that this delay was calling into question the rationale for the dam, Patel lost his temper. 'The Narmada Control Authority (the central body coordinating the project in Gujarat, MP, Rajasthan and Maharashtra) is to blame. Instead of facilitating, they are delaying.' Given the fact that the building of the canals was entirely Gujarat's responsibility and there was little any outside agency could do, the answer made no sense. Patel saw me preparing to ask another question. He got up and abruptly called a halt to the interview.

He had reason to avoid my question. The delay has indeed meant that the entire Sardar Sarovar Project is already a financial disaster. When the dam was first planned, rates of return varying from 12 to 18 per cent – well over the Government of India's minimum criterion of 9 per cent – were projected. But the actual rate of return will be far lower.

The official website for the project lists the benefits from the dam at Rs 2,175 crore a year from increases in agricultural production, power generation and water supply. These are hugely exaggerated figures, but let us pretend to believe them.

The costs based on the government's data suggest Rs 31,400 crore have already been spent as of March 2010. Of the total expenditure incurred, a sum of about Rs 13,000 crore has been spent on the irrigation network. Since only about 27 per cent of the irrigation canal network has been completed, building the rest could require another Rs 35,000 crore.

This means the total cost of the project will be at least Rs 66,000 crore, so that the benefit of Rs 2,175 crore amounts to an annual return of a measly 3.6 per cent – far below the minimum criterion for approving the project in the first place. If we use realistic figures for the benefits from the dam, annual returns barely touch 1 to 2 per cent.

In the simplest of terms, the returns from the Sardar Sarovar Project, irrespective of when it is completed, will never be enough to justify it. This project should never have been approved.

The people who worked out the justifications for the Narmada dams not only knew the arguments were wrong, they knew they had been concocted. They had created a complicity of lies that had been accepted even by the Supreme Court. The irony was that Arundhati Roy was duplicating their skill with numbers to create competing lies of her own.

~

From Ahmedabad I had called A.B. Patel, deputy executive engineer in charge of the stretch of the canal I was travelling along. I said I had got the number from the SSNNL office, which was true, and I had been told by the director that I was free to inspect the work on any stretch I wanted.

He took this to mean I had the director's ear. He was keen to talk. 'We have planned out the land acquisition, a survey has been carried out, but you know how complex the procedure is. On the ground there is no clarity between three brothers as to who owns which piece of the land. And then there is the revenue department, who knows how much time they will take? The sub-canals will take at least three years to conceive and build.'

'What can I do?' he said in response to my question about the frequent breaches along the canal. 'The canal supplies drinking water further ahead, so supply cannot be stopped even for routine maintenance. Parts of the canal have not been lined, others are decaying. In a few years, all of it may have to be done again.' The Gujarat water supply department, he told me, had failed to construct water storage tanks that could allow the canal to be shut for a few months.

The canal Patel looked after was breached at its source, where it branched off from the Saurashtra Branch Canal. When I told him about it, he laughed. The breach has been in existence for a year, he said, and then lowered his voice, afraid to say what, even so far from the SSNNL headquarters, was blasphemy. The branch canal, he told me, carries water against the gradient to Saurashtra. Five pumping houses are being built to transport this water by using over 250 MW of electricity. As a result, he said, the water going waste at the breach costs the state litre for litre 'as much as mineral water.'

A few days later, I relate this to Yoginder K. Alagh, now chairman of the IRMA (Institute of Rural Management Anand) board, and a former minister for power at the Centre. He had been one of the key proponents of the dam and had been involved in the design and the conception of the project from the very beginning.

He looks weary. 'The water for Saurashtra and north Gujarat was not part of the original scheme. We had carefully calculated the water available through the project. Once the system is in place, we will find that there is not enough water to provide for this part of the scheme. The water is simply not there and this will ensure the benefits of the scheme will go down.'

He likened the failure of the state to utilize water from the dam to putting a lot of money into the bank and not putting it to any use. 'The more the delays, the lesser the benefits, and the returns from the dam become very low. This is a real economic loss because there is a huge amount of investment locked up.'

~

I went to Khaingari village in Ahmedabad district because of the man who had been driving us along the canals, Mahendra V. Bharwar. He had moved from the village to Ahmedabad when he was still in his teens to join others from his Maldhari tribe who lived in the city. The Maldharis were nomadic cattle-herders, and like the men who had preceded him, he had taken naturally to the life of a long-distance cabbie, which often saw him on the road for days on end.

The northern part of Ahmedabad district lay not far from the Maldhari homeland in Kutch. Mahendra told me that the elders in the surrounding villages spoke of a time when they spent long days away from home as they set out with their herds of cattle, some their own and some belonging to the farmers they lived amidst, towards better pasture in Madhya Pradesh as the dry season set in. Herd after herd would mingle together in the migrating throng. Cattle, sheep, goats and camels would assemble in huge numbers, but the keen eyes of the Maldharis meant each could separate his herd from the others.

Along the way the farmers would welcome them, allowing them to settle for the night on their fields. Some would even pay for the privilege, the droppings from the herd providing much-needed manure for the crop to come. But over the past few decades this huge migration that circled through Madhya Pradesh has come under threat. The Madhya Pradesh government, running short of grazing land for the growing number of cattle within the state, started creating obstructions in the free movement of the herds. Slowly, the community in places such as Khaingari, who would farm the little land it had when men were not on the move, or work as farm labourers for the well-to-do Patels, began settling down or migrating to the city.

At Mahendra's house in the village, his family was expecting us. His elder brother Laxman took care of the little land the family had in the village. As we sipped tea from saucers, Laxman told me that there were about fifteen Maldhari households in the village. 'Now no one goes anywhere. We have all settled down.'

He had grown up seeing only one crop of cotton being farmed through the year in this area. 'Now we grow two crops, rice and wheat. The whole village is changing. The number of people here is increasing.'

We walked with him to the fields bordering the field canal that ran on the outskirts of the village, where we came across Rajubhai Waglibhai transplanting paddy in a field. He was running a diesel pump to irrigate the field. 'We had never planted rice here, but now we are worried. We have ten bighas under rice and we can't afford to lose the crop. We don't know when the water flows through the canal. Right now, it is running dry. We can manage a few days with the pump, but we can't save the crop without water from the canal.'

Just a few hundred yards further ahead, Meenaben Patel was sitting by the edge of the field canal. All she owned were two bighas of land. The paddy stood in a small plot by the field canal awaiting transplantation. She and her family had been carrying pots of water from a nearby tank to keep the crop alive. She thought we were government officials. 'Please get the water started, the crop won't last much longer.'

No one in the village had heard of a farmers' water user committee or a kisan samiti in the village, no one knew when the water would come and when it would disappear. These kisan samitis had been at the heart of the plan to distribute water to the farmers across the state. Out of the 4,680 needed for Gujarat in the Narmada command area, only 500 have been formed. Of these, very few do the work they are supposed to do.

For the farmers, even the unpredictable presence of water in this landscape was a miracle, but it was a small miracle in the face of the dislocation I had witnessed over the past decade. I remembered the awe with which Alagh had told me, 'Have you seen the main canal? It is beautiful. It is the largest irrigation canal in the world, like a river in high flood. No other irrigation canal in the world is even half the size. Never has so much water been available in the entire history of civilization in Gujarat.'

On the way back to Ahmedabad, I stopped by the main canal – a miracle of blue. Alagh was right, I had never seen anything quite as beautiful as the clear flow of sweet blue water in this parched landscape, or quite as tragic.

～

I was struck by the word Alagh had used to describe the canal. My repeated attempts to examine the progress of the work on the canal network had left me convinced that the beauty of the main canal may have been all that Narendra Modi, as chief minister of Gujarat, required of the canal system. The project, the dams and the canal network were conceived long before Modi, but the task of completing the network has been largely the responsibility of his administration. The Cabinet portfolio that oversees the work has been retained by Modi, so his responsibility is even more direct. It seems, for Modi, the aim of building the canal network was never meant to be the benefit it conferred, rather it was to show that he could bring water to this parched landscape.

As a hypothesis, this had the advantage of explaining the seemingly inexplicable pace of work on the sub-branch and field canals once the main canal had been built, and I had already found that there was something about bringing the waters of the Narmada to Gujarat that aroused a deep-seated atavistic impulse in many Gujaratis.

In Jabalpur, earlier in the course of my journey, I had gone looking for the house of Amrit Lal Vegad. The directions he had given me over the phone to his old colonial-style house were precise. Past the unlatched gate, the lawn and the garden were both a little overgrown but stopped short of the chaos of abandonment. I didn't have to wait at the entrance; Vegad was expecting me.

In person, in the old sprawling house that his family occupied, he was a short and wiry presence. I recalled that he had often written of his surprise at how well his frail frame had coped with the rigours of the river journey.

Having completed the parikrama piecemeal over a stretch of several years, he had written about the experience in Gujarati. The books had been translated into Hindi, and I had read these before I went to meet him. A year after my visit, a single volume had appeared in English. The title was simple and heartfelt, *Narmada: River of Beauty*. The narrative, like his journey, clung stubbornly to the riverbank, refusing to move away, whatever the obstacles. Through this stubbornness he achieved the unique and, thanks to the dams, unrepeatable feat of describing almost the entire parikrama route along the banks of the river.

There were other visitors around – a crew from the Films Division in Mumbai, making a film on the Narmada. His love for the river is part of his patrimony, he told them, his father was a lover of nature, with a passion for literature and long walks.

After college, he went to study at Santiniketan, the university set up by Tagore. The years he mentioned surprised me. He went there in 1948 and stayed on till 1953, that would make him well past seventy now, and he had still not stopped walking the banks of the river.

'Acharya Nandalal Bose taught me to paint, he gave me the eyes to see beauty,' he said, referring to one of the best-known painters of the Bengal school, a painter who believed you needed to step out of the studio into nature to learn to draw and paint.

'You can have the entire ocean before you, but if you don't have the vision, you will not see it. I was imparted this vision in Santiniketan. Now I understand, the creator was preparing me for the parikrama.'

Looking through the collection of collages he had pulled out for the cameras, it did seem that in those deceptively simple images, he had found a way to capture the simplicity and devotion of those who live by the Narmada, or walk its banks.

He took up the thread again. For the next twenty-five years, after his return from Santiniketan, he taught at an art college in Jabalpur, taking advantage of the long vacations to travel along the Narmada, sketch pad in hand. In 1977, in the company of a colleague and two students, he set off on his first stretch of the parikrama.

All this took a while, but after the crew packed up, we sat down for a vegetarian Gujarati meal, and afterwards he suggested that we go outside. We walked to a large swing, and continued the conversation to its gentle swaying.

'It was never a religious quest,' he told me. 'If I was a believer, I would reap the benefit of doing this in my next life, but I am already reaping the benefits in this life. The religious get a cheque when they undertake the parikrama, I have been given cash!'

It was only later that I recalled something he had written about a Diwali evening in Amarkantak. 'I asked the woman for a diya, lit it and set it afloat on the spring. Then, from the depths of my heart, I exclaimed, "Mother Narmada, I have lit a diya in your honour. In exchange, please light a diya in my heart. There is immense darkness within, and no way to dispel it."'

Claudio Magris, the writer of *Danube* and the patron saint of all chroniclers who venture on river journeys, seems to have known this feeling better than most. 'His little excursions to the springs was almost certainly a means of escape from that feeling of stalemate ... To distract your gaze from your inmost being, to apply it to analyzing the identity of others or the reality and the nature of things – there is nothing better.'

Now as I write, I wish I had spoken to Vegad about this. Instead, our talk veered off to the journey ahead where the dams awaited me on the river. It was a question he had thought about often enough and his answer sounded rehearsed. 'I had written in a newspaper that the dam is a necessity. The amount of water on this earth is limited, the population continues to grow, where is the choice? Rehabilitation of the displaced is a separate issue.'

Till this point, his argument was well thought out, he spoke in a fashion that aimed to convince, unsure as he was of my views. As I sat there in silence, nodding and listening, he took my silence for agreement, and the calm rationality with which he was making his point disappeared. 'Medha (Patkar) has taken money from foreign agencies, she even makes money from the fishing contracts at the Bargi Dam.'

I had thought that this man without faith, or with faith only in the river, with his apparent reasonableness would have reached the same conclusions that I had. But his belief in the dam seemed to connect with another part of him. 'Population is our biggest problem. It lies at the root of everything. It forces us to look for solutions. And in our blindness we want to run away from the fact that the Muslims are growing much faster than we are.'

Vegad, the atheist who sought the river for its beauty, did not seem to comprehend that modernity could not be taken piecemeal, the self-questioning rationality that went with it needed to extend to every premise. He had difficulty coming to terms with faith, but he had no difficulty in accepting on faith the crude propaganda that bolstered his prejudices. He himself had said that he remained a

Gujarati in Madhya Pradesh and he said it as if this was supposed to explain everything.

~

Even a single lamp dispels the deepest darkness. The simple message written on the wall at the entrance to one of the huts at the Sabarmati Ashram in Ahmedabad seems to suggest Amrit Lal Vegad was echoing Gandhi in his search for a peace that he appears not to have found.

The ashram is now a museum, hoarding memories of Gandhi's presence here. Even in this frozen space, so far removed from the context in which it was part of Gandhi's life, something of the man survives.

Gandhi's living quarters, the bare room with the charkha where he sat and spun while receiving visitors, perhaps deliberately echo the simplicity and the search for inner truth that connect him to the Quakers and Kabir the weaver.

I had picked a working afternoon, when there were very few tourists around. I found that there was something about the place that forced a quiet even on the group of young men in their tight jeans and dark glasses who seemed to have come by because they had nothing better to do, hoping, perhaps, to barge into a young couple or two for whom this was one of the few open spaces in the city safe from prying eyes.

I stepped out of Gandhi's quarters and stood in the shade of the tree overlooking the river, flowing blue with water as it may well have when Gandhi lived here. Parrots chirped overhead, squirrels darted around fearlessly. It was only the knowledge that I carried with me that made this setting seem absurd.

The Sabarmati River that flowed below had been perennial when Gandhi lived in the ashram. But soon after Independence, for the next fifty years or so, it had run dry for a good part of the year. As water began flowing along the Narmada Main Canal, Narendra Modi found a use for it that had never been anticipated by those who had planned the project.

212 HARTOSH SINGH BAL

The visuals of the main canal made for great publicity, but in reality the canal was just a very expensive alternative route for the Narmada to the sea. North of Ahmedabad, where the canal travelled through a tunnel below the bed of the Sabarmati, some of the water had been diverted to the river, which had become a third alternative route for the Narmada to the sea. What I was seeing, standing at the Sabarmati Ashram, was water from the dam that had displaced over a hundred thousand people. It had ended up providing a pleasant river-front view for the people of Ahmedabad.

From the ashram I could see a hum of activity by the river. Modi had another plan in mind. The Sabarmati/Narmada would be embanked and confined within the city, and the land so liberated on its banks would be used to construct a river front to match what London or Paris could offer. Dumper trucks and cranes were working overtime, but like so many of Modi's boasts, little attention was being paid to the reality of cost overruns, huge delays and the potential problems that stemmed from confining a rain-fed river. In the meantime, slums had been removed, people evicted – one more displacement in the name of the Narmada.

A few people had pointed out that embanking a monsoon-fed river had never worked anywhere in India. One sudden unexpected flood and the river front would flounder and be washed away. But almost no one had made the point that an occurrence far more certain would soon lay bare the absurdity of the project. Eventually, so long delayed that it would have made a mockery of the very purpose of the Sardar Sarovar Dam, the canal network would be finished and there would be no water to spare for the Sabarmati. When the high-rises finally took shape along the river, they would be staring at a dry bed for a great part of the year.

XVI

Every pilgrim who has circled the river must return to Omkareshwar to complete a parikrama of the island. This final act of pilgrimage not only recapitulates the larger journey, it also brings it to an end. These parikramawasis have already walked past the island twice, but forbidden to cross the Narmada, this is the first time they actually make the journey to the island. Most head to the southern bank of the island, either by boat or across one of the two footbridges that connect this bank to the island.

The island rises sharply from the river, and a cluster of buildings clings to the slope. From the steep ghats, stairs lead to several high-walled dharamshalas. The palace of the raja of Mandhata crowns the cluster, but it is the white Jyotirlinga temple that first catches the eye.

Of all the Jyotirlinga sites in the country, this is the only place where there are two contestants for the title, the Omkareshwar temple on the island and the Amleshwar temple on the southern bank. The matter has been resolved amicably, and pilgrims visit both the temples, secure in the belief that each temple represents one half of Shiva.

The busy street that leads to the Jyotirlinga temple on the island replicates the feel of any of India's better-known pilgrim towns. Shops sell items for pooja – agarbattis, coconuts, marigolds. Others sell

CDs and cassettes of devotional songs, as well as gaudily coloured pamphlets extolling Omkareshwar's virtues. What is missing here, at the end of the parikrama, as it is at the source of the river at Amarkantak, is the pleading hucksterism of the Brahmins.

Most visitors see no more of Omkareshwar than this, taking away the memory of a pilgrim town no different from many others in the country. Only the parikramawasis come away with the sense of a place that is unique even in a country with a surfeit of ruins and history.

If the Narmada flows through the centre of India, this island lies at the centre of the river's course. It is no coincidence that Sankara, who mapped the limits of this civilization in the eighth century, is believed to have gained enlightenment here. This is the nabhi, the navel of Hinduism. And at this centre, the meaning of classical Hinduism itself dissipates. The high art of the temple tradition collides with the vigour of tribal form, the Brahmin's right to officiate at temples collides with the tribal right to prior ownership, the meaning of Sankara's liberation itself becomes contested by other forms of the divine, from the feminine power of the yogini to the gods who until recently demanded human sacrifice.

～

During my visits to the island, a process of refurbishment was under way at the Jyotirlinga temple. From the foundations to the roof, everything at the temple was being looked at anew and redesigned. This was part of a much larger project, to redesign the island to make it easier for pilgrims to journey and bathe here.

The project had the approval of the BJP government in power which had declared Omkareshwar a pavitranagri, a sacred town. The actual implementation had been left to Jaiprakash Associates, or Jaypee as they refer to themselves, the same construction company that was building many of the major dams on the Narmada, including the one at Omkareshwar. Ironically, the company which is now among the largest construction companies in India, started in Rewa, a city named after the very river they are now damming.

On one of my visits, I was part of an NDTV episode that looked at the work being done on the temple. The episode includes a sequence where Sachin Gaur, the grandson of Jaiprakash Gaur, leads a camera crew around the temple. He comes across as a young man, very sincere, with little doubt that what his company is doing is not only necessary, it is a significant improvement on what existed on this island.

It never seems to occur to him that pilgrimage was never meant to be an act of convenience or that the hardship of the journey, its rigours and dangers, are part of the experience of the sacred, and in the name of convenience it is possible to destroy the very characteristics that make a place sacred.

At the temple entrance, Gaur points to the mosaic floor, and speaks to the camera. 'Earlier there was no proper lighting and ventilation in this area, plus we have done the flooring which was cracked. Earlier it was marble but it had been laid a long time ago, it was in very bad shape.'

The camera follows him, trained on the mosaic flooring, as he walks inside the shrine. He looks up and speaks again. 'We have fixed the ceiling. It was an old ceiling, it was all made of stone, there was no plaster or anything.'

The camera pans up to a false ceiling under construction, complete with inset ceiling lights. There are workmen on the roof; he asks a man who seems to be in charge of the work, 'What colour have you used?'

'Pink and white,' comes the reply.

Gaur keeps on speaking. 'Earlier the ceiling was very high, no one could get there and clean it, we had to fix it, make it more suitable.'

The camera pans up again, showing the intricacy of the stonework on the ceiling which will be hidden behind the pink plaster-of-paris roof.

He is asked about the people who are helping the company with the restoration.

With a confidence given to those inheriting a family business, Gaur answers, 'Our company is doing it in-house, the entire design is being done by us, the entire Omkareshwar project has been designed by us. We are already in the hospitality sector, where we have hotels and stuff, so we are used to doing these kind of things.'

At the heart of the river, in the heart of the country, with the backing of a BJP government which speaks in the name of Hinduism, the company building the dams on the Narmada has been busy reconstructing a Jyotirlinga temple in the image of a hotel lobby.

From the temple, pilgrims walk the parikrama path that leads to the western tip of the island, recreating the journey to the mouth of the river at Bharuch. For the first time in months, or even years, they are walking with the river to their left. They descend to the level of the river before beginning a steady ascent. Already within the first hour of walking there is a silence on the path, the throng at the temple seems far away. The path is cemented. As it climbs again, it moves away from the river, and amidst the lightly forested southern slopes of the island, an occasional ashram can be glimpsed through the trees.

The devout claim to see the divine symbol Om in the shape of the island, hence the name Omkareshwar. To my eyes it approximates a right triangle, the eastern and western tips the two vertices that mark the hypotenuse along the southern bank.

As the path curves short of the western vertex, pilgrims take a small detour to the tip of the island. Here they pay obeisance to what they believe is the confluence of the Narmada and a tributary that invokes the name of one of the sacred rivers of the south, Kaveri. The tributary actually meets the Narmada a few hundred yards upstream of Omkareshwar, and the dam stands between the confluence and the island, but the old belief survives – that the rivers do not merge at the actual confluence, rather they criss-cross, the Narmada flowing between the island and the southern bank, the Kaveri between the island and the northern bank, meeting downstream here at the western tip.

A set of thatched shops standing on wooden stilts line the path that once led to a small temple. The temple has disappeared, washed away by a sudden and unprecedented discharge from the dam. It is this unpredictability that people living downstream from the dams on the Narmada have learnt to fear.

On 7 April 2005, sixty-two people were drowned because of the discharge of water from the Indira Sagar Dam. They were bathing in the river on a full-moon night at one of the traditional fairs on the banks of the river. Yet, the Narmada Hydroelectric Development Corporation (NHDC) that operates the dams released 690 cusecs of water between 7 and 9 p.m., raising the height of the river by 1.8 metres and an additional 230 cusecs between 9 and 11 p.m., raising it a further 0.6 metres.

S.K. Dodeja, then chief of the NHDC said, 'It was the district administration's job to warn the pilgrims and the NHDC of the crowds congregating on the banks of the Narmada. Lack of coordination between the local authorities and NHDC had led to the misunderstanding.' It never seemed to have occurred to the NHDC that they needed to maintain an annual calendar of fairs on a sacred river, but then, this was just another instance of a body manned by engineers failing to factor in the possible impacts of a dam. Misunderstanding is a well-suited euphemism for drowning sixty-two people.

From the confluence the path gently ascends eastwards along the northern ridge. The Rin Mukteshwar temple complex is the first of the major temples along the northern bank. It dates back to the medieval period, but the application of regular coats of whitewash had made it difficult to separate the original structure from later additions. Ram Balak Das, who officiates as the priest, tells me he has been looking after the complex for eight years. The offerings for many of the temples go to the mahants who live here for part of the year, but those from the main temple, the oldest of all, go to a Bhil family.

Past the temple, the nature of the journey changes. Very few people can now be seen on the path. The terrain seems rougher, wilder, a considerable distance away from the noise of the pilgrim town. The path leads through two fort gates, huge and cavernous, and the climb eases up near the first of the temples.

The summit of the island was once a fortified city, dating back to early medieval times, though some of the temples seem to predate it. It was believed to have been thriving till Aurangzeb destroyed it after a prolonged siege. As the climb levels off, remains of the fort walls lining the northern ridge become visible. Along the path, stone foundations suggest rooms and barracks. The walk has eased up and soon the path touches the first of the temples on the summit, Gauri-Somnath. From the temple 247 stairs descend straight down the steep slope to the pilgrim town below. It is a rarely used route, shortening the pilgrim path to the summit.

The temple stands on a metre-high plinth and the sikhara encloses a double-storey structure, still gracefully intact. The garbhagriha houses a 6-foot shivling carved out of black stone. The lingam is said to have been transparent at one point of time. A myth, which occurs almost unchanged in the accounts of early British travellers, claims that at one time pilgrims could look at the lingam and see their future unfold before them. After Aurangzeb sacked the island, and his soldiers had mutilated every idol they could find, he stood before the lingam to behold his future. In the vast chain of births and rebirths that Hinduism promises each being, the emperor saw that he would reappear on this earth as a pig, that most unclean of animals in Islam. Enraged, he had the lingam set on fire, and the transparent stone turned black.

Even when it is rendered so crudely, reflecting a tension between two religious traditions that has really never been settled in India, Aurangzeb stands defeated in mythology. Unlike the battles he fought and the wars he won, this was not a defeat that could be undone.

The priest who shows me around the double-storeyed temple is from a Bhil family that has the rights to the offerings here. His name is Sunil Patel, and he says he really doesn't know much about the rituals of worship; he has been observing others in the family and imitating them. It happened to be his turn today because his uncle had to go into town.

Next to the temple, the ASI museum displays the sculptures found scattered on the island. Devi Singh Solanki, the sole ASI man posted here, tells me no excavations have ever been carried out. All the sculptures on display have been collected from the surface of the ruins. There are so many that those that cannot be displayed indoors are on display out in the open, the ones that remain lie scattered around within the museum compound.

The yoginis are in abundance, finely formed, full-bodied, ranging from the serene to the macabre, but even in the mutilation imposed on them by Aurangzeb's men, they are exquisitely worked, and the hideousness of the aesthetics of a giant Shiva statue that looms ahead along the pilgrim path, displacing the pre-eminence of the Gauri-Somnath temple on the island summit, comes as a shock.

The men at work on the statue mention that a media baron is paying for its construction. I am unable to verify this, but the statue is in keeping with the amusement parks he operates. It belongs to the world of Disney, not to the geography of this island. Meant to be over 90 feet high when complete, it is an act of desecration, much like Jaypee's attempt at restoring the Jyotirlinga temple.

Past the Shiva statue, the terrain wanders through another great expanse of ruins. Everything here seems to be devoted to the sacred. Temple ruins and vast sculptures dot the landscape. A fallen head, a torso, giant blocks of stone that once held up temples, line the path.

The cult of the goddess is evident everywhere. It seems that at the very core of the fortified city lay a sacred space devoted to a cult that has now disappeared. It evokes another sacred site by the Narmada, mentioned by Elkanah in his account: the temple of the eighty-one yoginis at Bheraghat, on the top of a hill adjacent to the

Narmada, a few kilometres from Jabalpur. The river flows below, the marble rocks lie immediately upstream. A steep flight of stairs leads to a semicircular structure, 125 metres in diameter, open to the sky. It resembles no other temple to any gods or goddesses; this is the home of the yoginis.

Less than twenty such temples exist in India, most of them in central India. This is the largest of them all. Along the circumference a covered, colonnaded walkway leads past the niches that provide shelter for the yogini statues. The niches originally sheltered the statues of eighty-one yoginis. No other yogini temple that exists today houses as many; the usual number is sixty-four. But even here, the puritanical zeal of a few rulers has been allowed to hold sway. The ruthless efficiency that went into such defacement – a nose broken, a breast sliced off, limbs severed, penises broken off – a sign of a monomania that verges on madness.

The historian Vidya Dehejia has traced the history of the cult in her book, *Yogini Cults and Temples: A Tantric Tradition*. The cult seems to have thrived between the eighth and the twelfth century in central India. At least three dynasties – the Chandelas who ruled from Khajuraho and built the well-known temple complex there, the oldest of which is a yogini temple; the Kalachuris of Tripuri, or what is Jabalpur now; and the Parmars of the Malwa – seem to have extended royal patronage. The decline and defeat of these dynasties seem to coincide with the retreat of the cult.

Dehejia argues that salvation or moksha was not an intended end, rather the intention was to acquire occult powers, gain success in this world. A text that dates back to the first millennium, *Sri Matottara Tantra,* describes how the practice of the yogini cult imparts the eight siddhis, the ability to become minute in size, the ability to become gigantic is size, the ability to become weightless and hence to leave the body and travel at will, the ability to become weighty and the power that comes with it, the ability to submit others to your will, control over the body and mind of the self and others, the ability to control the natural elements and the ability to fulfil all desires.

Such powers were not to be obtained easily. To begin with, they required alcohol. The yoginis are described as swaying with the intoxication of wine and delighting in its pleasures. They are consumers of blood and require the sacrifice of animals, in particular goats and buffaloes, offerings that Dehejia believes lead to one of the central rituals of the yogini cult.

The corpse ritual, as Dehejia describes it, is performed at the centre of the ring adorned by the yoginis and is dedicated to Bhairava (An incarnation of Shiva sent to curb Brahma's pride, Bhairava chopped off one of Brahma's five heads. For this sin he was forced to forever carry the head in his hand).

> The corpse must be a beautiful one, not injured in any way, and not defaced or marked in any manner. All its limbs must be intact and it should be a recent body that is still sweet smelling. It should have all 32 teeth, all the auspicious signs, and it should be perfect in every way.
>
> Bathe the corpse to the accompaniment of mantras and smear it with Kashmir sandalwood paste. Then, establish the shava in the centre of the mandala and recite the Bhairava mantra. All this must be done in the middle of the night. O sadhaka performing this rite, be strong-minded, courageous and free from all doubts. Hold the head of the corpse and, with enthusiasm, and disregarding the protruding tongue, cut off the head in one single stroke so that it falls to the ground.

Some of the yoginis in these circular temples are depicted holding a severed head, or adorned with a necklace of skulls.

Dehejia argues that the other main ritual of the yogini cult is maithuna or ritual copulation as practised by the Kaula tantrics. The initiates sit in a circle made up of at least eight persons, an equal number of men and women. Couples are paired, and within this circle there are no distinctions of caste. They drink alcohol and recite a mantra. In a carefully modulated sequence, the men touch their partners before copulating with them, imitating the divine act of Shiva and his consort, often depicted as yoni-lingam in Shiva temples such as Gauri-Somnath. It is then no surprise, as Dehejia notes, that the yogini temples existed on hilltops in secluded places.

In Omkareshwar, the yoginis are present not in arrays of sixty-four or eighty-one, they seem to be present in abundance everywhere. The museum has sculptures of the sapta matrikas, the precursors of the yogini cult; Varahi, boar-headed but elegant; Chamunda, one of the sapta matrikas but depicted alone, all ribs and bones, garlanded with skulls, a yogini who demands animal sacrifice and liquor as offerings; Mahishasuramardini, the slayer of the buffalo-demon Mahishasura, hence the sacrifice of buffaloes; and Katyayani Devi, another form of the Mahishasuramardini.

Only in this setting is it possible to see why one of the most popular hymns to the devi and her many forms, the *Mahishasuramardini Stotram*, was composed by none other than Sankara. This is also why I believe Dehejia is wrong when she suggests liberation of the self has little to do with the cult of the yoginis. The cult was born not in defiance of the serene intellectualism of Sankara's non-duality but in keeping with it.

Perhaps the basic idea goes back much earlier to the Buddha, to whom Sankara owes a great intellectual debt. The existence of absolute evil can only spring from a Manichaen belief. If there is a oneness, or a non-duality to be more precise, then the existence of death, intoxication and copulation are also aspects of this non-duality. If denial can result in the path to illumination, a denial tempered by self-control of the most extreme kind under the guidance of a teacher, then so should excess, if it is tempered by the same extreme of self-control taught by one who has experienced this path.

Further ahead, in the sacred heart of the city of Mandhata, an outsize depiction of Chamunda dominates the fort wall. She has been recently stained saffron, in keeping with the belief that she must be depicted in red. She appears again on the northern fort gate. An old myth suggests Kali, who fed on human flesh, and her companion Kaal Bhairon once held sway over the island. Finally, the ascetic Daryao Nath was able to seal off Kali in a cave below the Jyotirlinga temple, where, the belief goes, she stills lurks barricaded behind an iron grill, not far from the cave where Sankara is said to have meditated and gained enlightenment. Bhairon, however, continued to lurk on the island, periodically needing to be assuaged with human sacrifice.

The path passes through another gate, the larger-than-life goddesses look out, guarding against intruders. Just ahead, at the Siddhanath temple, Shiva in a calmer guise reclaims the island. Among the numerous shrines on the island, this is by far the most exquisite. It seems older than the others, and does not subscribe to the forms of temple architecture that were in place by the twelfth century. It is a colonnaded structure standing on a high plinth, about a metre and a half tall. The roof has given way; it is not clear if a sikhara ever towered above, but the architecture suggests a flat roof. The pillars are elaborately carved, as are the sculptures on the main structure. The plinth is lined with elephants carved out of red sandstone. In pairs they lock tusks and trunks, individually they seem to hold aloft the temple.

Amrit Lal Nayak, the temple custodian, insists he is a Bhilala, not Bhil, as were, he insists, all the other custodians I had met. 'We are,' he says, 'descendants of Rajputs who married Bhil women.' He knows the rituals of worship well, having learnt them from his father, who was custodian of the shrine for forty-five years.

'Till a few decades ago, this part of the island was thick jungle,' he tells me, 'the path barely existed. You could find snakes everywhere. The concrete path has only been built recently after Digvijaya Singh undertook the island parikrama. The families of those people who have settled on this side of the island have arrived recently. Earlier nobody stayed the night here. Now the jungle is slowly being cleared by people looking for firewood.'

I finish talking to him and wander through the temple complex. The open ground adjacent to the plinth slopes down, and all at once the far end of the island comes into view, and with it the dam. Even though I was prepared for its presence, it comes as a shock.

Silhouetted against the dam is the shell of an old temple, much as

Geoffrey Maw had described it sixty years ago: 'On the very edge of this cliff stand the last three pillars of one of the most ancient temples on the island. At the foot of the cliff, but out of sight from the top, a smooth flat rock stands waist high in the river bed. This is Bir Khila, Hero's Rock, and this is the spot where liberty to worship Shiva on the island was bought at the price of human sacrifice.'

Maw was not writing of a myth. James Forsyth has documented an eyewitness account by a British officer who observed such a sacrifice: 'In 1822, a European officer of our Government witnessed the death of almost the last victim to Kal Bhairava at this shrine. The island then belonged to a native State (Sindia), and our Government had not then begun to interfere with such bloody rites. The political officer who wrote the account of it was therefore unable to prevent it by force. I came on the description a few years ago in MS., hidden away among many other forgotten papers in the Government record room of the Nimar district. The concluding portion may be interesting as perhaps the only account on record, by an eye-witness, of such an occurrence.'

Forsyth does not name the officer, but the account is compelling, and the details seem to suggest it is genuine:

I took care to be present at an early hour at the representation of Bhairon, a rough block of basalt smeared with red paint, before which he must necessarily present and prostrate himself, ere he mounted to the lofty pinnacle whence to spring on the idol. Ere long he arrived, preceded by rude music. He approached the amorphous idol with a light foot, while a wild pleasure marked his countenance. As soon as this subsided, and repeatedly during the painful scene, I addressed myself to him, in the most urgent possible manner, to recede from his rash resolve, pledging myself to ensure him protection and a competence for his life. I had taken the precaution to have a boat close at hand, which in five minutes would have transported us beyond the sight of the multitude. In vain I urged him. He now more resolutely replied that it was beyond human power to remove the sacrifice of the powerful Bhairon. So deep-rooted a delusion could only be surmounted by force; and to exercise that I was unauthorised.

While confronted with the idol, his delusion gained strength; and the barbarous throng cheered with voice and hand, when by his motions he indicated a total and continued disregard of my persuasions to desist. He made his offering of cocoanuts, first breaking one; and he emptied into a gourd presented by the priestess his previous collection of pice and cowries. She now tendered to him some ardent spirit in the nutshell, first making her son drink some from his hand, to obviate all suspicion of its being drugged. A little was poured in oblation on the idol. She hinted to him to deliver to her the silver rings he wore. In doing so he gave a proof of singular collectedness. One of the first he took off he concealed in his mouth till he had presented to her all the rest, when, searching among the surrounding countenances, he pointed to a man to whom he ordered this ring to be given.

It was a person who had accompanied him from Ujjain. An eagerness was now evinced by several to submit bracelets, and even betel-nuts, to his sacred touch. He composedly placed such in his mouth and returned them. The priestess at last presented him with a pan leaf and he left the spot with a firm step, amidst the plaudit of the crowd.

During the latter half of his ascent he was much concealed from view by shrubs. At length he appeared to the aching sight, and stood in a bold and erect posture upon the fatal eminence. Some short time he passed in agitated motions on the stone ledge, tossing now and then his arms aloft as if employed in invocation. At length he ceased; and, in slow motions with both his hands, made farewell salutations to the assembled multitude. This done, he whirled down the cocoanut, mirror, knife, and lime, which he had continued to hold; and stepping back was lost to view for a moment. The next second he burst upon our agonised sight in a most manful leap, descending feet foremost with terrific rapidity, till, in mid career, a projecting rock reversed his position, and caused a headlong fall. Instant death followed this descent of ninety feet, and terminated the existence of this youth, whose strength of faith and fortitude would have adorned the noblest cause.

I walked to the edge of the island where the three pillars still stand. The fall is vertiginous but the river no longer flows directly below. Debris from the dam construction has piled up by the cliff, and later, when I walk below, there is no sign of Hero's Rock. The temple retains its aura, perhaps amplified by my reading. The dam rises from the river, almost as high as the cliff. Dumper trucks, which seem like a child's playthings from this height, ferry material to the construction site.

The two images, the two temples of India, stand in stark contrast. But at least the man who sacrificed himself so boldly, with so much fervour, had volunteered for the task. He was one of the faithful. The sacrifice demanded by the dams has been forced on those who have not volunteered, who have little belief in the faith that calls the dams into being.

Copyright
Acknowledgements

The author and the publishers are grateful for permission granted to use quotations from the following:

Dharwadker, Vinay, trans., *Kabir: The Weaver's Songs*, New Delhi: Penguin Books India, 2003.

Eck, Diana L., *India: A Sacred Geography*, New York: Random House, 2012.

Guha, Ramachandra, *Savaging the Civilized: Verrier Elwin, His Tribals, and India*, New Delhi: Oxford University Press, 1999.

Roy, Arundhati, *The Greater Common Good*, Mumbai: India Book Distributors, 1999.

Parts of the book have appeared in some form in *Open, Tehelka, Himal, The Indian Express, Asia Literary Review* and *The New York Times* Blog.

Every effort has been made to obtain permission from copyright holders. But any omissions brought to our notice will be remedied in future reprints/editions.

Acknowledgements

Companions on the road: John Bowles, Durga and Subhash Vyam, Venkat Syam, Ajay Jaiswal, Gopikant Ghosh, Prakash Hatvalne, Radhika Bordia.

Unstinting hosts: Pyare Lal, Gangaram, Ram Prasad Dhruve, Girija Shankar Agrawal, Rakesh Dewan, Yogesh Dewan, Teji Grover, Rustam Singh, Rano Titus, Raju Titus, Medha Patkar, Jayashree, Revati, Sarang and Amit Bhatnagar, Mahesh Langa.

Sympathetic critics: Chitvan Gill, Basharat Peer, Ramachandra Guha, Siddhartha Deb, Vatsala Kaul, Jaspreet Singh, Chitra Padmanabhan, Anand Narasimhan, Omair Ahmad, Hirsh Sawhney and Mitali Saran.

The political bureau at *Open* for picking up the slack: Jatin Gandhi, Rahul Pandita, Dhirendra Jha and Mihir Srivastava.

V. K. Karthika at HarperCollins for her forbearance.

Anne Thomason at the Earlham College library for her promptness and generosity in dispatching the Beard Diary.

My sisters, Ravtosh, for her incisive comments on the manuscript, and Manu, for the gray Maruti 800 which never failed me on the journey.

My father Amarjit (who did not live to read a manuscript that I feel would have been close to his heart) and mother Neena for decades of indulgence.

And Pamela for making it all possible.

Select Bibliography

An Officer in the Service of the Honourable East India Company, *The Pindaries*, London: John Murray, 1818.

Baviskar, Amita, *The Belly of the River*: Tribal Conflicts over Development in the Narmada Valley, New Delhi: Oxford University Press, 1995.

Berman, Marshall, *All That Is Solid Melts Into Air: The Experience of Modernity*, New York: Penguin Books, 1988.

Borges, Jorge Luis, *Collected Fictions*, New York: Penguin Books, 1998.

Borges, Jorge Luis, *Seven Nights*, New York: New Directions, 1984.

Bowles, John, *Painted Songs & Stories, The Hybrid Flowerings of Contemporary Pardhan Gond Art*, Bhopal: INTACH, Bhopal Chapter, 2009.

Central Provinces District Gazeeter: Hoshangabad, 1908.

Dehejia, Vidya, *Yogini Cults and Temples, A Tantric Tradition*, New Delhi: National Museum, 1986 edition.

Dharwadker, Vinay, trans. *Kabir: The Weaver's Songs*, New Delhi: Penguin Books India, 2003.

Eck, Diana L., *India: A Sacred Geography,* New York: Random House, 2012.

Farooqui, Amar, *Sindias and the Raj: Princely Gwalior C. 1800-1850*, New Delhi: Primus Books, 2011.

Fazl, Abul, *Akbarnama*, New Delhi: Low Price Publications, 1994.

Forsyth, James, *The Highlands of Central India: Notes on Their Forests and Wild Tribes, Natural History, and Sports*, London: Chapman & Hall, 1872.

Friere, Paolo, *Pedagogy of the Oppressed,* London: Penguin Books; 2nd edition, 25 January 1996.

—— *Teachers as Cultural Workers – Letters to Those Who Dare Teach,* translated by Donoldo Macedo, Dale Koike and Alexandre Oliveira, Boulder, Colarado: Westview Press, 1998.

Guest, Tim, *My Life in Orange,* London: Granta, 2005.

Guha, Ramachandra, *Savaging the Civilized: Verrier Elwin, His Tribals, and India,* New Delhi: Oxford University Press, 1999.

Kalidasa, *The Loom of Time (Meghdutam),* London: Penguin Classics, 1989.

Lethbridge, Roper, *The Golden Book of India: A Genealogical and Biographical Dictionary of the Ruling Princes, Chiefs, Nobles, and Other Personages, Titled or Decorated, of the Indian Empire,* London and New York: Macmillan and Co., 1893.

Lyall, Sir Alfred, *Verses Written in India,* London: Kegan Paul, Trench & Co. Ltd, 1889.

Maws, Geoffrey Waring, *Narmada: The Life of a River,* Rasulia: Distributed by Friends Rural Centre, 1991.

McEldowney, Philip, 'A Brief Study of the Pindaris of Madhya Pradesh', *The India Cultures Quarterly,* Vol. 27, No. 2, 1971.

Mehta, Gita, *River Sutra,* New York: Vintage, 1994.

Metteyya, Bhikku, *The Cynosure of Sanchi,* Maha Bodhi Society, 1946.

Müller, F. Max (ed), Georg Bühler (trans), *The Laws Of Manu: The Sacred Books of the East,* Part Twenty-five, Oxford: The Claredon Press, 1879.

Pande, Govind Chandra, *Life and Thought of Sankaracharya,* Varanasi: Motilal Banarsidass, 2004.

Rajneesh, *Osho's Life, An Anthology of Osho's Life from His Own Books,* http://www.oshoworld.com/biography/biography.asp.

Rambharos Agrawal, *Gond Jati ka Samajik Adhyayan,* Mandla: Gondi Public Trust, 2005.

The Rig Veda, London: Penguin Classics, 2005.

Roy, Arundhati, *The Greater Common Good,* Mumbai: India Book Distributors, 1999.

Rushdie, Salman, *Haroun and the Sea of Stories,* London: Granta, 1991.

Sleeman, W.H., *Rambles and Recollections of an Indian Official,* Delhi: Rupa Books, 2003.

Strabo, *The Geography of Strabo*, London: Loeb Classical Library edition, 19171932.

Syam, Bajju, *London Jungle Book*, London: Tara Publishing, 2005.

Sykes, Marjorie, *An Indian Tapestry: Quaker Threads in the History of India, Pakistan & Bangladesh, from the Seventeenth Century to Independence,* completed and edited by Geoffrey Carnall, York: Sessions Books Trust, 1997.

Taylor, Thomas, *Select works of Porphyry,* London: T. Rodd, 1823.

Vegad, Amrit Lal, *Narmada: River of Beauty*, New Delhi: Penguin Books India, 2008.

Willett, John and Ralph Manheim (eds), *Bertolt Brecht Poems,* London: Eyre Methuen Ltd., 1976.

Index

About the Author

Hartosh Singh Bal trained as an engineer at BITS Pilani and a mathematician at New York University before turning to journalism. He is co-author of *A Certain Ambiguity: A Mathematical Novel*, which won the Association of American Publishers' award for the Best Professional/ Scholarly Book in Mathematics for 2007. He is the political editor of *Open*, and has worked for *The Indian Express*, *Tehelka* and *Mail Today*.